Harry H. Johnston

The River Congo from Its Mouth to Bólobó

With a general Gescription of the natural History and Anthropology of its western

Basin

Harry H. Johnston

The River Congo from Its Mouth to Bólobó
With a general Gescription of the natural History and Anthropology of its western Basin

ISBN/EAN: 9783337240486

Printed in Europe, USA, Canada, Australia, Japan

Cover: Foto ©Andreas Hilbeck / pixelio.de

More available books at **www.hansebooks.com**

THE RIVER CONGO

FROM ITS MOUTH TO BOLOBO

WITH

A GENERAL DESCRIPTION OF THE NATURAL HISTORY
AND ANTHROPOLOGY OF ITS WESTERN BASIN.

BY

H. H. JOHNSTON, C.B.

WITH OVER SEVENTY ILLUSTRATIONS BY THE AUTHOR

FOURTH AND CHEAPER EDITION

REVISED BY THE AUTHOR

LONDON

SAMPSON LOW, MARSTON & COMPANY
LIMITED
St. Dunstan's House
FETTER LANE, FLEET STREET, E.C.
1895

To

HENRY MORELAND STANLEY

This Book is Dedicated

IN MEMORY OF GREAT KINDNESS SHOWN

TO ITS AUTHOR

PREFACE.

I BELIEVE a negro potentate once observed, with regard to the encroachments of the Anglo-Saxon race, that first came the missionary, then the merchant, and finally the British soldier. An almost analogous case to political conquest is the occupation by science of new fields of research. The pioneer is a man of the Livingstone or Stanley type, who rapidly traverses an unknown region, braves its dangers and endures its privations, and points out to his successors where his discoveries may be best taken up and worked out in detail. I trust, therefore, that as Mr. Stanley may claim to have been the great missionary of knowledge on the Congo, so I, in following humbly in his steps, may rank as the merchant who has brought back for the world's inspection some samples from the unworked mines of information, whose presence the great explorer could discover, but whose wealth he had perforce to leave behind him on his rapid march. I have not ventured to make this work a record of novel explora- tion, for I visited few places that were not already explored ; nor of scientific research, for I lack the necessary ability. I have merely tried to produce with pen and brush an ordinary guide-book to the Congo, which may convey to intending travellers or stay-at-home folks a fairly just impression of the main features of the great

river. All that is written or drawn within has been
directly done from Nature, and the faultiness in it arises
more from incompleteness of detail than from incorrect
outline. Nearly the entirety of the book has been compiled
in the midst of my studying-ground. Many of the
chapters here are reproduced exactly as they were jotted
down in pencil, either when stopping to rest in some
shady spot, or as I glided along the river in a canoe. All
the illustrations have been photographed directly from
my drawings, twenty-three of them being absolute *fac-
similes* reproduced by the Typographic Etching Company.

H. H. JOHNSTON.

LONDON, *February*, 1884.

PREFACE TO FOURTH AND CHEAP EDITION.

ELEVEN years nearly from the date of the first publication
of this book I am asked by the publishers to put my name
to a specially-prepared fourth edition which will be issued
at a cheaper rate. During these eleven years greater
changes have occurred in the Basin of the River Congo
than in any other part of the Dark Continent. The
African International Association has developed by
degrees into the Congo Free State under the Sovereignty
of the King of the Belgians, and finally into a Belgian
Colony. The Arabs have been conquered and almost
expelled from the Congo Basin. Stations have been
established on all the great confluents of the Congo
and on the main river itself up to within a short

distance of Bangweolo. Mr. Stanley, after completing his gigantic work in founding the Congo Free State, traversed that unknown country between the Congo and the Nile in his search for Emin Pasha, and then returned to England to marry and settle down in the enjoyment of a reputation which will be found in future centuries scarcely second to that of Columbus.

I myself have never set eyes on the Lower Congo since I left it in June 1883, though I have since travelled over that plateau in East Central Africa which gives rise to the main stream of this greatest of African rivers. A considerable portion of the Upper Congo has been placed under the British Flag and is now administered by the British South Africa Chartered Company. Our interests in this great river and in the welfare of the Congo Free State are now not only geographical but political. The Anglo-Congo Agreement has set at rest any rivalry or differences of opinion between the British and Belgian Authorities who are cordially working side by side in the suppression of the Slave Trade. By this Agreement the British are given a right to carry their Trans-Continental Telegraph line along the west shore of Lake Tanganyika and thence up to the British Protectorate on the Upper Nile.

This remarkable development, which has taken place in what is after all only a small slice of my own lifetime, may interest some few of my readers in this old record of my experiences on the Congo at a time when Stanley's work was first beginning. I have left this record but little altered, preferring that the public should read the somewhat artless descriptions of a very young man, rather than a remodelled and more staid treatise which might lose its sense of actuality. I have, of course, corrected all

obvious inaccuracies, and where it is useful I have adde
a little new matter written in the light of fuller knowledg
and I have also cut out most of the scientific appendice
as being out of date and no longer necessary in the muc
fuller knowledge which prevails of the fauna and flora
the Congo Basin.

I trust the book in its new shape may prove acceptab
especially to those who are just beginning to read abou
Africa.

H. H. JOHNSTON.

LONDON, *January*, 1895.

NOTE.

In the orthography of all the African words in this book, I have followed a simple phonetic system. The consonants are to be pronounced as in English, and the vowels as in Italian or Portuguese, viz.:—

a = ah ; e = eh ; i = ee ; ô = aw (o = oh) ; u = oo.

I have only diverged from this system where the proper names from long use have accustomed us to other spelling. Thus I write "the River Congo" and "Angola," because for several centuries the Portuguese have spelt these names in the same manner. Properly, they should be, according to the simplest system, "Kongo" and "Ngola."

LONDON

PRINTED BY WILLIAM CLOWES AND SONS, LIMITED,
STAMFORD STREET AND CHARING CROSS.

CONTENTS.

CONTENTS.

LIST OF ILLUSTRATIONS.

A JOURNEY UP THE RIVER CONGO.

CHAPTER I.

FROM SÃO PAULO DE LOANDA TO THE CONGO.

AMBRIZ—JOURNEY OVERLAND TO KINSEMBO—AN AFRICAN DINNER—
BOOKS AS AGAINST BRANDY—DESCRIPTION OF KINSEMBO—THE
CALEMMA—VEGETATION—JOURNEY OVERLAND TO MUSÉRA—A
CURIOUS MONOLITH—PHYTOGRAPHY OF SOUTH WEST AFRICA—
THE DESERT BOUNDARY OF THE TROPICS—AMBRIZÉTE—BAOBABS
—FLORAL BEAUTIES—THE TRADE ROUTE—THE NATIVES AND
ANNEXATION—CABEÇA DA COBRA—THE BUSH AT CABEÇA DA
COBRA—THE JASMINES—ASHIRONGO—THE CONGO—ITS MOUTH
—COLOUR OF THE WATER—BANANA POINT—KRUBOYS—KRU-
MANOS AND KABINDAS—APPRENTICESHIP AND SLAVERY.

IN the month of October, 1882, I left Loanda to carry out
a long-cherished idea of visiting the river Congo, to study
its little-known natural history, and to endeavour to por-
tray as accurately as possible the landscapes and inhabitants of lands which photography had not yet reached,
and where no student of nature had ever penetrated.

Having obtained a passage on board a Dutch trading-
steamer, I proceeded up the coast northwards to Ambriz,
the last possession of the Portuguese province of Angola,*
and lying distant from Loanda some sixty miles. When
we reached this place, early in the morning, I left the
steamer for a time, intending to journey some distance

---

* Since the date when this was written, Portuguese territory has
been extended from Ambriz to the mouth of the Congo; though all
the land north of Ambriz is placed within the Free Trade area of the
Congo Basin.—H. H. J.

along the coast by hammock, in order to gain a closer acquaintance with the character of the country that here borders the sea.   Carriers are not always easily obtained at Ambriz, and they were even more difficult to secure at this particular time, for they found such lucrative work in bringing coffee from the interior to the merchants' stores that they little cared for the more fatiguing task of carrying a white man in a hammock to Kinsembo.   The day passed in listless and hopeless waiting at the house of an English trader, and I began to think it would be necessary to resign myself to the disagreeable thought of passing a night with the fleas and mosquitoes which Ambriz lavishes on all new-comers; but as the sun began to sink very near the sea horizon, a sufficient number of men were collected one by one, a hammock was borrowed, and I gladly shook the dust of Ambriz off my feet, and settled comfortably into the half-drowsy state which the swaying motion of the hammock produces.   Our path lay for some distance along the seashore, right in amongst the foam of the breakers, whose deafening roar made the ears ring.   Here safe from their cruel force, on dear Mother Earth, I could look with wonder and interest on the irresistible roll and terrible rebound of the waves, which render landing on these unprotected coasts almost im-possible in anything but a surf-boat.   Half-an-hour's jog-trot on the part of the men brought us to the river Loge (Nloji), which at present (1883) is the northern boundary of the Portuguese possessions in Lower Guinea.   The clumps of mangrove which border its narrow mouth are very fine and picturesque, and afford shelter to many water birds, which were busily fishing for their evening meal whilst we waited to cross the river.   A native canoe came from the opposite side, and ferried us over in two journeys; and then, leaving the river, we passed through several black and fetid marshes, where the branches of the mangroves grew so low that they often took me by the chin and nearly jerked me out of the hammock.

As the ground grew more solid and strong, forests of " candelabra " euphorbias, ugly, bewitched-looking things,

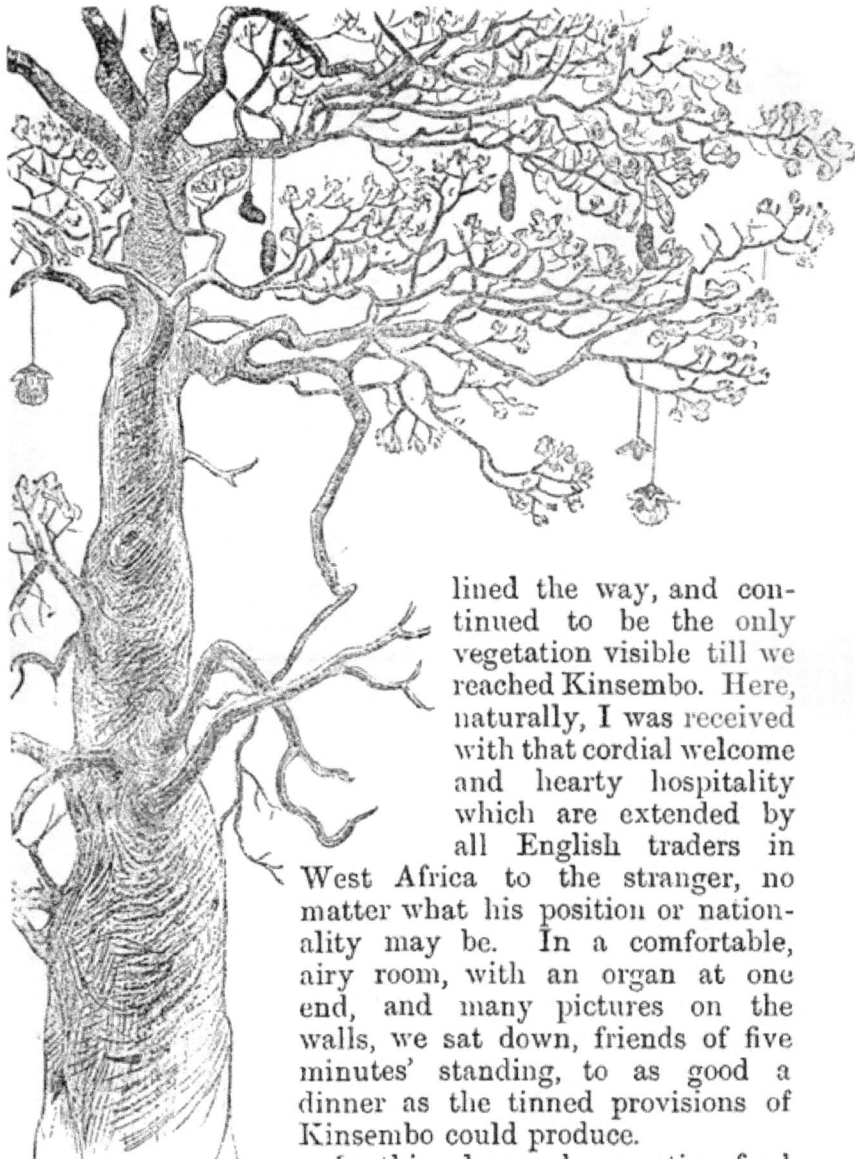

BAOBAB COMING INTO
LEAF AND FLOWER.

lined the way, and continued to be the only vegetation visible till we reached Kinsembo. Here, naturally, I was received with that cordial welcome and hearty hospitality which are extended by all English traders in West Africa to the stranger, no matter what his position or nationality may be. In a comfortable, airy room, with an organ at one end, and many pictures on the walls, we sat down, friends of five minutes' standing, to as good a dinner as the tinned provisions of Kinsembo could produce.

In this place, where native food is almost non-existent, save an occasional water-buck (*Cobus* antelope)

B 2

or a dish of little rock oysters, the European inhabitants
live nearly exclusively on provisions sent out from
England, and live well withal.   It takes a stranger to the
coast quite by surprise to see the excellence and variety of
these preserves ; and except that one longs occasionally
for a little fresh salad, the bill of fare presented by the
great purveyors of tinned provisions is quite an appetising
one in Africa.   On one of the evenings spent at Kinsembo,
we had a dinner much as follows, the *menu* of which I
append for the consolation of such of my readers as may
be proceeding to the West Coast of Africa.

Mock Turtle Soup.

Salmon Cutlets.

Lobster.

Curried Rabbit.

Roast Beef.   Boiled Mutton.

(*with preserved potatoes*).

Game patty.

Asparagus.

Plum Pudding.

Peaches.   _____   Strawberries.

Tea.   Biscuits.

All these things, except the rice eaten with the curry,
came out of tins, and the plum-pudding and asparagus
were especially good.

   All merchants on the coast do not live thus ; it is only
among the English trading-houses that the employers
feed their employés so well.   On the other hand, it is with
sorrow to be confessed that amongst the English traders
insobriety still lingers, although latterly this evil has been
successfully combated by the generous supply of good
aërated drinks, and light German beer.   In Africa alcohol
is less needed than anywhere else, and it is *good nourishing
food* that is required to restore the impoverished blood, not
fiery, fever-giving drinks.   The mental depression con-
sequent on the enervating climate is more healthily
dispersed by interesting and entertaining literature,

especially when this is enjoyed together with a cup of fragrant coffee, than by the continual glasses of grog, the "nips" of brandy, the "gins and bitters," the "mata-bichos," and "chin-chins," which, to react on the deadening senses, have to be continually increased in alcoholic strength. If, as one who has visited most parts of the West African Coast, from the Gambia to Mossâmedes, and enjoyed hospitality from many of the great African trading companies, I might give a word of advice to their managers in Europe: I would say, "Send out plenty of books. Remember that the mind in Africa runs more risk of being starved than the body, and that for those to whom the wonderful country in which they are residing does not itself seem a great book spread open for them to read by Mother Nature, the flagging spirits, the fatal home-sickness, and the dull depression of the brain are best diverted, not by constant sips of spirits, but by bright novels, by humorous essays, and by the fairy-tales of science that our current literature can so readily supply." Then, when the oil-lamp is lit, and the dusky African night is chased even from the windows by the bright reflections in the glass, the pale and languid European can forget the strange weird things outside—the marshes with their low, white, poisonous mist, the riotous "niggers" dancing round their fires, streaming and gleaming with perspiration, the great night-moths and the uncomely bats—in the beautiful creations and merry thoughts of our master-minds. In having chosen Kinsembo for the text of this disquisition I have not meant to imply that the worthy Englishmen there are more inclined to alcoholic consolation than elsewhere. Quite the contrary, in fact; and I am glad to say that it is for that reason a brighter place than many I know of farther north; but as it is one of the few great trading settlements that I encounter on my way to the Congo, I seize this opportunity of making known what, as an old African, I feel to be a distinct and easily remedied want amongst the English "factories" in West Africa—more books, less brandy.

Kinsembo is a flourishing place as regards trade, and has doubtless diverted much of the coffee, ivory, and india-rubber which should have come to Ambriz, for it was formed by the settlement of many trading houses who left Ambriz and Portuguese Africa in order to be free from import and export duties.

The different buildings of Kinsembo all stand on the summit of a range of high red cliffs, which end at the mouth of a little river in a long rocky point. This river, of course, has a sand bar, otherwise its mouth would form the harbour so sadly needed. As it is, both the landing and embarking of cargo is attended with considerable risk, as the breakers are almost more to be dreaded here than anywhere on the south-west coast. In the time of "calemma" (the Portuguese give this name to the great roll which every now and then comes across the Atlantic) the beach of Kinsembo is a grand sight to see—from the cliffs above. Wave after wave comes in like a race-horse, dashes itself on the beach, gathers itself up, and rolls back again to meet the one that follows. Sometimes these waves will come in one on top of the other, but generally it is every third wave which is the worst, and, after this giant billow has expended its force, there is an interval of comparative calm, in which the anxious boatmen strive to put off. Landing in a "calemma" is, I believe, less dangerous than putting out to sea. It is, however, a *mauvais quart d'heure,* full of suppressed excitement and anxiety. The great surf-boat, with neither bow nor stern so that it can go backwards or forwards at will, highly recurved at both ends, and like the crescent moon in shape, is steered by a man standing upright in the seaward end of the boat, and using as his rudder a long paddle. He approaches to within a certain distance from the shore, and then, after cautiously waiting his time, selects a big roller and rides in with irresistible speed on to the beach, where the boat is immediately seized by the rowers, who have jumped out, and hauled up out of reach ere the retreating wave can roll it back to destruction.

Kinsembo is not quite so barren as the Ambriz coast,

but vegetation is still very sparse. Hyphœne palms, however, make their appearance here as you approach this region from the south, and there are also strangely stunted baobabs (by some thought to be a different species) growing on the cliffs, and a coarse-looking convolvulus straggles over the sea-shore, intermixed with the Calabar bean.

The usual park-like scenery of the interior is some six miles distant from the sea coast. Kinsembo is one of the first points proceeding northwards from Angola, where the influence of the Congo region begins to be felt. The few native tribes more resemble the Ba-Kongo in their dialects than the neighbouring Ambundu people to the south.

The journey overland to Muséra, the next trading settlement, occupies about five hours' travelling on foot or in a hammock, but I spent some time longer on the way, as I stopped to sketch the curious pillar of Muséra, a great pointed stone, poised on a smooth slab of rock, and crowning the top of a small

Hyphœne Guineènsis.

eminence, from whence it is visible a long way off, both inland and out at sea. I cannot guess at the cause of this curious monolith, except that I think it improbable that it owes its origin and position to any act of man. There are many similar stones in different parts of the Lower Congo countries. There is a little vegetation at the base of the low hill on which the pillar stands, but it is the usual euphorbia and aloe mixture, and there is

no bush capable of affording shade, so I made my sketch
of the monolith as quickly as possible, and then hurried
on once more through the blazing sun. We passed by
many plantations of manioc, and emerged at last on the
sea-shore, where, sheltered by a few low jasmine bushes, I
halted for a short time to rest and refresh myself with a

PILLAR AT MUSÉRA.

frugal lunch; after which I started once more and reached
the Dutch factory * at Muséra in time for dinner.

The country round this settlement is much like Kinsembo in character. The same coarse grass, sparsely

* All the trading establishments on the West African Coast are
called "factories," more in the sense of the Portuguese word "feitoria,"
a place of business.

scattered bushes, and euphorbias; but here the rich vegetation of the interior is only three miles from the coast, and as the reader will notice, it is gradually approaching the sea, until at Cabeça da Cobra the last traces of desert influence will vanish and a tropical wealth of flora reassert its sway.

There are certain curious points in the phytography of South-Western Africa which are best shown in this accompanying map. I have endeavoured here to exhibit more clearly the distribution and comparative abundance of vegetation which may be observed in travelling over Western Tropical Africa, and more especially in the country lying between the river Cunéné and the Upper Congo. From Sierra Leone to the river Ogowé along the coast the one prevailing landscape is that of endless forest. This is, in fact, part of the forest region—the forest belt which has a distinctive fauna and flora, and which extends eastward, near the equator, more than half-way across Africa to Lake Victoria Nyanza and the western shores of Tanganika. This is the country of the anthropoid apes, which are found equally near Sierra Leone, and on the Wellé, and near the Upper Nile. But when the mouth of the Ogowé is passed, the forest begins to retreat from the coast,* and is gradually succeeded by more open savannah scenery, so characteristic of the major part of Africa, and so happily described by older travellers as "park-like," a designation which its open grassy spaces and formal groups of shady trees amply justify. Such is the country at Loango, Kabinda, and along the Lower Congo up to Stanley Pool. But a little to the south of the Congo embouchure the park-like scenery in its turn begins to retire from the sea, some-where about Cabeça da Cobra, a place I have already mentioned, and there follows a much uglier region of sparse vegetation and less abundant rainfall. Of such is the country around Loanda, where scarcely anything but euphorbias, baobabs, and aloes are growing, and where

* Except where it follows the courses of rivers.

there is often less than two months' rain in the year.
This harsh country continues along the coast for some
distance until about the 13th parallel, where it in its turn
trends off towards the interior, and absolute desert takes
its place and continues uninterruptedly as far as the
Orange River.   In a journey from Mossâmedes to the
river Cunéné, in 15°–16° S. latitude, you may successively
pass through these three last phases of scenery, and after
crossing a zone of absolute desert, enter a region of sparse
vegetation, and finally arrive at the beautiful undulating
country of scattered forest and grassy plains which only
reaches the sea as far north as the Congo mouth.   The
four districts I have just described may be said to vary
from almost absolute sterility to transcendent richness of
vegetation : perhaps the word sterility is hardly a true one,
as the desert soil is quite capable of producing ample
crops; it is merely the rainfall that is lacking.   The
sandy wastes between Mossâmedes and the Orange River
grow little but the strange *Welwitschia mirabilis* and a
few stunted *Bauhinias;* in the succeeding region the
euphorbias and aloes are the principal occupants of the
soil, with an occasional baobab, mimosa, or fig.   In the
park-like country the forest trees are too numerous and
varied to catalogue; but amongst them may be noticed
the beautiful Hyphœne palm, the oil-palm as far as 10° S.,
the cotton wood, the baobab, gigantic mimosas, figs, and a
variety of splendid trees belonging to the papilionaceous
order.   This is the most typical region of Africa, and it is
the country of the large game animals.   The rhinoceroses,
zebras, giraffes and many antelopes never enter the forest
belt that clothes so much of Western Africa, and which is
the grand climax of vegetable development where, with
ample space, continual rain, and an equatorial sun, plant-
life flourishes and rules supreme above the animal world.

There is a curious resemblance as regards sterility and
paucity of rainfall between the coasts of South-West
Africa, West Australia and Western South America.
They are all more or less of a desert character, whereas
Queensland, South-East Africa and Brazil are richly

endowed with vegetation. Further, it is an interesting fact, and one which can only be briefly noticed here, that in looking over a physical map of the world, one cannot fail to remark how, both north and south of the equator, the tropical is separated from the temperate zone by a more or less well-defined region of desert or barren steppe. The Sahara, the deserts of Syria, Arabia, Persia and Sinde ; the great desert of Gobi, and the barren wastes in China and Thibet separate the fertile regions of temperate Europe, Africa, and Asia from the zone of tropical rain, just as in North America, almost in the same latitudes, are salt plains, deserts, and the hideous lifeless tracts in Northern Mexico. South of the equator, we have in South America the desert of Atacama and the grassy steppes of the Gran Chaco, and of the northern states of the Argentine Republic ; the sterility of Central Australia, and finally, in South Africa, the Kalahari Desert which extends northwards to Mossâmedes, and makes its influence felt on the western coast line nearly to the vicinity of the Congo.

I rejoined the Dutch steamer at Muséra and proceeded to Ambrizéte, where there are many factories belonging to English, French, and Dutch companies. The inland scenery at about a mile from the coast is beautiful and park-like, though near the shore it is still a sandy tract with scanty vegetation. This soon yields to beautiful prairies, dotted with clumps of fine trees and radiant with many wild flowers, principally yellow ground orchids, white *Commelynæ*, and bright saffron-coloured convolvuli.

The *baobabs* (Adansonia) in the distance seem to be fine stout beech-trees in an English park, and their leaves are tender and green, just budding out under the October rains. From their branches, hanging straight down by a thread-like stalk, are the fair white blossoms with wax-like petals and a mass of feathery, filamentous stamens. These flowers soon drop, and their snowy whiteness is tarnished with yellow stains and bruises as they lie in heaps at the foot of the swollen, gouty trunk. The " calabash," the large fruit that slightly resembles the outer husk of the cocoa-nut in shape, remains on the tree simultaneously with the freshly opened flowers, and looks much like a large bat, folded in its wings and hanging to the branches. Thirsty with my noonday wandering under the sparse shade that the half-open leaves afforded, I jumped at a calabash, dragged it down and broke it open. Then I took out the pinky-white pith and chewed it, finding therein a most pleasant, thirst-quenching acid. The monkeys are very fond of this pith; so much so that the fruit of the baobab is sometimes called monkey bread. *Adansonia digitata*, the "Imbundeiro" of the Portuguese, the tree generally known as "baobab" (through whence this name comes, I know not), ranges over all Africa between the Sahara and the Kalahari Desert, and an allied species is found in Australia. Roughly speaking, it is a huge mallow, and is rather a gigantic plant than a tree, for the interior of its great swollen trunk is all spongy pith and not firm wood.

The candelabra euphorbias, so common on the Angola coast, still linger on about Ambriz, although they are handsomer and glossier in this more favoured region, and have lost that dingy colour and distorted form that characterise them farther south.* The aloes are all in blossom, and their tall, orange-red flower-spikes make a very pretty point amid the yellow orchids and the yellow-green grass. The river at Ambrizéte is picturesque, its mangrove woods are exceptionally fine, and as the ground rises to some height inland a fine view of the stream may be obtained as it meanders sluggishly through massive groves. On the snags by the water-side many aquatic birds are perched, and up the steep river banks there is plenty of greenery amid which stand out, like hawthorn in May, the snowy sprays of jasmine flowers which fill the air with such a balmy perfume. In the shallow pools and marshes are "mud-fish."† I notice them here for the first time so far south.

---

* The candelabra euphorbia (*Euphorbia candelabrum*) is never found farther northward on the south-west coast, or anywhere on the Congo.   † *Anophthalmus*.

The Ambrizéte River (which is properly called Nbrish) has rather a long course, and rises some little distance south-east of São Salvador on a plateau 2500 feet high, whence it descends in magnificent cascades, called the "Arthington Falls," into the plain below, and wends a tortuous way to the sea. Its upper waters were first visited and described by one of the Baptist missionaries from São Salvador, and he named its falls after a well-known English philanthropist.

As Ambriz is the great coffee port, so Ambrizéte is the outlet for the ivory trade, and has been for many years. As the reader will see farther on, the ivory road starts from Stanley Pool, passes through São Salvador and debouches at Ambrizéte. From Ambrizéte, or some neighbouring settlement, the pine-apple has been introduced along the trade routes far into the interior of the southern Congo region, and it is probable that limes, oranges, maize, sugarcane, manioc, and many other recent additions to native agriculture originally started from here, where the Portuguese traders brought them from Brazil, and, following the arterial trade routes, quickly overran these hitherto poorly-fed countries.

The natives of Ambrizéte are very turbulent,* and decidedly opposed to any idea of annexation or protection by a European power.† For this reason no white man is allowed to penetrate more than a few miles into the interior from Ambrizéte, and scientific explorations are indistinguishable in their eyes from political reconnaissances. In this way the region lying between São Salvador and the coast, vaguely named Ngoje, remains a terra incognita to Europeans. Wending my way northwards from Ambrizéte I touched at different spots where factories were established, but none of them offered anything worthy of note until I reached a small settlement about fifty miles south of the Congo, called Cabeça da Cobra (the "head of the snake"). This to my long-starved

---

* This is the opinion of the white traders, but the natives might say, on their side, that they only stood up for their independence.

† They have since (1885) accepted Portuguese rule.

eyes seemed a charming place. At last the hideous influence of the south coast was over, and a rich and varied vegetation grew down to the very waves.

There was a stretch of low-lying land about a mile or less in width, immediately next the sea, overgrown with dense bush, and, in fact, a sort of natural botanical garden with many specimens of the African flora displayed with prodigal abundance. There were groups of umbrageous trees (some of them handsome species of papilionaceæ with violet laburnum-like blossoms*) offering a welcome and unaccustomed shade, where, seated amidst a trellis-work of creepers on a dry carpet of fallen leaves and fading blossoms, you could dreamingly inhale the strong fragrant perfume which the ardent sun drew from the clustering jasmine that thrust itself into these pleasant arbours. There are apparently two species of jasmine growing here ; one has a somewhat pinky flower with shiny leaves and thorny stem, is very common throughout Angola,† and grows independently in large bushes, and the other has a much larger, pure-white, and stephanotis-like blossom, is without thorns, and seemingly a creeper in its habits,‡ clambering high up over the trees, and raining down its lovely star-like flowers in long trailing sprays.

In the background behind all this greenery the land abruptly rises, and seems to be a row of ancient cliffs from which the sea has retreated and whence the rain has washed down the loose surface soil that forms this verdant garden of the undercliff. Their summits are bare and worn from the constant denudation, but about half a mile inland a rich vegetation once more takes possession of the soil.

The natives in the neighbourhood of Cabeça da Cobra

---

* *Lonchocarpus* sp. inc. In some glades of the woods the ground beneath these trees was covered with a pinky-mauve sheet of their fallen flowers.

† I have never seen this jasmine (*Corissa* sp.) farther north on the Congo.

‡ Probably *Jasminum auriculatum*.

are *Ashirongo*,* a degraded tribe, with dull black skins and poor physical development, that extends to the Lower Congo as far as Boma, but principally inhabits the marshy country along its southern bank near the sea.

Some time before we reach the Congo the red cliffs, which are such a constant feature in the South-West African coast, sink lower and lower, and give place at length to mighty mangrove swamps of considerable extent. Then the sea becomes coloured by the sediment of the river, and the contrast is sharply marked where the cloudy river water meets the clear sea. The colour of the Congo water is dark-brownish red, and that of the sea transparent green; the temperature of the two waters is also different—that of the Congo registering 83° Fahrenheit, and the sea water 74°, a difference of nine degrees.

The mouth of the Congo is comparatively simple and undivided when compared with the great deltas of the Nile, the Niger, and the Zambezi. In fact, this is one of the first impressions which gives an air of "newness" to the river, and suggests that its present outlet into the Atlantic Ocean may not be of very ancient date. That the Congo in many directions is trying to force its way to the sea by means of smaller branches I am inclined to believe, as many of its so-called "creeks" between Boma and the sea, though at present remaining blind alleys, yet have gained in length in the memory of the European settlers on the Lower Congo, and it is the opinion of some who know the country that the river may ultimately force a way to the sea at Kabinda by means of a branch outlet from Boma (the present "Crocodile" river behind the settlement). The aspect of the mouth of the Congo with its two opposite points of Padrão and Banana is rather curious. They seem like the last fragments of the ancient coast-line through which the river has broken. Point Padrão is a spit of marshy land covered with splendid forest and fringed with breakwaters of mangrove and clumps of beautiful Fan palms.† Banana Point is a

---

* Possibly a corruption of *Ashikongo.*
† *Hyphœne Guineënsis.*

little peninsula of sand, which on one side is lashed by
the breakers of the Atlantic, and on the other meets the
brunt of the mighty Congo. Its existence is only saved
or prolonged by rows of stakes driven into the shore,
while the beach is raised and fortified by masses of large
stones. Why such an unmeaning name was given to this
sandy promontory by the Dutch, who first christened it, I
do not know ; certainly it is no longer applicable, for not
a banana is to be seen growing there. However, the name
sticks to it, and is known far and wide now, for Banana is
an important settlement, and is likely to become so in the
future development of the Congo, on account of being the
only good and safe harbour at its mouth. On this narrow
strip of land, where space is as valuable as in some civilized
cities, there are three separate factories of which that
belonging to the Dutch Company is by far the largest and
most important. On the ground occupied by this establishment many handsome palms are planted, to aid with
their roots in keeping the loose soil together. Where the
peninsula is joined to the mainland it is all overgrown
with giant mangroves and is very marshy in character,
being to all intents and purposes an island, for it is impossible to reach the high ground beyond, otherwise than
by water. On the inner side of the little promontory is a
deep and capacious inlet of the Congo, where there is
room for a whole navy to be moored. Here ships of
the greatest size can be anchored within fifty yards of
the shore.

The Dutch trading company of the Nieuwe Afri-
kaansche Handels Genootschap, occupies nearly half
Banana Point, and its site is healthy, for the narrowing
strip of land is swept by the sea breezes, and all the
washed-up refuse of the shore, together with the garbage
thrown out of the houses, is soon gobbled up by the scapulated crows. These useful birds are wisely protected at
Banana, and are in consequence very tame, assembling in
numbers on the sandy shore to demolish and consume all
putrefying matter that the land-crabs are too slow to eat.
The Dutch establishment is very large, and the white

CROWS ON THE BEACH AT BANANA.

employés are perhaps nearly forty in number. Kruboys, Krumanos, and Kabindas are used for all the ruder labour in the factories and steamers belonging to this company, and there are probably from three to four hundred of these "niggers" in the employ of the Dutch at Banana Point. There is a subtle distinction between *Kruboy* and *Kruman*, or, to use its Portuguese form, *Krumano*. The Kruboy comes from Sierra Leone * and the Liberian coast, and is much sought for throughout West Africa as an invaluable labourer well worthy of his hire. He is very independent and invariably returns home at the expiration of his term of service, and lives a rollicking life amongst his relatives before he re-engages. The "Kruman" is an artificial name given to the indigenous slaves of the country — men, for instance, of the Lower Congo tribes, that are sold by their chiefs to European merchants, who, in order to avoid shocking British susceptibilities, call them by the Portuguese rendering of Kruman (or Kruboy) — viz. Krumano. Then "Krumanos" are also obtained

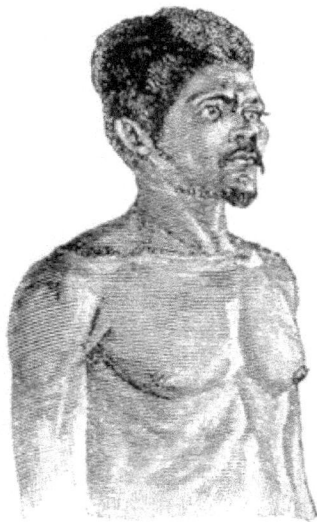

A " KRU-BOY."

by other means than payment. If a native in these countries steals from a white man, he is compelled to become his slave, unless his people are prepared to pay a large indemnity. Naturally, in nine cases out of ten, they do not care to do so, so the unhappy "nigger" who has been caught stealing a handful of tobacco or a piece of cloth (perhaps spread out as a bait) becomes the slave of the white man he has robbed. Such is the custom of the country, and one that seems to meet everybody's

* Those at Sierra Leone are rather a separate colony from the Kru country, which lies to the east of Liberia.

views just at present.   The native chief rules over a great
number of subjects, and can easily part with one or two
if " squared," and the white man stands greatly in need of
black servants—not independent freemen like Kruboys
or Kabindas, that will leave him to return to their own
country just as they are getting to know his ways ; but a
submissive slave that has no choice but to follow his

MANGROVE ROOTS AT BANANA.

master everywhere and remain with him always, knowing
well what he may expect if he runs away—and is caught.
Slavery certainly exists on the Lower Congo, as much as
it ever did ; * the only difference is that it is internal, so
to speak, and that owing to the vigilance of British

* This, of course, was written in 1883, and before the establishment of the Congo Free State. I let it stand as a picture of what
was.

cruisers and the absence of a lucrative market now-a-days, slaves are no longer exported from the Congo as in former days. And slavery will continue to exist, no matter under what name, as long as European merchants stand sorely in need of labour, and native chiefs are willing to "apprentice" or sell their superfluous subjects for an important consideration in gin, cloth, or guns. Any traveller who visits the factories on the Lower Congo— except perhaps in those belonging to the English—may see groups of slaves in chains who are so punished for having run away, and if he arrives at a time when a slave has just been recaptured—possibly by his own relatives, who have brought him cheerfully back, sure of a reward— he will have an apportunity of studying the application of the formidable cow-hide whips to the runaway's skin, and see the blood spirt from his well-flogged back. As a rule, I am bound to say the Krumanos are kindly treated. They are well fed, and have their wives and children often with them in their huts. If they were allowed to regain their liberty at the end of seven years of service, without being forced to renew their contract, there would not be so much harm in this system. The Portuguese method of government apprenticeship is one tolerably free from abuses, and would work well on the Congo.

CHAPTER II.

THE LOWER CONGO—BANANA POINT TO VIVI.

KISANGE—THE FOREST—*Lissochilus giganteus*—THE LAGOONS AND
THEIR INHABITANTS—A VEGETABLE VENICE—BIRDS—A NATIVE
VILLAGE—PETS—ANTELOPES—A CROCODILE ADVENTURE—PONTA
DA LENHA—THE RIVER FORMING ITS DELTA—BOMA—UNDER-
HILL—MUSUKA—HELL'S CAULDRON—A VISIT TO STANLEY—
BELGIQUE CREEK—VIVI—STANLEY AND THE NATIVES—THE
DINNER PARTY—ONE OF STANLEY'S STATIONS—LIFE AT VIVI.

EARLY in December 1882, I started to ascend the Congo
on a Dutch steamer, the *Moriaan*, and made my first halt
at Kisange, which is a small trading settlement some
twenty-one miles from the sea on the south bank of the
Congo, and admirably situated for a naturalist who wishes
to study the rich swampy region of the Lower Congo with
comparative ease and comfort. Here I spent three most
pleasant weeks, enjoying the kind hospitality of Senhor
Ribeiro at the Dutch factory. Indeed I have since re-
gretted the shortness of my stay, as there was such
abundant material for study, and at the same time so
many facilities for working in the midst of one's field of
research without undergoing privations or unnecessary
fatigue. Away from the temporary and feeble clearings
that the few commercial houses have made is grand
majestic forest towering up into the sky, and displaying
the most splendid effects which a rich and fantastic foliage,
a brilliant colouring of varied greens, and a weird architecture of contorted and massive trunks can produce.

Our adjectives are too puny to describe fitly the vegetation of such places as Kisange. We want to express
ourselves in the tongues of Central Africa, which have

Lissochilus giganteus.

sometimes seven different terms to express different kinds of forest. Beyond the actual inclosures of the factories here, there is a splendour of vegetable growth that defies an adequate rendering either with the brush or the pen. The hot sun and the oozy mud call into existence a plant life which must parallel in rank luxuriance and monstrous growth the forests of the coal measures, and reproduce for our eyes in these degenerate days somewhat of the majesty of the vegetable kingdom in bygone epochs.

In the marshy spots, down near the river shore, are masses of that splendid orchid, *Lissochilus giganteus*, a terrestrial species that shoots up often to the height of six feet from the ground, bearing such a head of red-mauve, golden-centred blossoms as scarcely any flower in the world can equal for beauty and delicacy of form. These orchids, with their light-green, spear-like leaves, and their tall swaying flower-stalks, grow in groups of forty and fifty together, often reflected in the shallow pools of stagnant water round their bases, and filling up the fore-ground of the high purple-green forest with a blaze of tender peach-like colour, upon which, I should have thought, no European could gaze unmoved. Yet the Portuguese merchants who lived among this loveliness scarcely regarded it, and laughed at the eagerness with which I gathered and painted this " capim "—this mere grass or reed, as they call it.

Clumps of a dwarf palm, *Phœnix spinosa*, which bears a just-eatable starveling date, hedge in these beautiful orchids from the wash of the river, and seem a sort of water-mark that the tides rarely pass : but the water often leaks through the mud and vegetable barrier, and forms inside the ring of dwarf palms many little quiet lagoons, not necessarily unhealthy, for the water is changed and stirred by each recurring tide ; and in these lagoons bordered by orchids and tall bushes, with large spatulate leaves, and white shining bracts about their flower-stalks,* by pandanus, by waving oil-palms, and by mangrove trees

---

* *Mussænda.*

KISANGE FROM THE RIVER.

poised on their many feet, and telling out against the
shining sky with their lace-like tracery of leaves—in these
quiet stretches of still water are the homes and feeding-
grounds of myriad forms of life : of blue land-crabs, whose
burrows riddle the black soil ; of always alert and agitated
" mud-fish," * flapping and flopping through the ooze ; of
tiny amethystine red-beaked kingfishers ; of kingfishers
that are black and white, or large and grey and speckled ;
of white egrets, of the brown and stork-like *Scopus
umbretta ;* of spur-winged geese ; and of all-devouring
Gypohierax vultures. A rustling in the vegetation, and
a large varanus lizard slips into the water ; or on some
trampled bank a crocodile lies asleep in the warm sun,
with a fixed smirk hanging about his grim muzzle. These
lagoons are places seething with life—life that is ever
stirring, striving and active—and when you suddenly
arrive, slipping and splashing in the watery footholds, the
sudden silence that greets you is rather the frightened
expectant hush of a thousand apprehensive creatures.
Beyond the lagoons and this strip of mud and water, rises
an almost impenetrable barrier of forest, nearly impossible
to pass by land, but which is fortunately pierced by many
little arms or natural canals of the Congo that intersect it
and penetrate to the firm dry land beyond. As you paddle
gently in a native canoe through the watery alleys of this
vegetable Venice, the majestic trees firmly interlaced
above and overarching the canal, shrouding all in pale
green gloom, the glimpses and vistas that you get through
the forest reveal many beautiful forms of bird and insect
life. Barbets† with red foreheads and large notched bills
are sitting in stupid meditation on the twigs, giving a harsh
and mechanical squeak if the too near approach of the
canoe disturbs their reverie. Little African woodpeckers
are creeping up the branches, deftly turning round towards
the unseen side when they observe you ; large green
mantises or " praying insects " are chasing small flies with
their great pouncing forelegs, and every now and then a

---

* *Anophthalmus.* † *Pogonorhyncus œogaster.*

blue roller-bird snaps up a mantis in spite of its wonderful assimilation to its leafy surroundings. Farther into the forest, the canal, a blind alley of water, stops, the soil becomes solid and well raised, and a native path is discernible, leading through the now more park-like and formal clumps of forest to a distant village, whence the crowing of cocks and the occasional shouts of the inhabitants can be heard. But the birds do not lessen because we are approaching the abode of men. Out of the bosky trees little troops of black and white hornbills suddenly start and flap their loose irregular flight to another refuge. Violet plantain-eaters gleam out in their beauty from time to time : golden cuckoos, yellow-vented bulbuls,* green fruit pigeons, grey ; parrots, parrots that are grey and blue and yellow-shouldered, green love-birds, and a multitude of little waxbills, a medley of diverse and beautiful birds enliven this walk through the forest along

Pogonorhyncus œogaster.

the black peat path with their loud cries, their lovely plumage, and their rapid movements. In the native village, which I thus reach, buried in the forest that over-awes a stranger with its majesty, there are many indications of the neighbouring fauna. These riverine natives along the Lower Congo find it a profitable employment to capture and tame every possible kind of mammal, bird, and reptile, which they then bring down to the English

* *Pycnonotus.*

steamers or the merchants at Banana to sell. Here, in this village near Kisange are young mandrils with their little leaden-blue faces gazing at you wistfully from the doorway of some native hut. In neatly-made wicker-work cages constructed from the light pithy wood of the baobab, many birds are awaiting the departure of their captors for Banana. Here is a green parrot,* green with a few red splashes on the wings, something like—perhaps somewhat allied to—the Amazon parrot of South America. Number-less little "cordons-bleus," waxbills, and weaver birds, are twittering in their really pretty cages. A poor little *Galago* lemur sits, huddled and stupid, in his wicker prison, stunned by the bright daylight to which he is exposed. The sight of all these living things is too much for me ; and although I know how impossible it is to keep live creatures when you are travelling, I yield to the clamorous natives, and buy a cage of rare barbets (one of which is illustrated on p. 28), five in a charming little cage for a shilling, or at least for a shilling's worth of cloth at the neighbouring factory.

Kisange is very nearly an island,† being encircled by two arms of the Congo which only dry up occasionally in the dry season ; on the mainland, where the land is really firm, more game is present than on the islands and marshy banks of the river. Harnessed antelopes,‡ bush-bucks,§ *Cobus* and *Cephalophus* antelopes are found in certain quantities. Crocodiles are not so numerous here as towards Boma, where they become a positive pest. As an illustration of their boldness and rapacity, I will cite the following incident which has recently been reported to me from this part of the Congo. A Portuguese merchant was descending the river in his large native canoe. He was seated on a chair in the bow, and, as the canoe glided along, he noticed a large crocodile keeping up with it, and swimming under water. He paid but little attention to the creature's movements, merely noting its constant

---

* *Pæocephalus robustus.*
† Kisange in Kongo means "island."
‡ *Tragelaphus scriptus.* § *T. gratus.*

pursuit to the canoe-men, who laughed at its persistence. Suddenly, however, the crocodile sprang from the water and seizing the white man by the leg, nearly dragged him into the river. The Kabindas, who were paddling, intervened with great decision and presence of mind, and beat the crocodile about the head with their paddles so severely that he moderated his demands, and went off with a foot instead of the white man's whole body. The victim was taken to an English merchant of Ponta da Lenha, who is skilled in surgery, and who, I believe, saved the life of the crocodile's victim by skilful treatment. , This should teach travellers on the Congo not to welcome the companionship of crocodiles, but fire at them in and out of season. Hippopotami are not so frequently seen on this lower part of the river, but become more numerous as we approach Boma. The carnivora here are represented by civets, lovely little genet cats and leopards, whose claws are used to decorate the caps of the chiefs on the Lower Congo.

The next settlement of importance is Ponta da Lenha, where steamers call for supplies of wood-fuel (whence the name in Portuguese—"The Wood Point"). Ponta da Lenha, forty miles from the sea, and just out of the district of the mangrove swamps, offers little of interest or note save its fine orange trees, the only ones to be found on the lower river. This place is barely above the level of the stream, and the shore has to be protected with piles, as the Congo is eating Ponta da Lenha away. Only a little while ago, a French factory disappeared completely into the water, which now flows twenty feet above it. In the ordinary course of events this place would long ago have disappeared without the intervention of man ; for the Lower Congo seems to be widening its bed year by year, and even striking out new issues towards the sea— at present all of them blind alleys; but the Congo is so ambitious of having a delta, that I am sure he will ultimately attain what his older fellows in Africa, the Nile, the Niger, and the Zambezi already possess.

Boma, once, and that not long since, the limit of

European extension on the Congo, lies about eighty miles from the mouth of the river, and is the site of many "factories" and trading establishments belonging to the English, Dutch, French, Portuguese, and Belgians. There is also a flourishing Catholic Mission here. The river at and below Boma somewhat resembles the Congo at Stanley Pool in its great breadth, its many islands, and the numberless water-birds that haunt its banks. The sinister influence of the barren stony hills and straitened stream that marks the Cataract region is over, and Nature expands in richness and luxuriance. No villages are found near the river until Vivi is reached. There is, it is true, a sort of native town near Kisange, but it is chiefly used for trading purposes, and is almost abandoned in the rainy season. Boma is, perhaps, the most unhealthy place on the Congo. The heat is excessive, and behind the European houses lie great swamps and fetid marshes, which not only give rise to much fever, but breed the most terrible mosquitoes for size and bloodthirstiness that I have ever known. Fortunately, both my visits there, coming and going, were of short duration, and I hastened to leave a place which, whether from fancy or otherwise, seemed to me eminently disagreeable.*

Ascending the river towards Underhill, a settlement of the Baptist Mission on the south bank of the Congo about 110 miles from the sea, where I had been invited to pass a few days on my way to the interior, I noted the increasing asperity of the river scenery. The rounded grassy downs of Boma became abrupt and jagged hills with great red patches of bare earth, and little forest remaining in their stony clefts. The graceful Hyphœne palms with their fan-like fronds gradually decreased in numbers until they finally and completely disappeared. Meantime the river narrowed, and wound tortuously with many whirlpools and sunken rocks amid the stern pre-

---

* Now (1894) Boma has become the administrative capital of the Congo Free State, and draining and clearing have made it far healthier and more suited for the great capital it will some day become.—H. H. J.

cipitous hills, hills that were fast becoming mountains. I
touched at Musuka, a point of departure for São Salvador,
and Noki, a trading station on both sides of the river, and
finally arrived at "Underhill," the site of a large Baptist
Mission, a place known by the natives as Tundua.
"Underhill" stands a few miles from Vivi on the opposite
bank, and is situated amid really picturesque scenery.
The great river takes a broad bend opposite the station,
and is shut in on both sides by the towering hills, so that
it resembles nothing so much as a beautiful mountain
lake lying in a profound gorge, save that the whirling,
racing current shows you on reflection, that there must
be a great river harassed and exasperated by the many
obstacles that incessantly beset its hurried course towards
the sea.   Caught in this great bend, the river tearing
down from Vivi has to pass through a somewhat narrow
passage, and then hurls the whole of its stream against an
immense and imposing cliff that really seems a great
mountain side shorn in half.   It rises almost perpendicularly from the water, which so boils, and whirls, and
seethes, and eddies at its base, that this loop of the river
has been called by the Portuguese "Hell's Cauldron." The
intense red colour of the earth, where the cliff has been
scarped and bared by the rains, and its lurid reflections in
the streaks of smooth water ; the dark purple-green woods
that nestle in the sombre hollows of the hills—hills that
seem pitilessly to enclose the scene and forbid escape—
the unquiet water and the ghoul-like vultures, always
soaring in black and white relief against the dark-toned
background ; all these details render the grim name
singularly applicable, though the scene to which it has
been applied has a savage beauty about it that redeems
the gloom.
    The little mission-house was building when I first went
there, the principal element in its construction being, as
in most of the temporary houses on the Lower Congo,
what the Portuguese call "bordão," and the English
"bamboo," but which really is the strong shafts of the
full-grown fronds of *Phœnix spinosa*, a species of dwarf

palm, growing abundantly on the river between Boma and the sea, in the marshy districts and flat mud-banks that border the widening river. The skeleton of the house is first formed by a scaffolding of stout poles cut from among the saplings of the neighbouring forest, and in between these the "bamboo" rods are worked, and make an excellent and firm partition through the chinks of which the air can freely penetrate. Underhill is a pretty station, but so shut in by natural obstacles that it is difficult to explore much of the neighbourhood in the absence of any path over the stony hills, where the strong grass, growing often six feet high, does not conduce to a pleasant walk.

I was preparing to make a little journey along the south bank of the river, hoping ultimately to reach Stanley Pool, when on the eve of my departure the *Belgique,* a steamer belonging to the African International Association, called at Underhill, and the captain gave me a message from the chief of Vivi station, inviting me to come over to see Mr. Stanley, who had just returned from Europe. I deferred my intended departure for a day, and accompanied the captain of the *Belgique* on his way up stream to Vivi. Several times before, I had seen this vessel pass the mission and then disappear, as it were, into the very mountain side, for the entrance to "Hell's Cauldron" was strangely hidden, so that to the great wish I entertained of meeting Stanley in Africa, and discoursing with him there on African things was added a vague curiosity to see what was "round the corner" of this great gorge in the mountains. What I did see, on turning a bend in the straitened and harassed stream, here flowing between precipitous hills of a thousand feet, was Vivi, which, as it rose bright and glistening under the afternoon sun, its white houses crowning a great, gaunt cliff, and gleaming out in their brightness like some Eastern city on a fortress-hill, did, indeed, hardly look a peaceful settlement, but rather the stronghold of some river pirate and the store-house of his booty. The little steamer, fearful in those days of struggling to the foot of Vivi Hill, where the last

D

strong rush of water was difficult to stem, put into a little
creek—Belgique Creek as it is still called—and here we
landed, and walked through moist woods and dank ravines
to Vivi, the last part of the way being an arduous ascent
along a red clayey road. As we neared the station,
increasing numbers of people were seen, till, arriving in
the centre of the great oblong space round which the
houses stand, it was like assisting at some huge African
fair. Two hundred and eighty Zanzibaris had arrived the
day before, in addition to those that were already at the
station, and then there were "Kruboys," "Kabindas," and
many of the natives from the vicinity; for, in addition to
the already numerous arrivals, several important chiefs
with their crowds of followers had come to hold a palaver
of honour, a sort of afternoon call, on "Bula Matadi," * to
welcome him back to his work on the Congo. Here he
was, seated on his camp-chair, his pipe in his mouth, and
a semicircle of grinning kinglets squatting in front of him,
some of them smoking long-stemmed, little-bowled pipes
in complacent silence, and others putting many questions
to "Bula Matadi" as to his recent journey to Europe—to
"Mpūto," the land beyond the sea, as they call it—and
receiving his replies with expressions of incredulous
wonder, tapping their open mouths with their hands. I
paused involuntarily to look at this group, for Stanley had
not yet seen me approaching, and was unconscious of
observation. Perhaps he never posed better for his picture
than at that moment, as he sat benignly chatting and
smoking with the native chiefs, his face lighting up with
amusement at their naïve remarks, while the bearing of
his head still retained that somewhat proud carriage that
inspired these African chieftains with a real respect for
his wishes, and a desire to retain his friendship. Any one
observing Stanley at this moment could comprehend the
great influence he possesses over the native mind on the
Congo, and could realise how that influence must tend
toward peace wherever Stanley's fame has reached, for to

* Stanley's Congo name, "The Rock Breaker."

attack a friend of Stanley's seems to the natives scarcely less futile than attacking Stanley himself. Stanley turned suddenly as the chief of the station introduced me, and welcomed me in a thoroughly cordial manner; then dismissing the native chiefs, who had examined me curiously under the belief that I was " Bula Matadi's " son, he sent Dualla for some tea. Dualla was a handsome Somali lad, son of the chief of the police at Aden, and versed in many European and African languages. He had been Stanley's body-servant on the Congo since 1879.

On the first night of my arrival we were a larger party —some twenty-seven white men in all—than the ordinary dining-room would comfortably contain, so, as the night was brilliantly fine and still, the long dinner-table was spread in the open moonlight near the edge of the jagged cliff, and here we sat long after the meal was over, calmly enjoying the balmy night, and listening to Stanley's always vivid descriptions of past African experiences, enhanced in this case by such a splendid *mise en scène* to his discourse as Vivi, the dark mountains, the rushing river, and the quiet moonlight could lend. Vivi station* is about 360 feet above the sea, and a clear 270 feet above the Congo. The projecting mass of hill upon which the station is placed rises higher as it nears the river, and is almost inapproachable save from the inland side, or by means of a road winding up from the river bank. On the left of this precipitous hill a little stream, dashing in tiny cascades through a series of small chasms in the blue-grey rock, gives rise to some vegetation, and, indeed, rather picturesque hanging woods, and fertilises the large gardens and banana plantations that have been made in the valley. This stream is very nearly perennial, but in the dry season it occasionally fails, otherwise it may be looked upon as the water supply of Vivi, for its water is more agreeable to drink than that of the Congo, which, though perfectly wholesome, is charged with sandy sediment and has often

* Vivi is no longer in existence. It was found to be a very unhealthy place, and the river approach was very difficult. The settlement, therefore, was removed to the opposite bank at Matadi.—H. H. J.

a taste of weak tea. On the opposite side of Vivi Hill opens another valley, full of richly-hued green woods, rising and falling till they reach the distant rolling downs that rise above "Hell's Cauldron." Behind Vivi a huge mass of rock towers up into the sky, scantily covered with tufts of vegetation, and surmounted by great blocks of stone that look like the remains of a cairn or some Druidical temple.

To describe one of Mr. Stanley's stations is no very satisfactory task, for, by the time your description is printed and published, the place may be utterly transformed, and indeed, so quickly do things march now on the Congo that Vivi, the most stable of all the establishments, is probably no longer as I knew it.* However, in the beginning of 1883, the arrangement of the buildings was pretty much as follows. On the summit, and near the riverward edge of the cliff, was a flat and level platform, nearly artificial, and about eighty feet square. Here were placed several important houses. The principal one contained an upper story, with Mr. Stanley's bedroom, and on the ground-floor a large sitting-room, surrounded by amply filled book-shelves, the doctor's room and laboratory, the bed-room of the second in command, a "store," an office or bureau, and a gun-room. This house was going to be removed and rebuilt—or rather, an entirely new building was to be put in its place, as it was hot and badly adapted for the climate; the double walls did not seem to render it much cooler, and moreover, had become the home of a colony of abominable little bats, whose squeaking, both at dawn and sunset, was most fidgeting; perhaps, however, on account of the bats, mosquitoes were almost absent at Vivi, a great and appreciable relief to those who suffer from their venomous bites. The opposite building to "Stanley's House" was a large sort of one-storied barrack, containing a number of bedrooms for the white residents, and a large dining-room open on three sides to the air.

---

* Is no longer in existence, as I have already pointed out.—H. H. J.

VIVI FROM THE ISANGILA ROAD.

There were also on this upper plateau, which might be called the fashionable part of Vivi, an observatory, a shower-bath, a pigeon-house, and the usual domestic offices. From the verandah that runs along the shady side of Stanley's house a most beautiful view of the Lower Congo, with its woody islands, its swirling rapids, and noble downs may be obtained. Here, also, are placed many comfortable seats and chairs, and in the warm afternoon hours it is pleasant to rest here, half dreamily, with a nice book from the well-furnished library, and let one's eyes wander from its pages to the sun-steeped landscape below the hill. From this raised square two broad flights of steps lead down to an oblong space of ground with a long garden in the centre, round which are placed houses for white men, kitchens, stores, piggeries, fowl-houses, and finally, apart from all the rest, a powder magazine. Beyond these, and generally below, for the " white " part of Vivi occupies the summit of the hill, all the settlements and little tidy cabins of the Zanzibaris, the Krumen, and the Kabindas are placed, each race forming, as it were, a little colony by itself. This "native town" is scrupulously clean, and some of the little compounds belonging to the headmen, or to those whose married condition entitles them to a more excluded way of living, are really very pretty and bright, with their tiny plantations, and flocks of chickens and Muscovy ducks. In any direction, if you want to leave Vivi, you must go down. The prettiest walk lies towards the little brook. Thence, at sunrise and towards sunset, the women wend their way with their pitchers balanced on the head, to bring water for their households. Lower down the stream, near where the road to Isangila crosses it, is the washing-place where, under the shelter of a few well-placed umbrageous trees, the women spend the noon-time over the linen. It is here that all the gossip is exchanged among the coloured ladies ; and it is here that, if your " boy " obtains a few minutes' leave, he comes to revel in the scandal of black society.

Life at Vivi had a certain monotony, and one day

passed much like another, save that on Sundays no work
was done, and an air of decorous dulness pervaded everything.   When I stayed at Vivi it was generally to obtain
a temporary rest, and therefore I led principally an
indoor life and devoted myself to arranging the facts I
had already collected in divers expeditions.   My time
passed much as follows.   In the early morning, about six,
my Zanzibari servant would come into my room with a
tray of light breakfast—coffee, bread and butter, sardines,
&c.   I dallied over this meal with one of the hundred and
fifty books of the station library, and then sauntered out
in pyjamas to the shower-bath just outside the house, and
after refreshing myself with a good douche, I dressed
and took a walk to botanise or sketch.   At noon we all
met at breakfast—or lunch—which was laid on the long
table in the nearly open-air dining-room I have already
mentioned.   This meal generally began with soup, and
then there would follow roast meat and boiled, the flesh
of sheep, goat, pig, or an occasional antelope ; chicken,
cooked in different ways, curry, and all the most dazzling
show that tinned-meats could offer—not very brilliant or
toothsome these latter it must be owned—and I myself
always preferred plain roast goat, however tough, to the
insipid contents of a tin, notwithstanding the attractive
title it might bear in the *menu.*

Lisbon wine and Bordeaux were always on the table,
and occasionally beer.   Breakfast wound up with coffee
and biscuits, and the meal finished, every one separated
to pass away the hot hours of the day either in siesta or
reading beneath the cool verandah.   This was the silent
hour, when scarcely even a Zanzibari was seen stirring,
and where the European perspired tranquilly in pyjamas.
About four, afternoon tea was about, or afternoon coffee
or chocolate, as you preferred it.   It was generally made
separately for you by your own " boy," and either drunk
in one's own room, or enjoyed amid a group of gossipers
in the common sitting-room.   Then work began again in
earnest.   The pickaxes of the road-makers, the hammering
from the carpenter's shop, the cries of the Kruboys

THE LOWER CONGO SEEN FROM VIVI.

unloading cargo from a steamer, the jabbering of the natives come to traffic their products against the white man's cloth, beads, wire, and gin, all formed the busy turmoil that rose from the awaking station, and which continued till the sun was down, and the bell had sounded for cessation of work. Then the cooking fires of the Zanzibaris and the Kruboys twinkled in the dusky bush, and the dinner-table was laid for the white men, with the

ORCHIDS.

pleasant glow of lamplight reflected on the white cloth and the knives and forks, like a glimpse of far-off civilization. Every one expanded at dinner-time. The anxious chief forgot his anxieties; those who thought they were going to die of fever seemed at any rate resolved to die with a full stomach; the doctor rubbed his hands and looked hopeful; people who had been "distant" with one another during the day became cordial; and after the meal was over, and the cigars and wine were placed on the table, we would grow so interested in discussions as to the relative merits of the governments, the journals, and the theatres of our respective lands, that in our conversation we were completely transported back to Europe. So much so, that when we bade each other good-night, it gave quite a revulsion to our thoughts to leave the brightly-lighted dining-room, the laughing faces and the eager talk, and walk off to one's bedroom through the warm and scented African night, where the Southern Cross rose above that great rushing river, and where the deep silence was only broken at times by the cry of a night-bird or the yelp of a distant dog.

CHAPTER III.

PALABALA AND YELALA.

LEAVING Vivi for a time, I returned to Underhill, to
undertake the journey along the south bank of the river
for which I had made previous preparations, with the
intention, however, of returning to Mr. Stanley's station
should I not succeed in my enterprise. I intended, at any
rate, to visit the interesting native town of Palabala,
which lay about six miles from the Congo, due south from
Vivi. Having mustered my few carriers, most of them
the riff-raff of Boma, I left Underhill in the sultry noon-
time and toiled at first up a steep and stony hill, most
exasperating in character, where my feet slipped back at
every step off the sharp-edged stones. Then as the little
groups of Mission buildings vanished behind, shut out by
the brow of the hill, a fresh stretch of the river Congo,
rolling swiftly along through narrowing banks, came into
view, with Vivi rising high above its north bank, a crest
of white houses surmounting a scarped red cliff. The
road winding down from this eagle's nest to the riverside
was very distinctly seen. The stream of the Congo here,

according to Mr. Stanley's soundings, is of immense depth, ninety fathoms, and in the rainy season flows at the

Mussenda grandiflora.

rate of nine miles an hour; but to any one not knowing this, it is hard to believe that this river, 500 yards broad at most, is the same stream as the great Lualaba.

As one descends the valley, the river finally disappears

from view. It is flowing from the north, and Palabala lies
nearly due east. The path thither leads you through two
or three native villages of a comfortable and prosperous
appearance, and suggesting here and there by certain
cunning shifts and contrivances that their inhabitants are
not bereft of *savoir vivre.* There are well-cultured plots

HEN-HOUSE.

of maize and manioc, here and there a lime, and even an
orange tree (these latter rare), papaw trees, and the
beautiful passion-flower, which gives the fruit known as
maracujà or grenadilla, is carefully trained over a framework of sticks. Little beds of earth are being assiduously
hoed, and are marked out with geometrical accuracy by

means of the same device as our gardeners employ at
home, a tight string tied from peg to peg, only that in
this case a sort of bast or fibre is used instead of string.
There are clucking fowls with small chicks about them,
carefully housed in large hencoops made of withes and
grass to protect the chickens from their many enemies;
and for the hens to lay in, and the fowls to roost in at
night, neat little hen-houses are raised on posts, out of the
reach of snakes.

CONGO HOUSE.

In a rough sort of shanty, constructed principally of
overlaid palm-fronds, are the goats and the sheep (the
sheep are of the usual Central African stock, with short
hairy coats, supplemented in the ram by a splendid silky
mane from his chin to his stomach); and even, rarely, we
may see a black high-shouldered bullock stalled in a not
ill-fashioned manger made of the same material.

The houses are well and neatly built, generally raised a
foot above the ground on a platform of beaten earth.
There is first of all a framework of stout poles, one
very long pole forming the apex of the slanting and
wide-spreading roof, and on this is fixed a covering of
thin laths and dried grass. The roof extends some
feet beyond the body of the house, and in front is

prolonged to a sort of verandah, further supported by two extra poles, and susceptible of any modification, from being the shady space of a few feet where the inmates of the house pass most of their time, to becoming the great reception-place and palaver-ground of kings. Here, as we pass, the inhabitants of each house are nearly always assembled. The women look up from pounding palm-kernels and show all their teeth in a grin at the "mun-dele" (white man); the men, squatted in lazy ease, take their large-bowled pipes from their mouths and call out a salutation, generally "Mavimpi," whilst, irresolute be-tween the threshold and the interior, large-headed, round-eyed children mutely and distrustfully regard the white man, who must in their eyes as much embody some notion of uncanny bogeyism as the traditional black man does to English children.

Around each village there is a grove of bananas, or plantains, a perpetual source of food supply to their cultivators. Two sorts of fruit are principally eaten here; the plantain, which has no sweet taste, but is excellent roasted and eaten with butter, and the richly sweet banana.

The style of scenery on the road to Palabala is typical of the cataract region of the Congo, a succession of stony hills, covered with rough grass, and rich, fertile valleys with luxuriant forests and running streams in their depths. About midway to Palabala, you have to cross by means of a native ferry the river Mposo,* a rapid stream that rises near São Salvador, and flows into the Congo exactly opposite Vivi. Beyond this the road is all up hill and down dale, till at length we descry a fringe of forest which marks the site of Palabala, on the crest of a great hill, 1600 feet high. As I pass through the native village, the people cry out "Mundele, mundele," and several come forward and salute me with "'Morning," a contraction of "Good-morning," which they have learnt from the

---

* *Mposo* means buffalo. Many African rivers are named after animals.

E

missionaries. The missionary of the Livingstone Inland
Mission, who was resident at Palabala, gave me a kind
reception, and a welcome meal was soon prepared for
me by his orders. There were delicious fried bananas,
pounded pea-nut sauce with roast chicken, "palm-oil
chop," and many other native dishes, supplemented with
a few European accessories. After dinner I attended
prayers with the missionary in the school-house, where

MOUTH OF MPOSO RIVER.

an English lady, one of the members of the mission,
was residing. Here some twenty people were assembled,
principally boys. There was a little giggling at our
approach, otherwise they were well-behaved. The
missionary prayed in Fiote (the language of the Lower
Congo) and in English, and also read a chapter of the
Bible in the same tongues. The subject in Fiote was not
wisely chosen, being a wearisome record of Jewish wars,

where familiar-sounding Bible names were strangely mixed up with unintelligible Fiote. All the while the black congregation (swelled this evening by my five porters) sat stolidly unmoved, although the missionary strove to infuse as much interest as possible into his discourse. After this followed a Moody and Sankey hymn in Fiote, in which I felt anything but at home, and could only make semblance with my lips to be following. Finally, a short prayer finished up the whole, and then began a ceremony which the natives would not miss for the world. Each one came separately and shook hands with the lady, the missionary and myself, accompanying the shake-hands with a " goo'-night, Sir," applied indifferently to either sex. We also retired to our rooms, and although mine was rather damp (there was a fine crop of mushrooms—alas! not edible, and waving grass growing on my bedroom floor), I had a comfortable bed and slept well.

It was very humid and wet at Palabala. Every morning and evening a thick mist surrounded everything and rendered the place clammy and unhealthy. There are four kings or chieftains in this neighbourhood, Kongo-Mpaka, Nikiangila, Tantia, and a small boy, whose name I forget. Kongo-Mpaka is the head king, and only owes allegiance to the king of Congo at São Salvador. A little while ago one of the queens of this king of Congo made a sort of progress through his dominions, and was received with great respect at Palabala. The local dialect here is a very pure form of the Fiote (Fiote really means the " people," the " mass ") or " Congo " tongue, which has been studied by Europeans ever since the days of Brusciotto (1659), Proyart (1776), and Canecattim (1806). The Portuguese has largely influenced this tongue, as may be seen by the vocabulary; and perhaps at Palabala there are even more terms of that language in common use than farther north; nor is this to be wondered at, when we consider that Portugal has for four centuries exercised a dominating influence, religious and political, over these lands.

At Palabala the natives were, at the time of my visit, disposed to be impudent and even aggressive towards white men, but during the last few months of my stay on the Congo, they modified their tone, owing to their commercial relations with Mr. Stanley's expedition.

They are very superstitious, and for every person that dies somebody is made "ndoki" (or "devil possessed"), and has to take the *casca* poison.* This is usually administered in such a way as to be merely a strong emetic, under the idea that the victim may "bring up" the devil, and cast him out with his bile. They think a great deal of their "*Nkimba*," and on the south bank of the river, where Mr. Stanley's influence is not as yet so firmly established as in the neighbourhood of Vivi, it is dangerous for a white man to offend these fanatics, who will severely beat him (as they did a young member of the Livingstone Mission) with their long wands or staves in return for fancied slights. The Nkimba are in all probability males undergoing circumcision, and initiation into the rites of marriage. They may be of any age, boys of eleven or men of forty; but generally the "Nkimba-ship" is undergone by young men. A fuller description of their ceremonies and observances will be found in Chapter XVI.

The people of Palabala may be said to "patronise" Christianity, a religion which, in my opinion, they are in their present mental condition totally unfitted to understand. When the missionary holds a Sunday service in King Kongo-Mpaka's house, some twenty or thirty idlers look in, in a genial way, to see what is going on, much as we might be present at any of their ceremonies. They behave very well, and imitate, with that exact mimicry which only the negro possesses, all our gestures and actions, so that a hasty observer would conclude they

---

* This "Casca" poison is prepared from the thick, hard bark of a large tree, *Erythrophlœum Guineënse*, from 40 to 100 feet in height, belonging to the tribe *Dimorphandreæ*, sub-order *Cæsalpiniæ*, Nat. Ord. *Leguminosæ*. See Monteiro, 'Angola and River Congo,' vol. i. pp. 61–65; and Oliver, 'Flora of Tropical Africa,' vol. ii. pp. 320–321.

were really touched by the service. They kneel down with an *abandon* of devotion, clasp their hands, and say "Amen" with a deep ventral enthusiasm. The missionary, on the occasion that I accompanied him, gave a short sermon in Fiote, well expressed considering the little time he had been studying the language. The king constantly took up the end of some phrase, and repeated it with patronising interest after the missionary, just to show how he was attending, throwing meanwhile a furtive glance at his wives, who were not pursuing their avocations outside with sufficient diligence. A short prayer concluded the service, and when the king rose from his knees, he promptly demanded the loan of a hand-screw to effect some alteration in his new canoe.

Round Palabala the vegetation is very rich. There is beautiful forest in the valleys wherein pine-apples grow wild, and the bracken fern gives a familiar air to the undergrowth in the woodland glades. The *Cucurbitaceæ* are very noticeable here, particularly one species that has most gorgeous fruits; they are egg-shaped, about the size of a pear, and covered with prickles. The outside is the most brilliant orange colour; when ripe, the husk splits into four sections, displaying the interior where the black seeds are lying enveloped in pulp of the richest crimson hue I have ever seen in nature. The commonest birds round Palabala are the grey parrot, the Gypohierax vulture, and a small black hornbill.

In my journeys beyond this place I reached to the river Lūfū, but the extortions of the local chief, the difficulty of procuring food, and the untrustworthiness of my carriers, who were secretly in league with the natives, rendered any further progress along this inhospitable route inadvisable, especially as Mr. Stanley's road to the north of the river was open to me, where I should be perfectly free from the exactions of the native chiefs, and have merely the usual physical difficulties of ordinary African travelling to contend with. In fact, in the end of 1882, this road along the southern side of the Congo offered many obstructions which have since been removed.

The negro can only be ruled by gentle firmness, and the long-suffering missionaries are the worst people possible to deal with him. A "rule of love" he takes for a confession of weakness, and abuses it accordingly. When I had once entered Palabala, where the Livingstone missionaries have been patiently working for three years, I could not leave it, either to go backwards or forwards, until I had paid the rascally old king, Kongo-Mpaka, in the missionary's presence, a present of gin to the value of 25s. The missionary felt humiliated at having to interpret the king's demand, but it was a case of *force majeure*, and my kind host was powerless in the matter, having been so often exposed to forced contributions himself. However, this is all altered now.* Mr. Stanley's agents have recently made treaties with the chiefs at Palabala and in the neighbourhood, and as a result of their efforts the southern road now no longer offers the slightest difficulty to even a solitary traveller. I returned to Vivi on the first day of the New Year, 1883, and was in time to participate in a very enjoyable dinner which celebrated the Jour de l'An. The succeeding week was occupied in making various excursions and in preparing for my great journey up the river, which was to take place with the help, and under the auspices of Mr. Stanley's expedition. Amongst the various shorter trips, however, which I made at different times to places in the neighbourhood of Vivi, was a visit to the celebrated Falls of Yelala, the greatest and first-known rapids of the Congo, which I will here describe because of their natural sequence to the country already treated of, although I did not actually see them until my return from the upper river.

The Falls of Yelala are only some nine miles from Vivi as the crow flies, but by the winding road it is a distance of thirteen or fourteen. I started amid the morning mists that marked the commencement of the dry season. The

* Still more so in 1892, when the people are semi-civilized, quiet and contented under Congo Free State rule.—H. H. J.

overarching grass, rank and high with the previous rainy-season's growth, was most fatiguing and difficult to pass through, and before I halted at the pleasant little village of *Nguvi Mpanda,* I was cut and scratched and slashed to such an exasperating degree that I was quite out of temper, the more so as myriads of little barbed seeds had crept down the back of my neck, and were pricking me at every motion of my body. At Nguvi Mpanda a few

CHIEF OF NGUVI MPANDA.

minutes of welcome rest in the verandah of the chief's house, and long copious drinks of creamy, frothing " palm-wine " just drawn from the tree,* restored me to equanimity, and I was enabled to reciprocate the profession of brotherhood on the part of the amiable chief with like effusion. He had not yet wearied of a whistle I had given him on a previous visit, and used it with unnecessary frequency to enforce his commands. I ought to remark,

---

* In this case, *Elaïs Guineënsis,* the oil-palm, but the sap of other palms, as will be seen farther on, is used as a beverage.

en passant, that the palm-wine was served in a silver-gilt jug, and drank out of a silver-gilt goblet. This will give you an idea of how civilization is acting upon Nguvi Mpanda.

The path leading to Yelala branched off from the Isangila road a short distance beyond this village. For some half mile we wandered through plantations of sweet potatoes and ground-nuts, and then emerging from the thick vegetation, stood on the brow of a great hill, from which an astonishing sweep of view was commanded. We looked right across a wide expanse of rolling grassy down and winding valleys, at a colossal mass of rising-ground, surmounted by a fringe of dark trees, where lay the distant village of Yelala. To the right bold ranges of hills on the other bank of the invisible Congo, and to the left more hills from whence the little river Loa takes its rise. The humpy valley at my feet seemed a long basin of dish-like shape, shut in by these many mountains. I call it a "humpy" valley, because it was very unequal in surface. Little hummocks or hillocks broke up its uniformity, and it was dotted and strewn with blocks of white quartz, which seemed as if they had been recently washed out of the crumbling hillside by the heavy rains. A grand view for space and aerial effect it was, and one moreover singularly characteristic of this part of the Congo; but withal ugly, inhospitable, and tame. All alike, hills and valleys were clothed with waving yellow-green grass, the monotony only broken by the intrusive blocks of quartz. Save in one or two sheltered valleys, where a few pitiful oil-palms clustered, not a tree was to be seen; and the little gnarled bushes here and there to be found were almost covered with the tall, feathery grass that was emphatically the king of the country. The only signs of animal life were very large grasshoppers, with green bodies and scarlet wings, that whirred across the path in a blaze of scarlet, and then settled down on some grass stalk and relapsed into a monotony of green. The country was not lacking in water, fortunately, and our immoderate thirst, after scrambling down the rocky hillside, was amply quenched in the cool limpid water that flowed through every valley and ravine.

It was with great relief that we left this country of grass and rocks behind us, and entered the village of Kaï, which was embosomed in rich vegetation. Here we paused to drink more palm-wine, for the thirst engendered by the terrible scramble over loose stones and through the rasping grass was overpowering, and fortunate we were to be able to quench it with freshly-drawn "malafu" (the sap of the palm tree), which, to my thinking, is nowhere so delicious as in the environs of Vivi. Good palm-wine resembles strong sweet cider, and is quite as heady.

Kaï is little more than a suburb of Yelala village, and the short distance between the two is filled up with plantations and banana

Dracæna Sapochinowki.

groves. The rich and rank vegetation that surrounds the neatly-built houses is most amazing, compared with the barrenness outside. I saw some remarkably fine clumps of euphorbias * as I entered the village of

* *Euphorbia hermentiana.*

Yelala, and further on, some handsome *Dracænas,* or
dragon trees, in full blossom, with graceful sprays of
small cream-coloured flowers depending from among the
spikey leaves, the general aspect of the plant recalling
the Yuccas, to which it is distantly allied. It is the
first and only time that I remember to have seen this
Dracæna on the Congo, and it seems curious to find it
preserved thus in a village. Indeed, it is an interesting
fact that so many plants should be found growing in the
villages in this part of Africa, which are never to be seen
in the open. The euphorbias, for instance, I have never
seen in a wild state, so to speak, but they exist in all the
villages on or near the Congo from Yelala to Bolobo.
Their native name in Congo is " Ndiza," but although they
are known and named, I never could ascertain that any
superstitious value or importance was attached to them
which would serve to explain their constant presence in
native towns ; perhaps the real solution of this fact, as also
of the presence of large trees and luxuriant vegetation
round the villages, is that all the uninhabited country is
periodically set on fire by the natives, and that only in
those places which the bush-fires do not reach can rich
vegetation and forest trees exist. It is evident—and,
indeed, the fact has struck Stanley, Schweinfurth, and
most observant African travellers—that the grass fires
must largely affect the "phytography" of Africa.

The chief of Yelala I discovered by chance in the act of
performing a very hasty toilet in my honour. He was
wrapping a piece of velvet round his loins, in exchange for
the dirty cloth that was his every-day dress. He added
to this a long livery-coat, which must have been splendid
in the days when it retained all its buttons, and then,
issuing from his palisaded hut, he greeted me most politely.
His name, he told me, was Ntété Mbongo, and he was
chief of Yelala, of Kaï, and of three other villages with
very long names that I forget. A long, conical shaped
head, like an Aztec ; a pair of very fine expressive eyes,

* *Dracæna Supchinowki.*

surmounted by strongly-marked eyebrows, a well-shaped
nose, and thin lips, made up an original and certainly
distinguished physiognomy; and though there were at
times passing glimpses of expression that suggested cruelty
and greed, they were dispersed by an unusually pleasant
smile for an African chief. After the usual exchange of
" Mbote, mbote " (the common salutation of the Congo),
and the inspection of my tent and my bed, the chief called
to his little son, who came running up with a splendid
fish laid upon a banana leaf. It was freshly caught, and the
bloom of life still hovered about its pinky scales. This,
and a basket of eggs, was the chief's present; and, as I
was very hungry, and had not tasted fish for many weeks,
the gift was welcome. The fish, indeed, was delicious,
tasting and looking much like salmon, and there was so
much flesh on it that I had, first, fish-soup, then boiled-fish
with egg-sauce, and then fish cutlets fried in butter, and
then, after I had thoroughly dined off him, there still
remained sufficient to satisfy the Zanzibaris. The next
morning, at an early hour, we started under the guidance
of the old chief to view the great Falls of Yelala—to view
them, not as my predecessors had mostly done, from the
summit of a high and distant hill, but to contemplate this
wonderful rush of water from so near a point that the
spray fell in fine showers over the waterproof I had
fortunately donned. The journey thither was very
fatiguing. At first the road led through plantations and
pleasant forest glades, but soon quitted this grateful
verdure and umbrageous foliage, and took us over a steep
and stony hill, where the rocks were disposed in ascents
which were almost stair-like, more resembling, however,
the sides of the pyramids, for each step was fitted for a
giant's leg to mount, being often three feet high. Faraji,
one of my Zanzibaris, hoisted me laboriously up each
successive block, while the agile old chief, having wisely
divested himself of his blue velvet, skipped up the steep
ascent like any goat. At length we reached the highest
point, and then—imagine my disappointment—instead of
looking sheer down on the river, as I had hoped, another

valley of waving grass, and yet another hillside, lay before
us. The descent was little less fatiguing than the climb
had been, for the legs grew weary and palsied with continual jumps of three feet from block to block. Then the
grass of the succeeding valley tore and scratched us, and
as I mounted the next, and what seemed the last, ascent,
I was convinced that the Falls of Yelala could never
reward me for such exertions.

However, we eventually ceased to ascend, and as the
path began to round the summit of the hill, we looked
down on an imposing scene, whilst the sudden turn in the
path brought to our ears a deafening roar of falling water.

It *was* a grand view, and the very position from which
we gazed on this scene was enough to render it more than
usually striking. The path hung just on the edge of a
conical hill, and here, where we paused, a great slab of
basalt jutted out over a terrible precipice. From this pro-
jection we looked down some hundred feet on the giant
Congo, leaping over the rocks and dashing itself wrath-
fully against the imprisoning hills. Several islands
bestrewed its stream, one especially remarkable from
being a mass of velvet woods. This was called the
" Island of Pelicans," for numbers of these great birds used
this inaccessible spot as a breeding-place.

Before the first fall took place the river came gliding on
so smoothly, with such a glassy surface, as if never sus-
pecting the terrible conflict before it, and when at first it
met the rocks and the descent it streamed over them
almost unresistingly until, exasperated by repeated checks,
in the last grand Fall of Yelala, it lashed itself into white
and roaring fury, and the sound of its anger deafened one's
ears, and the sight of its foam dazzled the eyes. I had
wished to pause long on this rock, and even make it the
limit of my journey, but the old chief, who was enterprising enough to personally conduct a party of Cook's
tourists (and who knows that he may not yet do so ?),
insisted on my completing the descent, and viewing the
falls from their banks. I really doubted whether I could
ever manage to do so without at any rate seriously

YELALA FALLS.

damaging myself in the perilous enterprise, or even tumbling headlong into the river; but somehow, by means of a rope and a stout rod, I managed at last to reach a ledge of rock, where the spray of the great waves fell, and thence I made my way to a series of little caverns in the wall of stone, whence I could view the Falls of Yelala at my ease.

In all probability the Congo never descends here more than twelve feet at a time, but the constant succession of falls and the obstructing rocks lash the water into a state of indescribable fury. It is a splendid race of waves. Some seem to outstrip the others, and every now and then the water rebounding from the descent meets the oncoming mass, and their contact sends a shoot of foam and clouds of spray into the air. The rocks near the water's edge are covered with a long, filamentous water-weed of intense verdure, and looking like masses of long, green hair. White *plumbago* and many bright flowers are growing in the interstices of the grey rocks, over which large blue and red lizards chase the flies that are half-stupidly basking in the sunlight. There is a great overhanging mass of rock which the shade never quite deserts, and where the native fishermen are frying the just-caught fish for their mid-day meal. The wicker-work fishing baskets and traps are lying about, emptied of their contents, of which such as are not being smoked or grilled are tied together in threes and fours, and put in the shade till their captors are ready to depart. Sometimes one finny monster, as big as a salmon, is lying apart by himself, still gasping with his poor expanding and contracting gills, as he lies in a death agony in the dry, hot air. Soon his red gills and his entrails will be torn out and thrown where other heaps of fish refuge are already lying—centres of attraction to the buzzing flies and the fly-hunting lizards, and an all-absorbing theme of contemplation to the hungry black and white vultures that perch irresolutely on the neighbouring rocks.

The chief, and most of the men who accompanied us, had stripped, and were bathing with much merriment and satisfaction in the little weirs and back-waters of the river.   After his bath the prince of Yelala went and sat on a cool ledge of rock under the overhanging grotto. Here he invited me to come and partake of an impromptu meal of grilled fish.   This I was in nowise loth to do ; so we got out some salt, and some young ears of green Indian corn, which the thoughtful Zanzibaris had brought with them, and ate a most appetising breakfast of roasted maize and grilled fish—fish that a few minutes before had been gasping in the wicker-traps, and that were now served to us with their tails in their mouths, precisely as whiting are at home.

When my sketches of the Falls were finished, I wished to return, and, in spite of the noonday sun, began to clamber up the rocks, and regain the mountain path leading to the village.   The old chief, wiser than I, tried hard to persuade me to rest by the cool river-side until evening ; but, somehow, a strange fit of obstinacy possessed me, and I ran a very near risk of getting sunstroke as a reward.   The fierce heat radiating from the rocks—which, indeed, were too hot to be touched without hurting the hand—and the exhausting toil up this succession of stone blocks were too much for me, and, by the time I reached the outskirts of the groves bordering the village, I threw myself down in the grateful shade utterly sick and faint. I only mention this unimportant fact to show you that some Africans are really susceptible of thoughtful kindness ; for, in this case, the old chief, seeing me exhausted and ill, became most concerned, and sent off one boy to the village to bring me some of his precious rum, and another to the nearest brook for a calabash of cold water. Whilst these messengers were absent, he cut a large banana leaf, and fanned me with it gently, looking all the time most sympathizing.   I revived long before the rum came, though unfortunately the old chief insisted on my taking a drain of this nauseous compound.   On my return to the village, he supported me carefully with one arm ; and altogether, though my slight indisposition was un-worthy all this attention on his part, the Chief of Yelala impressed me as a kind-hearted old man. I have met with so many incidents of genuine feeling and sympathy from the natives everywhere on the Congo, that I am sure they are people of finer natures than the degraded negroid coast tribes. That night, soon rested from my exertions at Yelala, I set off and walked back to Vivi, ten or eleven miles away; but this journey occasioned me no fatigue, for the sun was down, and the glorious full moon had uprisen in the soft grey air, shining upon hills, and rocks, and palms and native villages; while a feeling of absolute peace prevailed over all, and no noise was heard but the cry of the goat-suckers and the stealthy rustling of our footsteps in the herbage.

CHAPTER IV.

VIVI TO ISANGILA.

On January 7th, 1883, I left Vivi for Isangila, and Stanley Pool. Mr. Stanley was very ill with fever the day I started; but although he was burning and shivering alternately, he would not let me go forward without ascertaining that everything which could aid me in my journey had been placed at my disposal; perhaps the most valuable help he rendered me was to attach to my person, as escort, three of his favourite Zanzibaris, Faraji, Mafta yu Hali, and Imbono—and it will be long before I forget them, or cease to regret the almost affectionate service they bestowed on me.

Before I start once more in imagination on my long journey up the Congo, these three faithful servitors deserve a few words of individual description.

Mafta, you would at once call a thoroughly respectable person, and I was so soon impressed by his superior appearance that I made him head man of the caravan. He was perhaps approaching middle-age, and his well-made figure of moderate height was neatly dressed in white cloth. Though his face was nearly black, the features were well formed and very Arab-like. His eyes were quietly humorous, and though he rarely laughed,

CONGO GRASSES.

yet he could express much sedate merriment when his eyes twinkled and his white teeth gleamed in concert. The next one was Faraji, a young man in all the plenitude of physical development, a good-natured giant, with a power in his muscular form that his lazy intellect hardly wotted of. Then came one of those worthy characters, Imbono, who illustrated the proverb, "handsome is as handsome does," for his uncouthness was forgotten when you found what an untiring and never-grumbling worker he was. Mafta was a very religious Mahomedan, who never touched any fermented liquor and looked pained when his laxer companions did so. Both Faraji and Imbono, although nominally Moslem in faith, became sad backsliders on the Congo. They drank fermented palm-wine when they could get it, and became very forgetful of the hours of prayer. Laziness was Faraji's besetting sin, and he was a great framer of plausible excuses. Imbono had no fault as a servant, save that he was ugly.

Having assembled my sixteen porters, and sent them on in advance to the first camping-place, I bade my last good-byes, and turning my back on white houses and white faces, rapidly descended the red hill, crossed the little brook, mounted another hill, passed quickly through a native village, where the dogs and the people rushed out to salute us, and then, gasping with heat and exasperated by the stony ascent, I arrived on the top of a small mountain and paused inevitably to regain my breath. Thence we trudged along through high grass that very much circumscribed the view. It is terribly annoying that all-obscuring grass; one of the first and foremost of Africa's petty disagreeables. Some of this monstrous herbage scattered on us barbed seeds that were armed at one end by a sharp needle-point and surrounded with short reversed hairs, so that, once the seed entered the clothing it could only work inward and not backward. Soon our bodies were pricked and scratched and irritated by the sharp-pointed awns that had penetrated through the innermost clothing to the skin.

Nguvi Mpanda, the next village on the road, is surrounded, as are most Congo hamlets, by splendid forest trees and well-kept plantations. Before we entered it the path wound through many fields of manioc (which gives the edible root so largely consumed in these regions), and in these fields women, who are cleaning the weeds away with strongly made native hoes, look up and scream to one another, "Mundele, mundele," and disperse with shrieks of frightened laughter. The little wondering children forget to follow their mothers in their astonishment, and stand gazing at me, open-mouthed with awe, as I pass, but when I stop to pat, with kindly meant gesture, their little dolichocephalic shaven pates, their terror finds tongue, and they burst into prodigious roars of agonised fright, rushing with little pattering feet over the newly-tilled beds, never daring to look behind at the white bogey, nor to stop till they are in their mothers' protecting arms, where they are received with laughing sympathy. The chief of Nguvi Mpanda stops us as we pass his verandah, under which he sits smoking with the village notables, and proffers palm-wine with hospitable insistance; which I do not like to decline, so I hastily quaff the freshly drawn "malafu" from a narrow-necked gourd and then tramp on again behind the men through more plantations of manioc, ground-nuts, and Indian corn, till we arrive at another village, with another hospitable chief, this time wearing a very bushy beard and moustache. However, if we are to reach the river Loa that night, where the first camp is fixed, there is no time to dally on the road, so we hurry on, waving aside, with deprecating thanks, all offers of palm-wine which, as a beverage, palls with constant repetition. Then the winding path—winding for no apparent reason but the innate tendency of men to walk in curves—becomes disagreeably rocky, all sharp stones and sudden descents; then a little bit of marsh intervenes, and so we are in the valley of the Loa, or in the valleys, rather, for cañons and ravines intersect the hills in all directions.

It is not a beautiful country hereabouts. It looks seared and yellow on the hillsides, and spotted with un-

pleasant, scrubby little bushes, giving no shade, and
bearing unsightly, uneatable fruits. Along the little
stream, where I go to take a bath, through the tall rank
grass that borders the channel, buffaloes have passed and
browsed some few hours before, and left some traces of
their pasturing, the whole place being redolent of a farm-
yard smell. I undressed, and placed my clothes on the
stones. Oh! the woes of inexperience. All along the
road I had seen my men slapping themselves with leafy
branches to keep off the flies, but I, being clothed, felt no
inconvenience, and therefore drew no inference from their
actions. Now that I am naked myself, myriads of small
black flies settle on me, and raise little points of blood
wherever their needle-like probosces pierce the skin. My
bath is but a short one, and is, while it lasts, total im-
mersion, after which I hurriedly drag on my clothes, to
screen my smarting, itching skin. Black blood-sucking
flies, little creatures, smaller almost than a midge, are a
prominent annoyance in some parts of the "cataract"
region. They are not so noticeable either on the lower
river below the falls nor in the open forest country above
Stanley Pool. The first night, after an eight-mile walk
from Vivi, we camped above the little river Loa, in a
country that was somewhat harsh and stony, although in
the deep ravines there was thick forest. Here were
growing in abundance large, compact bushes of *Camoensia*,
a plant with a beautiful pendulous blossom of creamy-
white, with a golden centre, and the very delicate, un-
equally-shaped petals lined with a narrow bordering of
dark brown. Camoensia* is a member of the great
Leguminous or bean-like order of plants, but it has no very
near allies in Africa or elsewhere. It was first noted by
Welwitsch (the great German naturalist who so largely
contributed to our knowledge of South-West African
flora) in Angola, and he appropriately named so lovely
and tender a flower after the great poet of his adopted
country.† In the still, warm night, the clove-like odour

---

* *C. maxima*, in this case—see illustration, Chapter XII.

† Welwitsch was in the employ of the Portuguese Government.

of these flowers becomes almost overpowering, but there is nothing sickly nor narcotic in their perfume.

The next day I stopped to lunch in a large village, Sadika Banza, the last collection of habitations we should meet with on our route. It was a largish native town, divided into several great squares by hedges of euphorbia. The chief, although said to be somewhat cruel to his subjects—he is indeed suspected of keeping up human sacrifices—is immensely polite to Europeans, much resembling in this certain Eastern potentates who receive distinguished strangers with such hospitality that they feel obliged to overlook the sufferings of the potentates' own people.

The chief of Sadika Banza sent me eggs, bananas, and a fowl on my arrival. The fowl, a somewhat aged male, was not immediately needed, so he was tied by the leg to a tent-peg. While in this fettered condition, all the other village cocks took a mean advantage of him and advanced to battle. There would have been little left of my gift horse—certainly he was half-plucked—had I not intervened and carried him into my tent. Between this bird and myself a strange attachment arose. At first I deferred eating him because he was so tough and thin; then gradually he became a privileged pet, allowed to roost every night in my tent. During the daytime, when we were marching, he was tied up with the cooking-pots and carried on a Zanzibari's head, and directly the caravan stopped to rest, this Gallas Africanus was released, and trotted round the encampment, finding all sorts of inexpressibly delicious things in the thick grass, to which he lustily called the attention of a harem of phantom hens. In every village where we paused to rest he gave battle stoutly to the local chanticleers, and so identified himself with the honour of the expedition that when he was killed and half-eaten one evening by a tiger-cat, we felt we had lost a doughty champion. Sadika Banza is like nearly every Congo village, placed on a high hill, and the path which leads up to it is arched over and hidden by the immensely thick grass which grows ten and twelve feet high. The trial to one's patience occasioned by this terrible herbage is very great, and I am sure the grass produces more loss of temper, and causes consequently more nervous fever than anything in Africa. The act of continually pushing apart the intercrossed blades is alone very fatiguing to the arms, while the face is scratched and tickled by the seeds and awns, and the shins are bruised by constantly coming into contact with the stout, inflexible lower stalks. The grass effectually shuts out all prospects of one's surroundings, and harbours and conceals snakes, buffaloes, and hostile natives. I do not know a more despairing outlook than on arriving at the top of a hill in Africa to look down on a tract of waving grass. If it be a lake, you can either cross it in canoes or go round it ; or if you look forth on a sterile desert you feel you may hurry over its sterility and at least see your way before you. But grass ! How are you to know what dangers it does not veil ? Quagmires, pitfalls, human enemies, or noxious beasts ? Fortunately this part of the Congo region is not all grass ; the valleys are filled with fine forests, where you may walk pleasantly at midday in the cool, sweet shade, under the grandly overarching trees. And here it is that the African flora is best represented. On each side of the path are beautiful cannas, thickly growing, with their crimson flower-spikes and yellow-green leaves, telling out strongly against the dark purple-green foliage behind. In the interior of the wood may be discerned flecks of colour caused by the orange flowers of a species of *Jatropha*,* and by the delicate pinky-mauve blossoms of the *Amomum*. There are strange Arums and *Anonas* and many sprays of a scarlet *Mussænda*, which grows as a tall tree, and of a large white *Mussænda*, clematis-like, trailing over the bushes and undergrowth. Myriads of little blue *Commelynæ* deck the ground, and there are blue bean-flowers and white, purple *Emiliæ* and *Gynuræ*, mauve and white *Cleome*, and large yellow mallows, while for absolute gorgeousness nothing can

---

* *J. multifida.*

compare with the divers gourds and seed vessels of the many species of *Cucurbitaceæ*, which when ripe, split open to expose the crimson interior, where the black seeds are laid in tempting rows to invite the birds to assist in their distribution. Indeed the whole effect in floral colouring like this is to suggest a tremendous competition going on amongst the many plants for the favourable notice of birds and insects, as if the flowers were advertising their advantages, and saying to the bees, "Your patronage is earnestly solicited." Certainly every taste is consulted, and every bait is offered in the way of gaudy colour and attractive scent, and all to ensure the possession of large families of children, and to effect their dispersal about the world.

In tropical Africa, at least, is invalidated the theory of some naturalists, that the equatorial regions cannot offer flower-shows like those of the temperate zone.

As we near the little river Buzi, the forest comes to an end, and on the further side of that stream the country is harsh and stony. We camped out on the top of a small eminence, and were much troubled by horrible little black flies which settled in clouds on one's hands and face, and sucked blood until they fell off senseless.

The next day we reached the Bundi. This stream lies at the bottom of a very deep ravine, and though it is over thirty feet broad, it flows absolutely hidden under the magnificent forest that overshadows its tumultuous course. The descent and ascent of this ravine are extremely steep, and as the path lies through dank forest, and is on a clayey soil, the passage requires considerable care to avoid slipping and rolling head foremost into the river. Several of the carriers do come down now and again very sharply in a sitting posture, but as it is a point of honour not to let go their loads, no casualty happens to the luggage. As the river was swollen and extremely rapid, I crossed it on the shoulders of Faraji, who was supported both behind and before by the other two Zanzibaris, and beyond getting my feet wet, I reached the other side in perfect comfort.

Between the river Bundi and the Lulu lay a dismal
region. One might say, fancifully, that it was under the
enchantment of some ill-disposed wizard who had cast a
spell over everything; perhaps the evil genius of Africa
trying to discourage the penetration of white men into his
secrets. The grass is tall, sometimes eight and nine feet
high. When it is dry it cuts you like a razor. It slashes
you across the face and over the backs of your hands.
The blades intercross and bar your way like hostile sabres;
they insultingly whip off your helmet; they fetter your
legs and interlace themselves round your ankles; but,
like most African difficulties, they lose much of their
resisting power if boldly encountered. Squeeze your hat
on tightly, lower your head, put your hands in your
pockets, and charge through them, and they will yield
before you. But evidently the wicked genius, seeing this
does not deter us, calls another agent to his aid. About
midday, the sky being fairly serene, I notice near the
horizon little masses of blue-grey cloud, but, as they are
blowing away from us, I think them unworthy of attention; until my men, who better know the tokens of African
weather than I, look at them and say " rain," and although
I hope they may be wrong, gradually those little masses
of cloud creep round the horizon, lifting themselves up bit
by bit, and soon the whole heaven becomes covered with a
pall of awful black cloud. We have arrived at a little
camping-place under some shade, and here, in spite of my
ideas of the connection between trees and lightning, my
carriers advise me to stop. The rain had already begun
to hiss down, but fortunately my tent was soon pitched,
and my luggage brought under shelter. The ground,
however, was very dank, and oppressed by the gloomy
sky, I felt disposed to be miserable, especially as clouds of
horrible mosquitoes tormented me continually, and sadly
inflamed my hands with their bites. However, with that
adroitness which most uncivilised races possess of quickly
lighting a fire, my men had soon made a splendid and
comforting blaze out of the fragments of wet timber that
lay around, and I presently had water boiling and a

steaming hot cup of coffee ready. Then, when I had
hollowed out a round space in the centre of the tent, and
filled it with red-hot wood ashes, which diffused a grateful
sense of warmth and dryness, and at the same time routed
the many insects, and when my tent was firmly shut
against the rain, and I had sat down to drink my coffee
and read some old newspapers, my feeling of discontent
had completely vanished, and I passed a not unpleasant
evening writing and reading. It is thus, by taking a little
trouble to make oneself comfortable under unpromising
circumstances, that one may alleviate many African disagreeables, and avoid much ill-health.

But the next morning was prepared for us a still harder
trial. Each broad blade of grass was charged with huge
raindrops, and as we pushed through their interlacing
stems they showered on us a generous tribute of water.
In five minutes I was wet through, and with heavy clinging clothes had to pass on through the wet vegetation, the
water from the leaves "swishing" on me as I went.
Then followed worse still. The clayey path became interspersed with muddy pools, and soon it was a series of
black morasses, connected by an occasional isthmus.
Now, at last, the track frankly recognised the hypocrisy
of pretending to be a path at all, and for four miles re-
velled in a wide marsh. This I had to cross on the
shoulders of Faraji, who, if he had ever heard recited in
the cafés of Zanzibar the voyages of Sindbad the Sailor,
must have thought that I strongly resembled the "Old
Man of the Sea," by the firm way in which I clung to his
stout shoulders. However, he made little of his burden,
and strode and splashed on through water and mud and
sharp reeds, till at length, after the wearisome march,
came a little sandy tract, then clear water, and finally the
solid earth reasserted itself. The evil genius must evidently have regarded this as his severest trial, for the
water in parts reached to the chest of the tall Zanzibaris,
and the footing was slimy and treacherous. Perhaps he
was watching our difficulties under the form of one of
those weird, uncanny marsh-birds which ever and anon

rose from the stagnant ooze, and uttering a dismal cry, flapped its heavy-winged flight through the miasmatic air. It did not rain, but the atmosphere was charged with clammy moisture, and gloomy tiers of cloud shut out all glimpses of sunshine and brightness. When we at length reached firm land, the quaking marsh was exchanged for harsh rock and sharp-cutting stones. Nasty, ill-tempered looking little bushes, all gnarled and crooked with peevishness, and bearing lead-coloured, uneatable fruits, dotted the dull red soil. There was no sign of animated life—no birds or butterflies; all seemed deserted and lone. But the hour of our deliverance drew nigh; from a stony height by this time attained, I suddenly looked down on the river Lulu, which was rolling its brown flood through a beautiful and thickly-wooded ravine. We hastened towards it and were soon at its banks; but the sorcerer's power was not yet exhausted. The river was in full flood, and had swept away the rough suspension-bridge of lianas, which was used on occasions when the stepping-stones were covered. So I had to sit down and wait till the Zanzibaris arrived—for I always walked so quickly that I was invariably in advance of the caravan—and two of them carried me across the blood-red stream, charged with the red soil of the hills which the heavy rains of the preceding night had washed by many temporary rivulets into its swollen current. On the other side of the river Lulu every one seemed inclined to repose from their fatigues. The loads were all disposed round the camping-place, the tent was pitched, and the breakfast put in preparation. In the meantime the majority of the men went down to bathe. I took off my wet things and laid them on great boulders to dry, and also went to wash in the river. The water was refreshing and cool, but unfortunately the horrible little black flies were still here, and rendered any uncovering of one's person torture, for they settled in clouds on the naked skin, spotting it with little points of blood. After a good rest and an enjoyable meal, I started ahead once more with my Zanzibaris. The influence of the bad genius was clearly over, and that of the good fairy had begun. A different atmosphere reigned here. The lowering clouds were lifting and the genial sun was dispersing the general humidity. In the forest through which the little track or foot-wide path meanders, the universality of beauty fills me with quiet delight. Delicious, penetrating scents from the many flowers embalm the air ; the chirping of insects and the pleasant low cries of birds gently vibrate on the ear, and the eye is continually feasted with the displays of colour or the endless deploying of graceful forms. Looking up towards the sky, you see the cerulean blue chequered with a fantastic lace-work of leaves, and little specks and dapplings of sunlight are scattered lightly over the outer groups of foliage, but hesitate timidly before the great depths of solemn gloom in the heart of the forest. Much animal life is evident here. At almost every turning, the path introduces you brusquely to a happy family of monkeys, who have descended from the tree-tops to feed on the small ground-growing berries, or to plunge their greedy, wasteful fingers into the crimson pulp of the straying gourds. They bound up into the trees on your approach, taking refuge, well within gunshot, on large platforms and nests of twigs, which they seem to have constructed on the upper branches. It would be absolute brutality to take advantage of their confidence, and bring them down with a bullet from your Winchester, when you have plenty of provisions in your cases, and stand in no immediate need of roast monkey. Besides, if you are but discreet, and behave as becomes Nature's guest, your great hostess will show you many of her quaint and beautiful children. The green fruit-pigeons startle you in the trees with their strange cry, commencing with a whirring noise, two or three clucks, and ending up with a sweet and prolonged coo. The bee-eaters are swooping in eccentric circles on the many flying insects, and little hornbills sit in staid immobility on bare and exposed branches, watching the bee-eaters, as if they would like to imitate them, but felt that such great exertions were unbecoming. These hornbills, large or small, come to the ground to feed almost invariably, no doubt, because it is there that most of their food, such as grasshoppers and the exuviæ of animals, usually lies. Still they are a curious instance of an arboreal type of bird gradually becoming terrestrial again.

The great ground hornbill which is found pretty well all over Africa, except in the purely forest region, is a most exaggerated case, for it absolutely avoids the trees. Certain cuckoos, parrots, and woodpeckers become ground-loving birds in spite of their zygodactyle feet. I can imagine poor Dame Nature nearly losing her temper with, for instance, such a thing as a tree-duck. " Whatever," she must say, " made you take to living on trees when I had shaped and adapted your feet and your body for the water ? Why can't you know your own mind ? " But the tree-duck and the ground hornbills and parrots are influenced by the same cause that makes a man who has been brought up as a land surveyor qualify himself for the Stage—the struggle for existence, the necessity of finding a place somewhere in life's economy.

Some such thoughts as these beguile my way through many a mile of forest and hill, till at length, arriving on the Congo bank at Ngoma, my attention is effectually diverted to the imposing spectacle of the Ngoma Falls. The standpoint from which one best views them is a little platform or quay protected by a breakwater, and pro-jecting somewhat into the river. Here lately stood an immense mass of precipitous rock ; but Stanley, in opening a rapid route to Isangila, blasted the side of this cliff, and over the *débris* constructed a passable way. It was this that gained for him the name of Bula Matadi, or the stone-breaker, among the astonished natives. From this quay at Ngoma you command a splendid view. Nearly in front of you two branches of the Congo, separated by a long island, come rushing to a coalition, like two brothers whom a temporary obstacle has separated, or like two great political parties which, in view of the difficulties farther on, agree to coalesce, and carry off between them the lead that has hitherto been in the possession of a mild and temporising eddy. At the

end of the island, right across the river, are strewn hidden
rocks, but over these the two meeting currents leap
triumphantly, and the waves madly race with a joyous
clamour to their fraternal union. Some distance after the
junction, froth and roar are over, but a great and irresistible body sweeps on its course, letting no obstacle
stem its overwhelming tide. On the island the trees
bordering the water tremble and nod paralytically as the
great current strikes against them. but higher up the
foliage is massive, rich and majestic, and stands haughtily
unmoved by the racing flood beneath, like an unbending
aristocracy superciliously regarding the mad progress of
the democratic torrent that seems so far beneath it. But
the current, however madly, is flowing towards an end,
the Sea; and it either leaves the great trees far, far
behind it on its course, or, with cruel, overwhelming force
washes away their foundations, and carries them, poor
victims, to be dashed to pieces in the cataracts, and to
strew with their shorn fragments the distant shores where
the waves of river and sea may drift them.

The views of water, wood, and rock are so fine from
here, on this little quay, that in my imagination I see the
day when civilization shall have covered the Congo, and
when places like these will be the resort of tourists and
lovers of nature; when there shall be a railway from the
coast, a station a mile off, " Gare des Chutes de Ngoma,"
with omnibuses and touts—" Par ici, monsieur, pour
l'Hôtel du Beau Rivage;" "The Falls Inn, sir, very
comfortable, sir, splendid view," and so on. Then there
will be prospectuses and advertisements in the " Gazette
d'Isangila " and the " Congo Times." What embarrass-
ment one will naturally feel at having to choose between
the Falls Inn and its "twenty acres of tropical forest
attached," and the Hôtel du Beau Rivage with its billiards
and dancing casino!

As I left the spot where I was ruminating on these
possibilities, and entered the "twenty acres of tropical
forest attached," I could not escape a pang of regret at
the thought of the degradation and *banalité* that this

coming civilization would entail. How lovely the forest
looked in its virgin state ! Man had meddled with it
just enough to make a decent path, but no more. One
could look down, down, down through the mazes of green
leaves and grey boughs at the twinkling water, which
flowed under the massive trees in a still and quiet backwater. It was a beautiful semi-transparent screen between
me and the ardent sun, who, through the great and
spreading leaves, sent shafts of light and glorified whole
masses of foliage with an aureole of golden green. Up
above, in the dim purple solitudes of the forest, there were
mysterious possibilities, an endless field for conjecture and
for the flight of fancy. What strange creatures might not
live in its depths ? What sylvan tragedies went on there
at night, when the leopard made his descent on a family
of monkeys just asleep, and awakened the forest with a
momentary clamour. Perhaps, here at night you would
hear the great elephants tearing down saplings and
feeding themselves with juicy leaves and young shoots.
At any rate you know the vast green gloom stretches far,
far away in one direction, and that you will not come
suddenly upon a row of villas at the other end. And
when, satiated and filled with beauty, you do leave the
wood, it is quite comforting to continue your road along a
plain hillside which calls for no admiration. Beautiful
scenery is as overwhelming sometimes as the society of
very distinguished people—the incessant admiration it
calls for is fatiguing. We crossed a pretty little river,
and camped out that night on the rising-ground above it.
Everybody seemed contented and satisfied. I had a
well-cooked dinner, and sat long afterwards looking at
the southern constellations and the crescent moon. The
men chatted and sang round their fires in a happy state
of fulness, and I went to sleep that night convinced that
all the disagreeables of the journey were over, and that
to-morrow morning would see me comfortably settled at
Isangila. But on the morrow, alas ! the sky was lowering,
and soon after our departure the rain began. All the
pathways were turned into rushing brooks of red water ;

the descent towards the Congo became a terrible glissade
and soon I was thoroughly, hopelessly wet through as 1
half ran, half waded along the swampy paths, while a
continuous sheet of water acted on me like a shower-bath.
At last I turned a corner round the hillside I was descending, and there, conspicuous on a rising mound, was
the station of Isangila. The path changed into a broad
causeway, up which I walked, feeling, now that I was no
longer in the wilds, somewhat embarrassed by my dis-
reputable appearance. However it was absolutely necessary to change my clothes in order to avoid a rheumatic
attack, so I hastened to present myself to the chief of the
station, who fortunately would not wait for an explanation,
but hurried me off to a room, and busied himself so
effectively in serving out fresh garments, and in preparing a hot bath, that before many minutes were past, I
had quickly peeled off my soaked clothes, and had washed
and clothed myself in dry, if somewhat expansive, habili-
ments. I was seated at a comfortable repast, and drinking
endless cups of hot coffee as one by one my bedraggled
men came in, their burdens terribly soaked. I spent the
remainder of the day in learning the worst, but fortunately
although so unprotected my luggage had very little
suffered within. The rain, which had begun at six this
morning, lasted for twelve hours without intermission ; a
thoroughly hopeless, drenching, furious, persistent downpour, and not at all the violent, but fleeting thunder-
shower one imagines so characteristic of the tropics.

G

CHAPTER V.

ISANGILA TO MANYANGA.

The Isangila Fall—Position of the Villa ε—A Native Market—The Manioc—Cookery for Explorers—Ground-nut Oil—Toffee—Captain Tuckey's Expedition—Journey to Manyanga—Riverside Scenery—Islands—A Whirlpool—The Pratincoles —Mbote—Lieutenant Nilis—Disturbance at Manyanga—Different Mediums of Exchange—A Native Diet—Woman in Africa—Mlongo-Mlako—Ntombo Mataka Falls.

Isangila is a pleasantly situated station on a commanding bluff almost overhanging the river. From the terrace of the dwelling-house one of the grandest views on the Congo may be obtained. Right in front across the river there is a great towering cliff like that above "Hell's Cauldron," which I have previously described, a hill cloven in twain, its scarped sides showing the bare purple red earth; but its sombre look is relieved by the bright green grass that clothes the little knolls and irregularities varying its sheer descent towards the Congo, and the graceful crown of forest which lends a pretty finish to its somewhat gaunt head. At its base, the river, which has hitherto been gliding onwards with deceitful smoothness and a glassy surface, suddenly breaks into white foam and frothy waves, but only that part of it near the base of this cliff; the other half of the great river goes rolling on smooth and unruffled, still mirroring the clouds and the hills, till at length the whole stream takes one great bound over some hidden ledge of rocks, and the mass of this mighty current is lashed and churned into a terrible conflict of waves. Right across its breadth seethes a zone

of dazzling foam, and from the constant oncome and recoil
of the masses of water rise tall columns of spray into the
air, descending in glittering drops on the tree-covered

Baphia nitida.

islands, and forming under the sun's rays fitful gleams of
rainbow colours that at first seem hallucinations of the
eye. Below this great Isangila Fall (rapid is almost a
better word) the harassed river breaks away into many

little far-off bays of quiet water where it seems to dally
and rest amid the wooded islets, pausing to collect itself
for another rush towards the ocean. At this opportune
spot the river Lūfū, come from a great distance southwards, ventures timidly to join itself to the great Congo
stream, and fortunately finds it in a placid mood, smiling

FIRST ISANGILA FALL.

at the sky, and gently lapping the shores of its verdant
archipelago.

Isangila station is on a well chosen and healthy site, and
the beautiful views around it alone render it a pleasant
sojourn; but hitherto it has suffered some disadvantage
from being a long way off the native villages and markets,
which are situated at some little distance from the
river, and along the native roads in the interior. The fact
is, that from Stanley Pool to the coast the native trade—
or ivory—routes do not closely follow the river Congo
but rather diverge from it right and left, taking a more

direct route to the coast. The southern road goes from Stanley Pool to São Salvador and debouches on the sea at Ambriz and Ambrizéte; and the route along the northern side of the Congo runs also at a distance of several miles from the river's bank, and divides into two principal branches, one going from Manyanga to the river Niari-Kwilu and the sea, and the other rejoining the Congo at

SECOND ISANGILA FALL.

Boma. Consequently, the real village of Isangila is situated on this important trade route and at a distance of six or seven miles from the river. This renders it somewhat more difficult to procure plenty of fresh food from the markets; but by degrees the natives, never long in finding out where their best interests lie, are shifting their great weekly market nearer to the newly-found station.

One of these native markets is a curious and interesting sight to see. They are generally held every four or every

eight days, either weekly or fortnightly, for the native
week is of four days only.   One of the days of the week
often bears a distinctive name of "selling," or "market"
day.   The natives will often come a hundred miles to
attend one of these big markets, and there are generally
over a thousand present.   They bring sheep, goats, pigs,
Muscovy ducks, and fowls for sale or barter, the fowls
most carefully packed in long wicker cages, fastened
between two stout poles converging at each end.   Eggs are
usually carried in large finely-plaited baskets; indeed
some of their basket-work is so tightly made that it will
hold water.   At the markets between Isangila and
Manyanga five hundred eggs may be bought at a time.
The natives also sell fresh vegetables, pumpkins, sweet
potatoes, and even a wild cabbage, bananas, plantains,
pine-apples, ground-nuts, sugar-cane, maize, kola-nut
tobacco, and "Kikwanga."   Kikwanga needs a word of
special mention, it is such an important article of con-
sumption in the Congo dietary.   The root of the manioc,*
or cassada, a very ancient introduction from Brazil, is
taken and pounded into a fine white pulp.   This is left to
soak for about twenty-four hours in running water (possibly
to rid the substance of a certain acid poison attributed to
the root), and is then allowed to ferment.   When worked
up into a consistence of stiff dough it is divided into
portions, and each portion is wrapped up in a large green
leaf until wanted for cooking.   Kikwanga tastes and looks
like sour dough, but it is highly nutritious.   The best
way of eating it is to cut it into very thin slices, and to
fry these in butter, or if butter be not procurable, in
ground-nut oil, easily extracted from *Arachis hypogœa*.
Perhaps a simple receipt for doing so might interest
intending African travellers who are reading these pages.
Take a bushel of ripe ground-nuts that have previously
been dried in the sun, pound them to a pulp, and put
them in a cauldron of boiling water.   The oil will rise to
the surface, and can easily be skimmed off and put apart

* *Manihot utilissima.*

into a vessel. The residue is excellent fattening food for
fowls, and the oil itself is almost indistinguishable from
the best olive in taste. Indeed most of the olive-oil we
use in England *is* nothing but the oil of ground-nuts,
which are exported largely from West African ports to
Marseilles, to be there manufactured and flavoured into
various salad oils christened by different names. This oil
of ground-nuts is excellent as a kitchen grease and as a
lamp-oil. I will even give you another recipe in which
this substance may be advantageously employed. Take
a quantity of sugar-canes, some nine or ten sticks, peel
them, cut them up into small cubes, and mash these to
a pulp, straining off the abundant liquor into a large pot;
put this over the fire to boil, and at the end of an hour
and a half you will rejoice to find the sweet syrupy liquor
reduced to a considerable quantity of gluey barley-sugar.
If you find yourself as I did for several months without
any other form of saccharine matter, this will make a
useful addition to your daily fare, and when mixed and
cooked with the right proportion of ground-nut oil will
give you a most toothsome toffee. Little expedients and
shifts like these serve considerably to lighten the explorer's
lot, and to render palatable many forms of native food.

An African market with so many commodities to sell
and so many eager sellers and loungers, is a most animated scene. The din of voices may be heard afar off,
and when you enter the great open square, where, under
the shade of great trees, perhaps a thousand people are
disposed in little chaffering groups round their heaps of
wares, it is worse than the parrot-house at the Zoological
Gardens. The women are the keenest traders, they
haggle and scream and expostulate, and chuckle aside
over their bargains, whilst the hulking men lounge about
in good-humoured listlessness, or squat in rows stolidly
smoking. Although the strife of tongues is great, few
real quarrels occur. There is in most cases a chief of the
market, perhaps an old Fetish man, who regulates all
disputes, and who so heavily fines both litigants that all
are chary of provoking his arbitration. This babel lasts

but one day, and then for the rest of the "week" or "fortnight" the market-place is void and desolate; only the old wicker baskets, banana-skins, corn-shucks, feathers, and egg shells remain to witness to the great assemblage which has taken place. Of such a kind is the great market near Isangila, and there are similar gatherings at Manyanga, Lutété, and in proximity to most of Mr. Stanley's stations.

Before I leave the subject of Isangila to proceed with my description of the river, I might mention that this was almost the farthest point reached by Captain Tuckey's expedition, and was called by them "Sangalla." Some of them did, indeed, penetrate nearly as much farther as about where "Baynesville," a station of the Baptist mission, is situated, but the general researches of the expedition may be said to have been arrested at Isangila. Poor Captain Tuckey here thought that the greatest difficulties were vanquished, and imagined that the comparatively tranquil stream which he saw before him indicated the absence or unimportance of further cataracts. Had he not broken down and died at that time would he possibly have been able to struggle past the greater difficulties beyond, with a fiercer population opposing his advance? I think not, and his expedition appears from the very first, hopelessly and sadly foredoomed to those who read its records with the fuller knowledge of to-day.

The journey* to the next station, Manyanga, may be made by water, the rapids on this part of the Congo being just passable in a stout boat, or by land along the north bank of the river; but this route is most fatiguing, and occupies at least eight days, whereas by water it is only four or five. I left Isangila on January 16th with my three Zanzibaris, to go up this part of the Congo in a little steam-launch the *Royal*, now removed to the upper river, and forming part of Mr. Stanley's flotilla. The scenery along this section of the Congo is at first very pretty. A fine papilionaceous tree, *Baphia sp.*, was abun-

---

* A distance of about 86 English miles.

dant, and its blossom sent forth a delicious fragrance.
The banks were generally richly forested, and masses of
creepers overspread the riverside trees. Sometimes they
appeared like a green cloth thrown lightly over the
foliage, showing its masses and forms distinctly marked
underneath. Sometimes they formed a delicate green
cobwebbery, or seemed great walls of vegetation, looking
as if carefully trimmed into uniformity of surface, but
often scarcely a foot in thickness. I can hardly give a
just idea of these beautiful examples of vegetable architecture. Often these creepers would stretch out as it were
a fresh series of constructions, their long, straight lianas
acting as scaffold poles. Then would come the horizontal,
interlacing arms, which soon formed a giant lattice-work,
and on this foundation the beautiful and uniform foliage
breaks out, until soon great walls and enclosures are
made, generally round some monster tree. How lovely
these arbours seemed to rest in! What an idyllic life one
might fancy it possible to lead amid these fairy mazes like
tenderly veiled transformation scenes, where the brilliant,
glaring sky and its rudely positive white clouds are so
crossed and recrossed by the boughs and liana ropes that
the glory of daylight seems to shine afar off beyond the
meshes of our fairy realm, into which the sun's rays filter
through the leaf-masses in varying intensity of greenish
golden light. Beautiful indeed it is, where the monotony
of verdure is enlivened by the mauve convolvuli with
crimson centres, by the pale yellow flowers of the creeping
cucurbits, whose orange-red gourds shine like little lamps
amid the diapered foliage. The giant-speckled kingfisher
and his little active black and white brother haunt the
secluded creeks that these walls of upright vegetation
enclose; and on the gaunt, bare branches, forcing their
way through the tender interlacing creepers like wild
protesting arms trying to rid themselves of a clinging and
deceitful embrace, on these gnarled and whitened boughs
the fishing-eagles perch, greeting our approach with cheerful boisterous screams. A "giant" heron, too, sat on a
branch amid sombre shade, where he would have remained

quite undistinguishable from the grey boughs and boles around him, but overcome with a spasm of tardy fear, he flounced out from his retreat, nearly knocked against the funnel of the steamer, and flapped his huge wings with frightful strivings to get away.

Here and there the Congo became strewn with rocky islets, sparsely crested with trees; and in and out of these the stream was whirling and eddying and bubbling over the hidden rocks. We stopped at one of these islands, and at this spot the lighter we had been hitherto towing

THE GIANT KINGFISHER (*Ceryle maxima*).

had to be made fast alongside the steam-launch, for together we were to cross a formidable whirlpool. When we turned the island we saw the vortex with great flakes of foam like balls of cotton-wool dancing madly in a perpetual round. Full pressure was put on, and in we went —wurra!—and out again, almost at right angles, so that some of the balls of foam, like bewildered captives in an enchanter's magic circle, are set free by our sudden breaking through the meshes and go gaily floating down the stream.

Sometimes there are long stretches of low rocks in the river, looking like rows of slates stacked in a builder's yard; and on the shore of the stream and along the island beaches would show banks of dazzling white sand, apparently above flood-mark, since numbers of pratincoles had made their nest there. These pretty little birds, called scientifically *Glareola*,* are really small waders allied to the plovers, with, perhaps, even a far off relationship to pigeons and sand-grouse; but to a superficial observer they seem merely large, stout swallows, and certainly resemble these birds by the way in which they pursue the insects over the surface of the water, flying low and catching their prey in mid-flight. On the Congo, between Isangila and Manyanga, they are found in flocks of over a thousand at a time, absolutely covering the isolated rocks on which they perch.† Perhaps their presence in such large numbers is the reason why in this stretch of the river mosquitoes are so happily absent.

In the broader parts of the Congo, groups of trees stand in the very middle of the river, stemming its rapid flood. They must mark the sites of rocks and banks uncovered in the dry season, or, more probably, of newly submerged islands, for otherwise the seedling tree could hardly have attained sufficient growth in one dry season to withstand the river's flood. Some distance beyond the Itunzima Falls, which are not very striking, the Congo broadens greatly; but nearing Manyanga, the scenery of the river becomes in the highest degree commonplace. Low red hills, streaked and spotted with dull yellow-green, and fringed at their bases with scanty forest, border the great watercourse, which itself seems to have renounced all its high spirits and to have assumed a wearisome platitude of expression.

Groups of natives on the south bank are squatting on the sand, with their fishing-nets put up to dry. Their

---

* Probably *G. Nordmani*.

† In the 'Last Journal of W. A. Forbes,' whose death was one of the greatest losses British science has sustained (he died on the Niger, in January, 1883), I find the following extract referring to his journey up the Niger (p. 514, 'Ibis,' Oct. 1883). "On one of the banks, *Glareola cinerea* in *thousands*, with a few of a darker one (? *Nordmani*), one of which I got. . . ."

dogs are prick-eared and spotted yellow and white, exactly like those in a Noah's ark. They salute us with load cries of "Mbote," a frequent polite salutation pronounced in English, "Mbawtay"), which means "good," "well," "smoothly," and, in fact, all sorts of conciliatory things, and is commonly used along the Congo, between the coast and the Equator. "Mbote" is a most useful term to acquire, and only practice can teach the different meanings which varied modulations of the voice may give to it. On the Upper Congo, beyond the Pool, when entering a strange village, and seeing rather suspicious looks directed at my uncanny white face, I would say in inquiring tone "Mbote, Mbote?" and then the natives would either relax into a grin and repeat the word volubly, or in obstinate cases scowl more determinedly, and yell "Mbote ve, Mbote ve!" (ve, pronounced vay, means "No"). It can be made a very pretty word; and when a smiling native says to you rapidly, "Mbote, Mbote, Mbote," it is like patting you on the back, and is, indeed, often accompanied by that caressing action.

On the morning of the fifth day after leaving Isangila we arrived at Manyanga. This station is decidedly "a city set upon a hill," and people with weak lungs or unsteady hearts may well stand appalled at such an ascent as lies before them up that winding red road, nay, even hesitate as to whether they will not sooner seek hospitality at the snug little Baptist Mission which lies embosomed in trees by the water side. But generally the hospitable chief of Manyanga station descends from his eyrie to meet his guests, and aided by the stout alpenstock which is lent you, and beguiling the steep ascent with a pleasant interchange of question and answer, you forget to murmur at its steepness, and find yourself quite unexpectedly before the verandah of the principal dwelling-house.

I had pleasant days at Manyanga* whenever I stopped there. Its chief, Lieutenant Nilis, was a charming and an

---

* I believe this station no longer exists now, or has passed into the hands of the French, who acquired the north bank of the Congo from Manyanga to the Ubangi River.—H. H. J.

intellectual man, who knew how to make life at his station most agreeable for his guests.

To his initiative the entire present construction and arrangement of the buildings are due. There are three houses for Europeans, many capacious brick-built stores, and quite a large "coloured" town of Zanzibari, Kabinda, and other native huts. The making of sunburnt-bricks from the surrounding soil has turned out very successful, and the bricks thus made are better adapted for the construction of durable buildings than wood, which is so liable to the attacks of white ants, or stone which is both costly and damp-retaining.

Manyanga was the scene of the only serious disturbance which has as yet taken place between the expedition of Mr. Stanley and the natives. While the former was away at Stanley Pool, dragging his boats to the upper river, the numerous natives of this well-populated district picked a quarrel with the little garrison of the station in the hope of finding it an easy prey. The dispute is said to have first arisen in a "question de porcs." That is to say, that the natives complained that the pigs of the station played havoc with their fields of manioc and maize; perhaps they did, but the chief of the station (the predecessor of Nilis) was quite willing to indemnify the natives for any harm his pigs may have occasioned to their crops had they not taken the law into their own hands and carried off the pigs. It was, in fact, for them nothing but an excuse for a general plunder they had long been meditating; for we are no longer in the district of the "Congo" people proper —the gentle, indolent race of Vivi and Isangila—but in the country of the much fiercer and more energetic Basundi, the country of "Sundi" heard of by Tuckey, a tribe who long stood between the races of the interior Congo basin and the traders of the coast. However, they in this case found out their mistake. The besieged garrison sallied out with spirit, drove away the host of attacking natives, and burnt down their villages in reprisals. Then the natives, quickly recognising the only thing they bow to—superior force—came to terms, and paid a fine in land imposed on them as a war indemnity. Three months afterwards they were the best of friends with the white man, and were the first amongst the Congo tribes to furnish of their own free will hired porters to transport the goods of the expedition. Now Manyanga is so entrenched and fortified that probably none but a European army could capture it, and its communications with the Congo are so admirably arranged that the river acts as a continual basis of operations, whence supplies may always be obtained by steamer from Isangila.

Manyanga is built on a narrow plateau surmounting a precipitous hill of perhaps four hundred feet in height. There is a slight bay, or inlet, of the Congo at its base where boats can be safely moored in a little backwater of the Congo. On either side of the hill is a deep ravine with nearly precipitous sides, so that it is nearly impregnable on three sides, and only the narrow neck of the level plateau which connects with the hills of the interior has to be defended. Through the ravine on the right hand of the station tumbles a little stream of clear water, much haunted by crocodiles in its lower course. On the further side of the stream, at a much lower level than the station, is situated the Baptist Mission, very bright and pretty in outward appearance, embowered in fine groves and close to a charming little creek of the river, but for all this unhealthy, I believe. It is one of the few places where I have heard of dysentery on the Congo. One of the Baptist missionaries recently died from that disease, contracted at the mission station of Manyanga. On the other hand the sanitary reputation of the plateau is undoubtedly good, and there is a freshness and breeziness in the air that you miss down below by the river side. I am convinced Mr. Stanley has done wisely, apart from strategic reasons, in placing all his stations on the highest ground attainable.*

* I am afraid, both Mr. Stanley and myself afterwards arrived at a different opinion. The stations set on a hill all proved unhealthy, on account of their exposure to the cold night winds, and were nearly all abandoned after several years.—H. H. J.

THE RIVER CONGO SEEN FROM THE PLATEAU AT MANYANGA.

Manyanga is a great food centre. I have already hinted at its abundantly supplied markets, where eighty or ninety fowls, fifty goats, troops of sheep, and hundreds of eggs may be purchased at a single time. The favourite medium of exchange here is blue glass beads, and hand-kerchiefs and stuffs will scarcely be taken at any sacrifice. Indeed it is quite a false idea to imagine that you can go anywhere in Africa with any sort of bead and any kind of cloth. Each district has its peculiar tastes and fancies to consult, and you might starve in one place with bales of goods that would purchase kingdoms in another. In one part of the Congo basin red is the favourite colour, in another blue, in a third green, and I have come across some tribes where white cloth far outvalued coloured or patterned stuffs. Between Vivi and Isangila you will find red handkerchiefs, striped cloth, brass "tacks," gin, and wire useful. At Manyanga blue beads rule the market; at Stanley Pool brass rods. On the Upper river, besides most of the articles already mentioned, "cowries" come into use, and are used freely as small change.

At Manyanga, owing to the abundance of native food, and the scarcity of nearly every European article of diet which then existed, we were able to test the possibility of living solely on the products of the country, a state of affairs which, owing to the expense and difficulty of transport, is very likely to occur, and must eventually largely influence the conditions of colonization. On the whole I had little to complain of. We had no tea, coffee, cocoa, wine, sugar, butter, or bread, it is true, but with a little ingenuity substitutes were found for many of these adjuncts to European living. The goats gave plenty of milk, and we drank it hot, and "made believe" it was tea. Palm wine was our only intoxicant, and "Kikwanga" in some way took the place of bread. Palm-oil fried our meats, enriched our stews, and fed the lamps that lighted up our evening meal. We had superb desserts of massive pine-apples, bananas made puddings that were richly sweet, and plantains took the place of potatoes. I never ate with better appetite and rarely lived more happily.

H

The daily arrivals of natives at the station were always an amusement. Sometimes they would come with a baaing and protesting goat or sheep for sale. One day a party of men arrived with a very stout lady of whom they wished to dispose for her value in blue beads. She was quite the thing for me, they were convinced, and would make an excellent lady-help for my next expedition. There was no end to her catalogue of graces and

MLONGO-MLAKO, KING OF DANDANGA.

accomplishments. She wore moreover a handsome nose-ring, which would be given in to clench the bargain. Unfortunately the price asked was quite beyond my means, nor was Nilis able or willing to acquire her services, so, in common with some goats and fowls we had also declined, she was reluctantly returned to her relatives. There is no doubt that if the native porters can be induced, as is not infrequently the case, to bring their women with them, these latter prove a valuable adjunct to the expedition. They carry burdens nearly as heavy as those borne by their husbands and brothers, and carry them much more cheerfully. They wash and cook better than the men, and have a way of preparing manioc for food that seems beyond masculine knowledge or skill. In steady hard work and endurance of fatigue they certainly excel the other sex; they ask less pay, they eat less food, and, in short, I should seriously recommend the utilization of female labour in the formation of all African expeditions. Many Zanzibari women accompanied their husbands across Africa in Stanley's great journey, and he writes, touchingly, in the 'Dark Continent,' respecting their patient endurance and dogged perseverance.

The fact is, woman in Africa has not emerged from her proper status—her proper *African* status, I mean. When this great continent is fairly civilized, is traversed by railroads, and intersected by canals, when all the rough, hard, coarse battling with natural obstacles is over, then man—African man—can afford, if he will, to indulge in a more delicate and finer-natured spouse, who is worthy to be conceded the privileges which chivalry grants to the artificial weakness of her sex. At present the women lead a harder life than the men, and they are consequently inferior to the better-nurtured males in mental development and physical beauty. Conscious of their lower grade in society, they are thus ever anxious to merit by their assiduity in well-doing the approbation of the nobler sex.

There are several native "kings" round Manyanga. One of them was a constant visitor at the station, and a terrible beggar, always on the look-out for cloth and beads. His name was Mlongo-Mlako, and he was chief of a town or district called Dandanga. Shortly after my arrival, he made a call on us, avowedly to see the new white man, and probably also with the idea that there might be a little "cloth" to be given away. His majesty of Dandanga nearly fell a victim to the superstitions of his people a short time ago. A wife of one of his sub-chiefs fell ill and died; and, as is always the case in this

country, the medicine-man was called upon to say who
had " bewitched " her.   He assembled a sort of coroner's
inquest, and they came to the unanimous conclusion that
King Mlongo had killed the woman with his sorceries.
The wretched monarch would have had to take " poison-
water " had not an English missionary opportunely
arrived at his village, and laughed the people out of their
foolish superstition.   To please the white stranger, the

THE " WIDOWED ONE."

king was pardoned by the fetish man, but pardoned
reluctantly, for his real sin was not having bewitched
a woman, but being a terrible miser.   Avarice amongst
these people is considered the blackest of crimes, and had
king Mlongo been in the habit of freely lavishing his gin
and his cloth on his subjects, his loving people would not
have fixed upon him as a sorcerer, nor the heir-apparent
have been so active in the prosecution.   He was very
little grateful to his benefactor, however, and immediately

presented himself at the mission, not to thank its head for saving his life, but to demand a piece of cloth *because* his life was saved. On the occasion of this particular visit to the station, he was accompanied by the widowed chief whose wife he was supposed to have bewitched. They were now on the most amicable terms, and the widowed one, having daubed his ugly face with charcoal in sign of mourning, gave himself up to unlimited merriment, and was thinking, he told me, of marrying again.

Above Manyanga all further navigation of the river ceases, and there are quite close to the station the great falls of Ntombo Mataka, where the successive descents of the Congo, as nearly as anywhere, approach cascades in appearance. Seen from the heights above, these falls appear like two great " steps " of water, and the river here descends perhaps some thirty feet in all. The roar of the cataract can be heard miles off, and the backwater it creates is so powerful, that at the sides of the river the water persistently flows with a strong stream in the reverse direction to the central current. It needs some care to cross the river near the station lest the boat be drawn into the backwater, to be carried forcibly up into the cataracts, whirled round and dashed to pieces.

To reach Stanley Pool therefore, from Manyanga, you leave the Congo, and follow the native roads either to the north or south of the river. The southern route is by far the easier and safer to follow, as the hills are less steep, and the natives are pleasanter and kindlier people to deal with than the cantankerous Ba-bwende to the north. In either case the distance to be walked on foot is about one hundred miles.

Some few miles behind Manyanga, one of the much-used native tracks passes from Stanley Pool to the upper waters of the Niari and its tributary the Ludima, and thence to the sea. This useful alternative route has been thoroughly mapped and surveyed by Mr. Stanley's agents who have founded a chain of stations along its course.*

* Which was afterwards given up to France,

CHAPTER VI.

MANYANGA TO LÉOPOLDVILLE (STANLEY POOL).

ROAD TO LUTETE—THE CHIEF LUTETE—RAVINES ON THE ROAD TO STANLEY POOL—THE EDWIN ARNOLD RIVER—A SUDDEN STORM—KINDNESS OF THE ZANZIBARIS—AN ORGIE OF PINE-APPLES—TRAPPING BATS—A FETISH-HOUSE—CROSSING THE INKISSI — A LEOPARD'S FOOTPRINTS — CARVED LOGS — THE WA-MBUNO—NGOMA—LÉOPOLDVILLE—THE MISSIONS—THE FOOD QUESTION—THE FUTURE OF LÉOPOLDVILLE.

As usually happens in this country—whenever you have got everything ready for a start—the morning I was preparing to leave Manyanga for the Upper river with a hastily formed caravan of Zanzibaris, the rain came pelting down, and kept us waiting vainly for its cessation. At last, towards evening, just to make a start, I availed myself of the kind offer made by the Baptist missionary then in residence at the little Mission below the hill, and packed the men, the goods and myself in the large and roomy Mission boat, while the missionary himself steered us over the difficult passage. I camped out that night opposite Manyanga, intending to start by the early dawn along the southern road to Stanley Pool, viâ Lutete. The weather was miserably wet, and the ground on which the tent was pitched became a sort of morass, into which the iron legs of my bed gradually sank under my weight, so that I found myself and my bedclothes nearly level with the muddy grass. However, I arose the next morning with nothing worse than a severe sore throat, which the continuous exercise of the long day's walk quickly dissipated.

The general scenery on the road to Lutete is interesting

A WILD PINE-APPLE.

in character, and offers many beautiful landscapes, which, however, are all of the same type and grow somewhat monotonous in feature. A great stretch of valley, filled with rich forest, with a sounding stream that is seen flashing through the trees, is bounded by boldly-shaped hills, between each of which lesser valleys lie, that seem, as it were, tributaries of the great one, some of them mere crevasses in the mountains, but each with its tiny stream, its cascades, and its velvety woods. Occasionally, especially near Lutete, patches are cleared in the valleys, and the rich soil which the rain is always washing down from the hills is planted with manioc, tobacco, ground-nuts, and bananas. This gives, at times, a strangely civilized look to the country, and suggests the idea that in the future, when colonists flock to occupy the Congo territories, these lowlands will become true golden valleys, bringing forth all the products of the tropics ; while their hill-sides, terraced and planted with vines, will be surmounted by many a fine-built habitation, from which the Neo-African may complacently look down on his rice-fields and his gardens, or his plantations and his sugar-brakes, which lie basking under an equatorial sun, irrigated by a never-failing stream. And what a future studying-ground for scientific men ! When people have conquered their unreasonable fear of the Congo climate, and some medical man has deigned to study the local hygiene, and so instructed us as to what we should eat and drink, and how we should live that we may best become acclimatized—when transport is facilitated and communication with the outer world easy and assured, then let the scientist come and found his botanical garden in one valley, and his vivarium in another, whilst in his comfortable brick-built house, built of the bricks that are locally made, and exposed to the dry and healthy breezes that assail the hill-tops, he may prepare his specimens, and arrange his accumulated facts as much at his ease as if he were in Kew or the British Museum.

The rounded hills that encircle these luxuriant valleys are covered with strong coarse grasses of several sorts, of

SCENERY NEAR LUTETE.

which the flower stalks often attain the height of fifteen feet, and with gnarled and stunted trees, bearing leaden-coloured, almost uneatable fruit. I should omit the qualifying "almost," were it not that I have seen the Zanzibaris occasionally gnawing them. These trees are spread in a sparse manner over the hill-side, and give it from a distance a spotted appearance. This difference in richness of vegetation that exists between hills and valleys in this part of Africa is not due so much to the relative abundance of moisture as to the prevailing grass fires in the dry season. These sweep over the hills at times, destroying all the finer trees, so that only these stunted shrubs and the rank grass spring up from their roots anew and flourish for a season. Therefore it is that around the villages whose plantations are protected from the ravages of the flames, as far as may be possible, rich forest invariably exists, and their presence may be infallibly detected in this country by the groups of fine trees and patches of purple forest growing isolated on the many hill-tops. Again, in all shut-in valleys and river-courses, where the fires are choked, there vegetation of the most wonderful character riots in all the wild luxuriance of its unchecked growth. I have already alluded to this subject in my description of the villages at Yelala, and shall make some further remarks in treating of the forest region beyond Stanley Pool.

Lutete is a pleasant little station, situated about eight miles from the Congo, on a high plateau, and commanding the great ivory route which runs from Stanley Pool to São Salvador and Ambrizéte. This important native road gradually diverges from the Congo to the south-west. Already at Lutete it is over eight miles in a direct line from the river bank. The bit of connecting road between Lutete and the landing-place opposite Manyanga, has been wholly or partially constructed by Mr. Stanley's assistants. That, and the short bit of road between Vivi and Isangila, round Ngoma falls, are all the engineering his expedition has at present undertaken, although with time and men Mr. Stanley hopes to construct a carriageable road from

Vivi to Stanley Pool, to be perhaps followed by a railway.

Lutete Station takes its name from a powerful young chief in the neighbourhood, who has built a large village, and named it, as is the custom, after himself. His town contains finer-built houses than any native settlement for miles round, and Lutete himself is a most enterprising young fellow, often accompanying his caravans of ivory down to Ambrizéte, on the coast, whence he returns with all sorts of trophies of civilization, such as coloured plates from the 'Graphic' and bottles of soda-water. The latter, he is half frightened of, and calls them "devil-water;" but he generally makes a present of them to the chief of the station, who, of course, handsomely acknowledges the gift with more than its equivalent in cloth. The coloured pictures from our wide-spread illustrated papers are proudly stuck up in the chief's own house. Whenever Lutete wishes to impress some uncouth savage chief from the interior, he takes him into his palisaded hut and shows him Cinderella with her broom, or 'Goody Two Shoes,' telling him, of course, bombastically, that they are special presents from "Mputo" * (beyond the sea), and the wondering savage goes away much impressed by the power and influence of Lutete. Shortly after my arrival Lutete, who was ill, sent his head wife to call upon me instead, and she brought me a large jar of palm wine as a present. This lady was extremely plain, but she was Lutete's favourite wife because she has borne him many children.

---

* "Mputo" literally means, "agitated water," and is in that sense primarily applied to the rapids of the Congo, where they seethe and foam. Then further it is used to describe the sea with its troubled billows, and in a still wider sense means all that comes from the sea. The natives of the Lower Congo believe, or used to believe, that all white men came up out of the sea, and that our clothes were made of the skins of sea animals. Consequently, "Muene Mputo" means "chief of the sea" viz., chief of all the white men, and not, as the Portuguese would have us believe, "the King of 'Puto' or Portugal." If the natives wished to say "Portugal" they would call it "Poltogale," not "Mputo." Further up the Congo, beyond the Pool, the natives, knowing little or nothing of the sea, call us "Sons of the Sky," or "Sons of Heaven."

Having passed one day at this station to rest, I again started with my caravan of thirty men to journey on towards Stanley Pool. The country we passed through, immediately before and after leaving Lutete, was of rather a peculiar appearance. Here and there were deep gullies, ravines, gulches, canyons—I know not what to call them—huge clefts in the land, either made or modified by water eating into the soft red soil. They are similar to the same strange valleys and ravines round about Loanda, in Portuguese Africa. Their depths, however, here are filled with the richest, most fantastic forms of vegetation, and to judge from the cries and noises that ascend out of the gulf of green, these glorious forests are peopled with many birds and monkeys. Any one of these ravines would be a rare hunting ground for the naturalist.

Some distance after leaving Lutete, on attaining a high plateau which is traversed by the native path, a grand view may be obtained of the Edwin Arnold River, as it comes leaping in tremendous cascades into the Congo. The waters of this tumultuous stream look exactly like a white cloth laid at intervals over the purple-wooded hills, for the distance at which you are standing does not permit you to see the motion of its stream, and the sheet of white spray is apparently as still and picture-like as if photographed.

The second night of my journey a disaster occurred to me, but one of such a common type in African travel that I venture to retail it to you here, so that you may take the good with the ill, and not imagine a Congo traveller's experience all sunshine and brightness. We were camped in a village as usual, and my tent was to all appearance carefully and correctly pegged out. I had eaten a well-cooked little dinner with keen appetite, and then had enjoyed the unwonted luxury of a novel over a cup of coffee. When at length I grew tired of reading, I got into bed, leaving my book open, and most of the things lying unpacked and in disorder. I reckoned that there would be plenty of time to pack up in the morning. As I lay on my comfortable bed, soothed by a delicious sense of repose, I heard the rain beginning to pat down on my tent in great drops, while the rising wind soughed mournfully through the neighbouring trees ; but this dismal state of the weather outside only accentuated the sense of comfort and security within the snug tent, and I was quietly falling asleep in a self-satisfied mood, when suddenly the wind rose like an angry devil, and puff! my tent was whipped up over my head, and laid flat on the ground a few yards off. In a second all was changed, and I was being brusquely awakened from my reverie, and half-drowned by the drenching rain, which was mercilessly streaming down on all my treasures. My bed-clothes were soaked, my novel—I remember it was Alphonse Daudet's ' Les Rois en exil '—was reduced in no time to yellow pap, everything was going to ruin and dissolution —the rain even beat the ground up into thick mud which engulfed most of the smaller articles ; and all this time I was too paralysed by the sudden shock and the cold *douche* of rain to call for help. At last, however, I found my breath, and applied it lustily to a small whistle round my neck. In a minute the Zanzibaris had rushed from an adjoining cottage, and seizing me up in their arms, carried me swiftly into shelter. Here, by the side of a blazing fire, I dried myself and my bed-clothes, and slept soundly on a native bed of matting. It was really wonderful the number of things that were saved from the wrecked tent and dried by the fire, and my losses were limited to the novel afore described, and some trifling odds and ends too mixed up with the mud to be detected. However, in future I always endeavoured when passing the night in a native village to borrow a house to sleep in. It is much more comfortable than sleeping in a tent, as you have greater space and freer ventilation, a tent always being abominably hot and close, whereas the chinks between the matting in the sides of the house allow of a thorough circulation of air. Then, too, the roof is rain-tight, and cannot, except in very rare circumstances, be blown away by the wind, and you have a perfectly dry and hardened floor.

I more than ever appreciated after this catastrophe the admirable qualities of the Zanzibaris, who are never at a loss, and who are often most unselfish servants. It quite touched me to see, when I staggered into the hut where they were sleeping, how one man gave up his bed, another his mosquito-curtains, and a third his blankets, in order that the "Little Master" might not catch cold while his things were being dried, and this not only from my own men, between whom and myself a real attachment subsisted, but from Zanzibaris I had only seen and known for three days. The Arab mixture in the Zanzibari men has not only given them finer features and more refined manners, but it has also implanted in them an unselfishness which is seldom found in the true negro.

The succeeding day, a bright sun dried up the remaining dampness in the ground and atmosphere, and we trudged along merrily through beautiful scenery. We are here following the great trade route from Stanley Pool to the coast, and the sides of the way are strewn with the top leaves of pine-apples, which, when the fruit is eaten, are thrown away, and, taking root in the rich red soil at the side of the path, serve to spread this plant along the whole route between Lutete and Stanley Pool, in some places, especially in the dank, moist ravines, forming an almost impenetrable hedge on each side of the narrow path. The inhabitants come to these narrow valleys, and fill their long wicker-baskets with the beautiful golden fruit which forms now so large a part of their diet. In one village we came to, there was a perfect orgie of pine-apples going on. The people were too indolent and careless even to sell them, and one woman, with whom, from pure habit, I was disputing the price of her basketful, said in a languid way to Faraji, "Here, take them; as he does not want to pay he can have them for nothing." The dogs, the cats, the pigs, the goats, the fowls, and the children, all lived on pine-apples. The very people had a golden tinge about them, as if from the absorption of such quantities of mellow fruit, and the fowls I bought here had a flavour that was quite inexplicable save for this theory of an exclusive pine-apple diet. Here it was quite impossible to resist halting; we arrived at about eight in the morning, and for two whole hours we sat and ate pine-apples. A few brass rods paid for the entire feast, and the generous natives, moreover, brought us a heaped-up basketful to carry on our journey. However burdened the men might be, this was an extra load they never refused.

Everywhere along the road here, are what seem to be rude imitations of telegraph posts, tall straight poles, with lines of fine string stretched from pole to pole; but from these strings descend numbers of loops or nooses, with a slip-knot. These I took to be for catching birds, as you sometimes see in English orchards similar traps for catching fieldfares and other fruit-eaters; but on inquiry I found they were set for bats, which fly against them in the dusk and are thus frequently caught to be eaten by the natives. Whether a bat is good for food I certainly doubt, the insect-eating ones would not seem to be so, and those that only subsist on fruit have an offensive smell of musk. But the people here seem to appreciate them. About this region the bracken fern, apparently of three or four varieties, become very abundant, absolutely covering large tracts of land. Where the region is at all marshy, along the banks of streams, this is rivalled by beautiful lycopodiums of most exquisite fern-like shape, and sometimes with a bluish tinge about their fronds. Curiously enough, the natives, who have very fair elementary notions about natural classification, do not recognise the bracken as a fern, but, on the other hand, include the lycopods in that order, to which, in their language, they give a generic name, "Manselele" (plur. of Nselele).

In the midst of the forest we came across a little fetish house. It was built of a framework of laths and the roof was thatched. On the projecting stakes of the roof plates and dishes of European manufacture were "spiked," that is, by some ingenious means a hole had been roughly pierced through their centres, and they were hung on the end of the sticks protruding from the thatch of the roof. Inside the hut was a circular mound of worked clay, on which many different patterns and designs had been traced by means of various coloured pebbles, white stones and even beads. On each side of this mound stood two statues about four feet high, representing separately, in the frankest manner possible, the male and female principle. The sex of either figure was so much *en évidence*, that according to our views they would be decidedly obscene, though there was nothing intentionally indecent about them, and they merely represented to the native's mind in a crude manner the, to him, mysterious power of generation or creation. The great resemblance these figures bore to native men and women, and the clever manner in which they were carved and painted, testified to the wonderful artistic faculties of this so-called savage people. At the feet of these statues were mugs, plates, and specimens of native crockery. All these articles were slightly broken, either to disable them for future use, and thus prevent temptation to rob the sanctuary, or, as seems more probable, with an idea that a broken plate or vessel " dies," and so goes appropriately to the land of the spirits.*

About noon on the third day of our journeying we came to the banks of the Inkisi, and had to cross that swift, rolling, turbid stream in native canoes. The natives always land much lower down the river than where they embark, for the current is so swift that it is impossible to entirely withstand its influence. It is here about as broad as the Thames at Windsor, and probably rises in the mountains eastward of São Salvador. For navigation it is quite useless, owing to its furious current and many falls; on the further side of the Inkisi, the woods are beautiful, and the path winds through enchanting scenery, over little brooks where green mossy rocks stem the impatient, foaming little streams, and under the grandly over-arching trees, festooned with mazy creepers and

---

* See chap. xvi.

I

beneath whose shade the humid soil is covered with a
carpet of ferns.   On the little sandy shore of one brooklet
where the restrained water, quitting its barrier of velvety-
green stones, whose severity is tempered by the tenderest
covering of moss, spreads itself out with pride to twice
its previous width, on the crisp white sand were deeply
imprinted the footmarks of a leopard.   Perhaps but a
few minutes before he had come there to slake his thirst;
he had stolen from his lair amid the dense brushwood to
this quiet bay of the brook, where he stood in soft grey-
green shade lapping the stream near where it fell in white
streaks over the moss-carpeted stones.   Long sprays of
maidenhair tickled his forehead, great knotted lianas
bumped against him as the slight breeze swayed these
vegetable ropes backwards and forwards. Little *pæocephalus*
parrots mocked at him, and yellow-vented fly-catchers
shrieked out his crimes; still he laps on with greedy
thirst, soothed by the soft-whispering shade of trees and
ferns in which he stands, with a background of intensely
vivid sunlit verdure, where the forest breaks open to the
sky.   But the distant sound of men's voices has disturbed
him, and as they push their noisy way along the woodland
path, crunching the dead twigs under foot and swishing
back the pendent boughs, he softly slinks away into the
untracked solitudes of dead sombre green, and leaves but
the trace of his footsteps on the sandy shore of the little
brook to attest his recent presence.

Again the forest lies behind us, and we toil up the hill
path as the sun is sinking, and enter a fine large village,
some five hours' march beyond the Inkisi river.   Here you
get a good idea of Central African life.   There is a general
aspect of tidy prosperity, and the people are unusually
sportive and merry amongst themselves.   I even witnessed
what is rarely seen amongst these races—amorous toying
and loving caresses between a fine stalwart husband and
his plump little wife.   Children, pretty little children,
were playing together and making dirt pies, one child
looking on and carrying a baby as big as itself.   One
infant had the whooping cough, and another was playing

with a beautifully made rattle. A hen and chickens, with that steadfast obstinacy that is so characteristic of fowls, would insist on retiring for the night in the house which had been assigned me as my lodging; so two capable little boys caught the ten chickens tenderly and conveyed them to a place of safety, the old hen naturally clucking and protesting behind. An immense quantity of pumpkins, with the ripe fruit and the great yellow blossom growing on the same plant, and the waving fields of manioc which I saw in the bright morning light, lent an air of prosperity and plenty to the tidy groups of houses. In this village, in front of many of the habitations, lay huge logs of wood, roughly trimmed tree-trunks. At one end they exhibited but little handling from the operator, but at the other they terminated in a rudely carved and painted head, executed with little finish indeed, yet the few strokes that wrought the semblance to humanity had been given with a certain decision and skill. There was, in fact, a good deal of character and expression in this sketched-out face, which, besides, bore much resemblance to the prevailing type of man in that neighbourhood. Whether these logs, of which many were lying prone before the cottage doors, were " house-idols " in disgrace, or merely ornamental settles, I could not ascertain; but when I mentioned the word for "idol" and pointed towards them, the men and women gathered round and laughed contemptuously. I might mention that the natives here call themselves "Wa-mbuno." The plural prefix " wa " again replaces the more classical " ba."

Beyond this village all was magnificent, grandiose forest. The path goes down, down, down into its depths, and the tree-tops shut out the sky. The long straight lianas, like plumb-lines and scaffolding depending from the branches, sketch out a sort of fantastic architecture. Large white jasmine flowers shine out like stars in the gloomy depths of foliage, and down at the bottom of the deep ravine a brown stream catches a few glints of green light as it hurries along.

On the evening of the fourth day, after leaving Lutete

we stopped at the village of Ngoma.* Here an old fetish-man and some young disciples were performing a sort of dance, in which they hopped about like frogs, squatted on their heels, and waved their hands downwards from the heavens. I was told they were calling down the rain—surely a most superfluous appeal to the clerk of the weather, who took care to souse us every day. Other of the inhabitants, more indolent, or conscious of the inutility of supplicating Providence, were reclining in different postures in lazy ease, having their hair dressed by women.

From Ngoma it was a trying march of fifteen miles to Léopoldville, and as I was suffering badly from an ulcer on the ankle, the road seemed doubly long; and when at length I limped into the station, I was in need of the kind reception accorded me. A late breakfast was soon got ready, and they gave me a splendid cucumber grown in the station garden.

You do not get a glimpse of Stanley Pool until you are quite close to Léopoldville, and it is then, on turning round the hill-side, that the magnificent prospect of it bursts upon your view.

Léopoldville, like most of Mr. Stanley's stations, is placed on rising ground,† but it does not occupy for its site the exact summit of the hill, being built on what may be called a semicircular ledge round the slope which faces the expanding Pool.

The principal edifice of the station is a large two-storied house made of wood, bricks, and a sort of mud plaster. The roof is of thatch, for the sake of coolness, and all the framework of the house is composed of huge beams of wood, apparently of great strength, but really a source of weakness, as the wood is being constantly eaten through by the white ants and other insect pests, so that frequently a beam gives way, and is renewed only just in time to save the structure. This house contains a large dining-

---

* Ngoma means "*drum.*" It is a word often applied to a sounding fall of water.

† And is very unhealthy in consequence.—H. H. J.

room, a store, and three bed-rooms on the ground-floor ; and on the first story a long, low-pitched chamber, which is generally Mr. Stanley's private sitting-room when he comes to Léopoldville. In his absence, it is occupied by the chief of the station. Behind the house, and apart from it, are the kitchens and domestic offices, and in front spreads a fine open porch, as I may call it, for want of a better word, which is really a large open apartment, in addition to the dining-room, projecting on to the esplanade, and forming a delightfully airy spot in which to sit during the daytime. In a row with this big house are two other buildings. One has a series of apartments for the white men, and the other a large supplementary store. Both above and below these European dwellings are many little houses for the Zanzibaris, and the natives attached to the station. Beneath the esplanade, which runs along the front of the " white " part of Léopoldville, and leading down towards the port, the Zanzibaris' houses make quite a neat and orderly looking town, each cottage having its garden and enclosure round it. The esplanade, which I have already mentioned, is really a flat terrace cut artificially in the slope of the hill, and is in continuation with the road arising from the interior. From this promenade views of great beauty may be obtained over the distant Pool and the neighbouring forest, and in the cool evening-time it forms a pleasant walk to stroll on whilst waiting for dinner. Here, too, in the early morning, the chief of the station passes all the Zanzibaris in review.

A quarter of a mile away, on the top of the hill, is the little Baptist Mission, which enjoys, perhaps, the finest situation of any building in Léopoldville, the view from its verandah embracing almost the whole extent of Stanley Pool. The Baptist missionaries have, besides, a large garden down near the banks of the Congo, and they rent altogether from the Expedition about two-and-a-half acres of land, paying for it the merely nominal sum of £10 per annum.

Above, below, and around the station are extensive gardens, banana groves, and plantations of manioc. They already begin to furnish no inconsiderable amount of food both to the black and the white inhabitants of Léopoldville, and of course in future, together with the stock-breeding establishments for goats, fowls, sheep, pigs, ducks, and pigeons, ought to completely nourish the station and its normal number of residents, so that only what may be termed "luxuries" need be introduced from Europe. There is no reason why many even of these should not be produced and prepared on the spot. The sugar-cane, for instance, is largely grown by the natives, and its pulp may in the simplest, most elementary way be boiled and strained down into a thick toffee-like sugar, quite suitable for all ordinary sweetening purposes without further refinement. Then, as we know, coffee is indigenous to most parts of tropical Africa, and if it does not actually grow wild on the Congo, it would certainly yield on these fertile slopes around the Pool the finest results under cultivation.

It is the food question that is the real difficulty of Congo exploration. Though the soil is richly productive, the natives grow only just enough to live upon in plenty themselves, but are not equal to a sudden drain on their resources. Mr. Stanley has long since understood the necessity of making his Expedition self-supporting, both from the expense and difficulty of importing preserved provisions from Europe, and from the inability of the natives to adequately supply anything like the amount of food which is daily needed for the nourishment of each station. Consequently, almost before he built houses, he laid out gardens, he planted bananas, and commenced the cultivation of manioc, and whenever he made an inspection of a newly-founded station or revisited an old one, his first care was the local husbandry.

Léopoldville boasts of a convenient little harbour in front of the station, protected by a spit of woodland which projects into the Congo. Here all the falls are over, or, rather, following the course of the stream, have not yet begun—the first takes place close to Léopoldville, a little behind the station—so that navigation from this port is open and unchecked for nearly a thousand miles eastward up the Congo. In fact Léopoldville, situated at the western entrance to Stanley Pool, is destined to be the great Empire city of Central Africa. From its shores there are, according to Stanley's calculations, 4,520 miles of free navigation north, and south, and east, into the heart of Africa. It will one day be the terminus of a

THE PORT OF LÉOPOLDVILLE.

railway from the coast and the starting point of a river journey half across Africa. The ivory, copper and iron; the spices, the wax and the gums of the interior will meet in its mart the costumes of London and Paris and products of the manufactories of the old world. Or, in another sense, the raw material which is poured into Léopoldville from the interior will return to it from the exterior in

other forms.   Its sugar will come back in the daintier
shape of Parisian bonbons, its india-rubber will be reim-
ported as highly necessary goloshes and waterproofs.
Congo spices will be mingled in English and American
sauces, and over the counters of its toilet shops the
merchant enriched in the ivory trade will purchase ivory-
handled brushes which are made in England from the
tusks that his firm has exported.   Who knows, even, that
the only note-paper in use amongst the fashionable world
of Léopoldville may not some day be manufactured from
the very papyrus which so thickly grows around the
woody islands and the reedy shores of Stanley Pool ?

CHAPTER VII.

STANLEY POOL.

SCENERY OF THE POOL—DOVER CLIFFS—BRAZZAVILLE—KALLINA
POINT—DEATH OF LIEUTENANT KALLINA—THE CHIEFS ROUND
STANLEY POOL—NGALIEMA—BOAT VOYAGE TO BOLOBO—A KIN-
SHASHA VILLAGE—A CONVERSAZIONE—HYPHŒNE PALMS—
SMOKED FISH—AN AFRICAN RAIN-STORM—IMPORTANCE OF
DIET—HIPPOPOTAMI—GREY PARROTS—KIMPOKO—A CLIMBING
PALM.

STANLEY POOL is a great expansion of the Congo, about
twenty-five miles long and sixteen broad. There are
seventeen islands of some note, the largest of them being
thirteen miles in length. Many sand-banks strew the
waters of the Pool, alternately covered and uncovered,
according to the season of the year, and there are also
floating reed and papyrus islands, formed of these masses
of aquatic vegetation, which are so strongly interknitted
by their fibres and roots that a man can stand on them.
These floating islets are occasionally of some extent, and
may be taken for real islands until their motion with the
current is observed. White egrets and many waterbirds
frequent them, and the hippopotami play round their
reedy shores. The large islands* are resorted to by
elephants and buffaloes, which creatures swim backwards
and forwards from the mainland with ease. Innumerable
waterbirds, storks, pelicans, cormorants, herons, egrets,
sacred ibises, spur-winged and Egyptian geese, terns and

---

* These vary in size and number according to the season. In the
rainy months they are subdivided into two or three each, with shallow
channels between. In the dry season the number of islands is much
diminished by the retreating waters.

THE *Calamus* PALM IN DIFFERENT STAGES: WITH FRUIT.

plovers, frequent the thick tangles of high grass and the many sand-banks, where they form strange groups with the crocodiles, who are wont to lie basking in the sun in a state of semi-conscious beatitude.

The Pool forms, as it were, a great cup-like basin, with an incomplete rim formed by sierras of peaked and picturesque mountains, ranging on the southern side from 1,000 feet to 3,000 feet in height. The banks of this great expanse of water offer considerable variety in character. At the northern, or north-eastern end, where the Upper Congo enters it through a somewhat narrow

FLOATING REED ISLAND ON STANLEY POOL.

passage, the scenery is very beautiful. High woods rise so steeply above the water that, as you sail beneath their shade, they seem to mount indefinitely towards the sky. It is a wall of forest. Then, almost opposite, following the northern bank, are the "Dover Cliffs," * their scarped sides white and glistening, and their crowns being covered with soft green grass. They more resemble, however, the scenery round Lyme Regis, in Dorset and Devon, than the harsher and more rugged cliffs of Dover. Then on both

* Their geological formation is a white, sandy, somewhat crumbling soil, not chalk.

sides of the Pool, the shores dwindle down into flat
forest land, the encircling girdle of mountains trending
off towards the interior, and when you reach Mfwa or
" Brazzaville," the coast is low and nearly on a level with
the water. It is here that De Brazza claims to have
secured a cession of territory to the French Republic, nine
miles in length. As you may see by the illustration,
" Brazzaville" consists of a very few native huts, half
buried in bananas, and backed by thick forest.* On the
left hand side, facing the Pool, there is a small creek,
which might be developed into a tiny harbour, and there
is a fine and fertile island, as yet uninhabited, save by

" BRAZZAVILLE."

chance fishermen, which might be successfully developed
by the French; but save these two advantages, not rare
anywhere in Stanley Pool, it is difficult to discover any
favourable point in this situation, or even to avoid the
conclusion that it is a badly chosen site for a station.
About this low-lying part of the Pool, ague is prevalent,
and in the rainy season I should say Mfwa would become
a rheumatic swamp. Had De Brazza fixed his intended
station anywhere on the high and breezy " Dover Cliffs,"
he would have done well, and, remember, the whole basin
of the Pool was open to him when he first arrived, for he

* No doubt very much changed now.—H. H. J.

reached it long before Mr. Stanley had been able to transport his goods and his men thither to found a station, so that the Franco-Italian, as it were, had the first choice of a site. I can only suppose that, in spite of the affection the natives bore him, they did not place much ground at his disposal, and that De Brazza fixed on Mfwa because he could not get anything better. He may also have looked across at Kallina Point, and hoped to secure that some day, and then be able to shut up the mouth of the Pool if necessary. This promontory is a red cliff, rising abruptly some fifty feet from the water, nearly opposite Mfwa, on the southern bank of the expanding river. Kallina Point might from its commanding situation be called the Gibraltar of the Pool, as from its easily fortified summit artillery could sweep the narrowing end of this lake and render the further descent of its waters by an enemy well-nigh impossible. Of course in conjunction with "Brazzaville," its possession by a hostile party could completely interrupt water communication between Léopoldville and the upper river.

A fearful current races round this cliff, difficult to stem even in a steamer, but really dangerous for native canoes going against the stream. Here, in December, 1882, Lieut. Kallina, an Austrian member of the Expedition, was drowned. He would insist on ascending the Congo in a small native canoe, being too impatient to explore the mysteries of the unknown to wait for the departure of the monthly boat which revictuals the stations of the upper river. As he was a very tall man, and for some reason chose to seat himself on a large chest in the stern, he rendered the balance of the canoe very unstable. The little craft was badly steered, met the rush of the current broadside as it whirled round this point, and was instantly capsized. Lieutenant Kallina was drowned, and his name has since been given to this redoubtable headland.

The people inhabiting the shores of Stanley Pool belong to the Ba-teke race, but they would seem to be comparatively recent arrivals, and to have dispossessed the older inhabitants and driven them into the interior or absorbed them as slaves. Where the Ba-teke have settled, on the south or eastern bank of the Congo, they form merely riverine colonies, and never extend their settlements many miles from its banks.

The principal chiefs round the Pool are Bab Njáli, who rules over Mfwa and the lower course of the impetuous Jué river; Ngaliéma, the chief of Ntamo and the territory round Léopoldville; three more important chiefs at or near Kinshasha, of whom one, Bankwa, is very averse to Europeans; and finally there is a great chief, fortunately of another way of thinking, at Kimpoko, where the Expedition possesses a flourishing station. Ngaliéma is the chief with whom Mr. Stanley has come most into contact, for Léopoldville is built on land bought from him, and he is the nearest, and not the most agreeable neighbour of the station. At first he tried to act the bully, until he saw how inadequate his strength of one hundred and fifty guns would prove in any attack on Léopoldville. Now he is by turns a whining suppliant, a sulky neighbour, or a crafty intriguer. He is a man of rather strong character and decided will, having raised himself from the position of a mere slave to that of a powerful chief of slaves. This town of Ntamo or Kintamo (the prefix Ki rather implies "district"), was founded and colonized by him, and he has since enriched himself immensely by ivory trading. Nearly all the ivory brought down by the Ba-yansi traders from the Equator (whence they receive it from the Ba-ngala, who in their turn get it from some still more remote tribe) comes to his market, and passes through his hands to Lutete and São Salvador.

I left Léopoldville, towards the end of February,[*] in a large lighter or whale-boat, rowed by a sturdy crew of Zanzibaris, to ascend the Congo as far as Bolobo, a large native village about 220 miles beyond Stanley Pool, where the last station of the Expedition had recently been founded.

Our departure, as usual, was signalised by a downpour of rain that was almost exceptional in its force and dura-

---

[*] The height of the rainy season.

tion, and which quickly showed me how ill-prepared we were for the exigencies of a tropical rainy season. In a large open boat, with absolutely no shelter but a hastily-slung sail which merely received pools of rain-water in its bosom to launch them on our heads when the violent wind gave it a twist; with no place of dry stowage for the luggage which just lay about in the bottom of the boat, or if floatable, floated here and there in the rain-water that in spite of the men's efforts of constant baling, lay often 6 inches deep in the middle of the lighter; circumstanced thus we had no course when it rained, but to stop rowing, run the boat aground, and seek for some temporary refuge wherein we and such of the cargo as was likely to spoil by constant soaking could await in shelter the return of fine weather. In this instance, we had scarcely rounded Kallina Point when the torrential rain forced us to make for the southern shore of the Pool, where the villages of Kinshasha were situated. The Zanzibaris, knowing well the indications of the weather, and foreseeing an entire day of rain, wished me to descend here, and seek refuge in a native hut, but miserable as I felt, with the rain streaming down my mackintosh, and my feet an inch deep in water, I hesitated, for here, only a few days before, the chief of Léopoldville, come on a friendly mission and camped out in the village, had been obliged to leave in the middle of the night, turned out by hostile natives who regarded the arrival of any white man in their district with irritable suspicion. Would they greet me any better, much less afford me a refuge from the rain? I asked myself, and supposing they not only refused us hospitality, but even ventured to rob and attack us, should we be in a position to resist? However, my scruples soon ended. The prospect of quietly soaking all day and getting rheumatic fever, or else returning humiliated to Léopoldville, was more disagreeable than adventuring myself amongst the capricious natives, who perhaps themselves might be depressed and softened by the weather. So I left the boat, took a few necessary articles of luggage, and walked up through the long wet grass to the village, where to my pleased surprise the natives received us most hospitably, and at once invited me into an inhabited hut, where I could remain and dry myself until an unoccupied dwelling could be found and placed at my disposal. The other inmates of the house, excepting the many and constant visitors, were a middle-aged man, with his hair *en chignon*, his wife, suckling a baby, whose forehead was ornamented with a band of scarlet pigment, and an old man, who might have been a poor broken-down uncle of the family.

After the drenching rain and sodden dampness outside, the dry warmth of this interior was a most pleasant contrast, and I sat down on a large raised bed of matting with a sense of comfort and resignation. There was a wood fire in the centre of the floor which served to dry my clothes, but the smoke coming from the burning wood made my eyes smart considerably. Seeing this, the woman removed the burning brands and only left the clear bright ashes on the hearth. The house was clean and tidy, and round the walls were ranged many neatly made articles. There were long pipes with little bowls, a clarionet, a white mug (these last presents from " Mputo "), a musical instrument like a guitar, but with five strings, a collection of skilfully made little pouches, containing I know not what, hippopotamus harpoons, fishing nets, horns, and a multitude of odds and ends, only to be classed under that convenient term *et cetera*.

I opened my case of provisions, laid the cloth on the bed, and sat down with considerable appetite to a frugal repast. The sight of the tinned condiments excited a considerable amount of half-fearsome interest on the part of such natives as watched my proceedings. They tapped their mouths with their fingers—a favourite mode of expressing surprise—when they saw Faraji cut with a "tin-opener" into what they imagined a solid block of steel, and produce little fish (sardines) floating in oil. But when I offered them some to taste they withdrew affrighted. It was "Nkisi" magic, white man's food—poison, and some of them were so alarmed at my proffering part of my lunch that they hurriedly left the hut. But curiosity soon

called them back, and visitors were continually flocking in.
Many children, some of them pretty little things, had
made friends with me, and were wonder-stricken at my
ticking watch, which they fully believe to be a little
animal imprisoned in a cage. Then to this paradise of
rest and calm came the tempter, a wicked old gentleman
with a wife and two marriageable daughters. He was
most anxious I should become his son-in-law, "moyennant"
several "longs" of cloth. Seeing my hesitation, he mis-
took it for scorn, and hastened to point out the manifold
charms of his girls, whilst these damsels waxed hotly
indignant at my coldness. Then another inspiration seized
their father—perhaps I liked a maturer style of beauty,
and his wife, by no means an uncomely person, was
dragged forward while her husband explained with the
most expressive gestures, putting his outspread hand
before his eyes and affecting to look another way, that,
again with the simple intermediary of a little cloth, he
would remain perfectly unconscious of whatever amatory
passages might occur between us. However, I evaded
these embarrassing proposals as delicately as possible, and
hinted with many smiles and "Mbotes," that were I otherwise circumstanced an alliance with one of the first
families of Kinshasha might have been within my means.
As it was, the honour seemed too costly. However, we
parted excellent friends, and the elder lady, with the
practical-mindedness of mature affection, presented me
with a fine large fish, which came in very handily for my
dinner, whilst her younger companions brought such
girlish offerings as eggs, corn-cobs and bananas. I, in my
turn, presented them with gaudy handkerchiefs, and
general satisfaction reigned.

Seeing that the hopeless downpour would never cease, I
made arrangements for the loan of a house to pass the
night in, and one was soon found--dry, clean, and spacious,
in which I and my impedimenta were quickly established.
It was then proposed—evidently by the village notables
—that an evening *conversazione* should be held in my
apartment, and the proposal was carried unanimously

K

Consequently, to my secret annoyance, an ever-increasing number of able-bodied people pressed into the little house, the men gravely seating themselves on the floor, each with his long pipe, quite prepared to spend a cheerful evening, and the women, as became their inferior position in society, standing about the doorway, and effectually blocking up all ventilation. A resolution was forthwith carried and presented to me by one who appeared to be the chairman, that my watch should be again exhibited to the ladies and gentlemen assembled. Sorry as I was to disappoint these harmless souls, I felt an effort must be made to secure a little quiet and repose, especially as my dinner was nearly ready ; so I managed to convey to them the idea that the white man was tired, hungry, and wished to be alone. The men then rose most courteously and quietly, shook hands with me, each one in turn, and with many "Mbotes" left the house, pushing the protesting women before them, so I was practically once more in the solitude I loved. I took off my wet boots, made myself comfortable, and turned with pleasure to the dinner and the novel that Faraji had just placed on a large chest which served me as a table. The mosquitoes here, however, were very abundant, but trumpeted despairingly round my mosquito-curtain. As the village sank to rest, the weird noises from the river rose into prominence, with the grunting of hippopotami and the cries of night-birds.

The next morning I left my Kinshasha friends, and again pursued my journey across the wide waters of the Pool, which now began to open into all its magnificent breadth. On many islands the Hyphœne * palms were growing, apparently a different species from the *Hyphœne Guineënsis* of the coast and the lower reaches of the Congo. This Hyphœne was a most beautiful and majestic palm, from thirty to sixty feet in height, with broad fan-shaped fronds of glaucous green, and clusters of bright orange fruit. Just below the crown of leaves there is a curious swelling or bulging of the stem, a not uncommon charac-

---

* *Hyphœne ventricosa* (Kirk)?

teristic of Borrassine or Hyphœnoid palms, and which adds strangely to the grace of the pillar-like stem.

The vegetation which clothes the shores of these islands is rich and pleasing in colour. It is brightened by masses of yellow cucurbit flowers, lilac-coloured papilionaceæ and mauve convolvuli. Beautiful scarlet seed-vessels of a *Cnestis* form blazing clusters of gorgeous effect amid the tender green foliage. Immense numbers of grey parrots. small flocks of them going together, flutter and play about

HYPHŒNE PALMS.

the tops of the tall trees, whistling and screaming joyously all the time, while on the many snaggs that rear their withered branches above the waterside, numerous little birds have for safety's sake hung their pendent nests of grass, and there is thus a constant twittering and fluttering of dainty forms round the gnarled old trunks and whitened twigs.

At one of the many islands, we stopped to eat some breakfast. The remainder of the fish presented to me by the lady of Kinshasha was re-cooked in a stew with some

sweet potatoes and manioc and turned out delicious.
Whilst this was being done by Mafta, I endeavoured to
make the tour of the island, but as more than half of it
was marsh, this was hardly practicable. Everywhere the
soft soil was imprinted by the hoof-marks of the hippopotami who at present were occupied with their mid-day
bath. Their loud grunting might be distinctly heard, and
as we sat in the boat eating our breakfast, many an uncouth head was raised with a snort and a jet of spray to
regard our proceedings. There was little of note to see in
this particular island. The hippopotami and the circling
kites had it pretty well to themselves. There were, however, some fine groves of the large and handsome papilionaceous tree, a species of Baphia, (which I have already
mentioned and illustrated in Chapter V.,) and the strong
fragrant scent from their white blossoms made the whole
island fragrant. In front of us, on a sand-bank, some
natives were smoking their freshly caught fish over a wood
fire, preparatory to disposing of them in the markets of
the Ba-teke. In all probability these men were Ba-yansi,
for this tribe does an immense trade in smoked fish
between the Equator and Stanley Pool. As they descend
the river with ivory and other articles of trade, they spend
much time fishing on their way, and frequently stop at a
sand-bank or island to smoke what they have captured.
The fish thus treated last a long time in good condition,
and are in some request amongst all the riverine natives
as an article of food.

I have sometimes found them excellent—I might almost
say delicious—white of flesh and flaky, with few bones,
and retaining from the smoking process a faint but very
pleasant flavour. On the other hand, at times the natives
have palmed off on me some that were evidently stale, for
on breaking them open, they were a mass of wriggling
worms within.

Hitherto, throughout this morning, the day had been
glorious, and all the time I sat at breakfast, watching the
hippopotami and the fishermen, the sky was radiantly
blue, blue as it only is during the rainy season in Africa,

for in the rainless months the sky is mostly covered with a whitish haze; but now, distant mutterings of thunder were heard from time to time, and threatening clouds · began to shadow the broad face of the still Pool, which erewhile reflected nothing but unsullied azure. Then rose suddenly a fearful inky black mass, rendered more weird by two flecks of pallid white cloud that seemed the eyes of the storm-fiend. Vivid zigzags of pink lightning played over the still water, and the thunder rumbled and tumbled as if they were moving colossal furniture in heaven. Yet the storm did not immediately burst on us, but rather crept round and round the horizon, as if playing with its victims. At one time I had lost all fear of it, thinking it seemed quite resolved to go off to the west; when, suddenly, a puff of wind sprang up in the opposite direction to the prevailing breeze, and in two or three minutes the cruel clouds were swept upon us, and a deluge of rain was hissing down. Useless to put up a sail shelter, the scornful wind whipped it off, and we could only sit patiently and soak.

This is the dreary part of an African rain-storm. The first beginning of the tempest is most awe-striking and impressive. One is half inclined to think that some great natural catastrophe, some appalling conflict of physical forces is at hand. The purple-black clouds that rise in fantastic masses, which an imaginative eye could resolve into unearthly beings overshadowing the earth and its frightened children; the dazzling snowy-white of their colossal heads rising up into the blue zenith and accentuating the inky darkness round the horizon; the jagged lightning, the first skirmishing attack of the storm, and the sudden bursts of roaring, deafening thunder—all this is grand and imposing, and fascinates the attention while it lasts. This is the "stagey" part of a tropical storm, and one which scarcely any book treating of the tropics fails to describe. But what does not seem to be equally noticed after the wonderful effects of thunder and lightning have had their due description, is the dreary persistent downpour which ensues, when the sky becomes a uniform drab and the rain descends for hours, not in "bucketsful," nor in "sheets," nor in any interesting or exceptional manner, but in a steady soaking drizzle with little hope of intermission. I have frequently known it to rain for twelve hours at a stretch in Tropical Africa, and on this particular occasion the rain lasted continuously for an even longer space of time.

We repaired to a sandy island, landed, and erected the tent. Never had I felt more miserable in Africa. It took an hour before the wet wood could be coaxed into a blaze ; and as the gloom of evening fell, with its dark mists and dismal obscurity, bands of hellish mosquitoes, worthy subjects of Beelzebub, king of the flies, swarmed round us, rendering it impossible to keep oneself in immobility. The poor Zanzibaris went stamping about on the sand and swearing in a meek way. As for me, I hastily swallowed some soup and a timely nip of brandy, and sought refuge in bed beneath my mosquito-curtains. Here, amid damp rags and clammy coverings, I passed a miserable night, fighting the hosts of mosquitoes that managed somehow to penetrate my muslin "moustiquaire."

The next morning I arose, feverish and ill. After a little hot soup, however, and some coffee, I began to feel better and to forget the dismal impressions of yesterday. And here I would pause to recommend to all intending African travellers the desirability of taking nourishment as soon after rising in the morning as possible. It is an excellent plan to save some of the soup or bouillon of the night before, and have it heated in the early morning, and drink it before leaving the tent. So much ill-health is incurred in Africa by carelessness as to nourishment, and by what is still more idiotic, an idea that it is more heroic to conduct yourself like a martyr, undergo long periods of fasting, and generally pay little attention to how much or how often you eat and drink. On the contrary, the whole question of success in Africa depends on regularly and amply nourishing the body with as good food as can be got. Let nothing, if you can help it, interfere with your meals : eat whenever you are hungry and abstain when you are not. Moreover, do not forget that in Africa a cosy cup of tea or coffee and a little light refreshment often comes in most opportunely and soothingly in moments of despondency and trouble, and that it "keeps people up" somewhat as proverbial cake and wine was supposed to do before a funeral.

As we left our sand-bank camp of the night before, the sun shone in but a half-hearted manner and more rain fell, but I was expecting momentarily to arrive at the newly founded station of Kimpoko, near the north-western end of Stanley Pool, where, at least, we should find rest and shelter for an hour or two. We saw many bands of hippopotami this morning, nine or ten generally going together. They approached the boat with a boldness and confidence which showed they had been little shot at by white men. However, the natives here hunt them assiduously with the harpoon. Indeed, in one creek, where the hippopotami were indulging in their uncouthest gambols, we ourselves saw a group of men some twenty yards from their prey, actively preparing for the chase. The tameness of these huge beasts is wonderful; one could almost fancy oneself in the enclosure of some vaster Zoological Garden : and when they opened their huge mouths, from time to time, displaying their glistening tusks, I sought involuntarily for the bun of my childhood to deftly throw into the pink chasm that yawned before me.

Flocks of grey parrots* flew across the sky, alternately screeching and whistling melodiously. I have seen it stated erroneously that the grey parrot never whistles in a wild state ; on the contrary, it does so very sweetly and with a great variety of note.

The newly-appointed agent at Kimpoko had seen us

---

* These birds are found in incredible quantities on Stanley Pool. If Cross or Jamrach established themselves here, parrots would soon be advertised in England at half-a-crown a-piece. I earnestly hope they may not, and that the Expedition, in acquiring such control over these territories, will extend to the wild things of nature the same protection from rapine as they promise to the indigenous men and women. ,

coming from afar and had prepared a welcome breakfast.
Underneath a roughly-made awning, in the middle of a
grove of Hyphœne palms, with a circle of natives eagerly
watching our strange doings, we sat down to a meal which
proudly exhibited the resources of the Kimpoko commissariat. First of all, as a pick-me-up, a good glass of
malafu, made from the sugar-cane ; then fried fish not
unlike grey mullet, a splendid eel with creamy flesh and
a very delicious flavour ; then various meats skilfully
cooked with native sauces, followed by a banana pudding

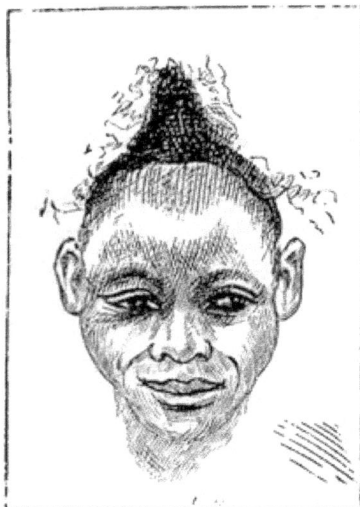

AN INHABITANT OF KIMPOKO.

and pine-apples. This was
not a meal to be grumbled at
anywhere, and many a similar
one may be enjoyed in Africa
if the traveller cares to forage
for its component parts. How
many people residing on the
Congo take the trouble to
fish for themselves ? And
yet what sport they might
have ! No, they languidly
dawdle about their verandahs
and leave it to native enterprise to occasionally provide
them with a fish course to
their dinner. And if no
natives come, then they are
content to live perpetually
on tinned provisions, a most
costly form of nourishment and one that is only excusable in barren places like Kinsembo, where hardly
any native food is to be got, and where there is no
interior transport to be paid for. The people of Kimpoko that surrounded us during our meal were good-
humoured and well-behaved. They had a great variety
of modes in dressing their hair, which is certainly much
longer and more abundant than in the coast races. The
chief of Kimpoko paid us a visit after breakfast. He
seemed a very gloomy, sulky person, and, I believe, was

rather offended at my many questions through the interpreter, and my constant habit of sketching the attendant wives who were with him. It is sacrilege, seemingly, to see the king drink, so before satisfying his thirst he shrouds his face in his mantle, gives a few quiet gulps behind it, and returns the glass empty as if he had been performing a conjuring trick. The chief seemed to think this ceremony would a little impress me, and looked out of the corners of his eyes to see if I was attending, but I felt in an irreverent mood, and let him know that I had frequently seen chiefs perform just the same precautions against sorcery or poison when about to drink. Indeed the peculiar rites and observances which attend the act of drinking among the chiefs of certain African tribes are very complex and curious, as will be seen in a future chapter, but their origin is, I confess, somewhat obscure, and the explanations offered by the natives are improbable and inadequate.

A QUEEN OF KIMPOKO.

As one approaches the farther —the northern—end of Stanley Pool, the scenery really becomes very beautiful. On the left-hand side is a range of bold and picturesque heights, their sides clothed with purple woodland. In the middle distance are groups of fine and spreading trees, standing out well against the blue hills, in all their vivid summer green ; and here and there the always graceful fan-palm seems to balance itself on its slender stem above the water, so symmetrical in shape that it appears planted for artistic effect. On the right hand, the narrowing stream is shut in by splendid hanging forests, rising to a great height sheer above the banks of the river, and casting their sombre reflections on its placid surface, where a white line of ripples becomes a positive relief to the eye. But as to relief in this study of purple and green, what can be finer. than a flock of egrets crossing the river with their fanciful irregular flight! Their plumage of perfect white, which gains them the qualifying name of "candidissima,"* their yellow beaks, and their graceful forms tell out so strongly against the sombre forest, that an effective picture is formed at once.

The banks here begin to be most markedly festooned and trellised with a curious *Calamus* or climbing palm, the fronds of which are prolonged into a bare creeping stalk,

THE NORTHERN END OF STANLEY POOL.

furnished with curiously reversed hooks, so that once the frond falls against a branch it attaches itself securely by means of these recurved thorns, and thus climbs higher and higher, often fringing the top of the forest with graceful heads of swaying fronds which with their waving whip-like terminations point straight skywards as if seeking for greater heights to climb. The motto of this palm should certainly be "Excelsior," and it might also be taken as a vegetable type of ambition. Beginning in the lowliest form

* I find this is the name of the American species; it is, however, quite as applicable to the egrets of Africa.

—the young palm looks like a broad-leaved bamboo with divided leaves—suggesting strongly its poorer and simpler relations, it soon begins to aspire, and from being first a ground-growing shrub, it throws out a long flexible stem rising far above the first humble set of fronds, and by means of its sharp hooks making use of every support in its way to climb higher and higher. Soon the leaves or fronds become more elegant. They split up from their previous bifid condition into many filaments, and at length the once lowly, feeble thing, by making use of everything that comes in its way and can give it a lift, looks proudly forth from the top of some giant tree, and, for a while content with the attainment of its ambition, has time to pause and throw out its flowers, which turn to bunches of scarlet dates. Its fruit has a thin sweetish pulp around it which seems harmless, at any rate to man, but I have never noticed any bird or beast devouring it. The colour of the leaves is a yellow-green, and it forms a decidedly bright addition to the river landscapes. The curious thing is that it is nowhere to be seen on the Congo between Stanley Pool and the coast. With the rapids it comes to an end, and therefore, as one of the first striking additions to the flora of the Congo which is met with on Stanley Pool, see p. 122.

We camped out after leaving Kimpoko in a beautiful spot near the end of the Pool, in a forest clearing. Unfortunately the mosquitoes swarmed to such a dreadful degree that all comfort was out of the question, and I had to take my meals as hastily as possible, stamping and swearing meanwhile at each successive bite; and with reason, for whether these mosquitoes were distinctly venomous, or whether my impoverished blood was easily poisoned, either for one reason or the other every bite turned to an ulcer, so that my ankles and neck were in a few days covered with disagreeable little sores, remaining comparatively painless, but quite incurable until I left the coast of Africa. It was little use, even, on this occasion to seek shelter inside my mosquito-curtains, for somehow or other many blood-suckers contrived to enter, and I

passed a miserable night. The myriads of disappointed
mosquitoes which remained outside kept up a continuous
and sonorous humming, so irritating in its unvarying tone,
that the occasional snorts and grunting of the hippopotami in the neighbouring grass-fields proved quite an
agreeable interruption.

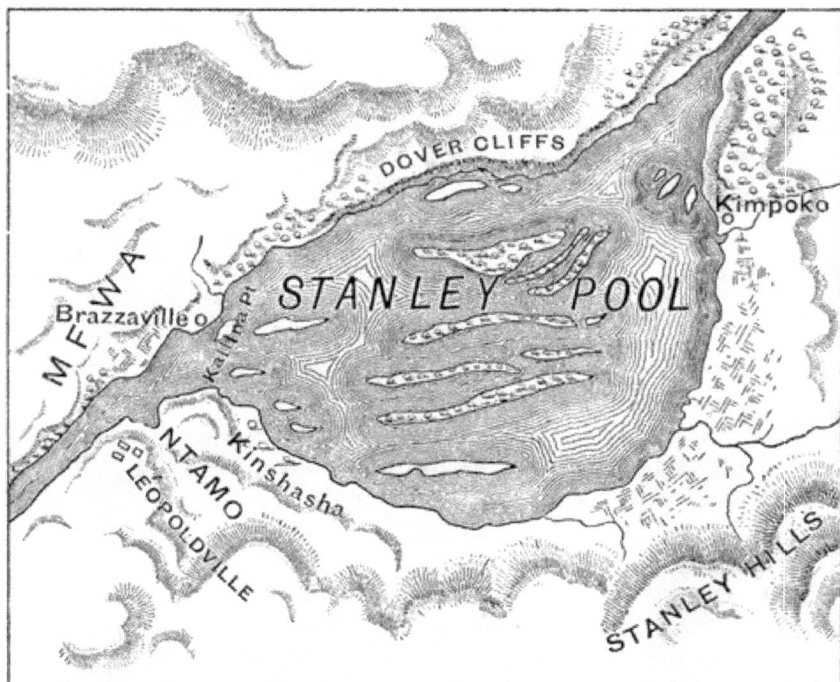

CHAPTER VIII.

STANLEY POOL TO THE KWA RIVER.

NATIVE CANOES—BUTTERFLIES—FLORA AND FAUNA OF THE RIVER-
BANKS— BANANA-COOKING—NGUI — NARROW ESCAPE FROM A
HIPPOPOTAMUS—THE BIRDS—THE NATIVE DOGS—LIEUTENANT
JANSSEN—MSUATA—A BAYANSI VILLAGE—NATIVE HAIRDRESS-
ING—PERSONAL DECORATION—A SACRED TREE—MYSTERIOUS
SLAVES.

SOME extracts from the diary kept during my fortnight's
voyage up the river beyond Stanley Pool will perhaps
most exactly give the impressions made on me at the
time by the aspect of things on the Upper Congo.

February 23rd, 1883.—I rose early, as soon as the least
diffusion of cold light was observable, and left my bed and
tent precipitately. The mosquitoes rendered one's toilet a
maddening torture, and I was thankful to repair to the
boat and eat some fried bananas there over a pleasant
book. As we left the great expansion of the Pool and
entered the narrower Congo, the forest scenery became
extravagantly rich, and many vegetable wonders were
displayed before our eyes. Farther on, the face of this
wild African nature has a little changed. On the north,
or more properly on the western, bank, the high wooded
hills continue, but along the other side stretches flat and
sandy woodland, with occasional tiny rills of delicious
water that is much preferable to that of the Congo for
drinking purposes. A little while before sunset, we
suddenly see some native canoes approaching, heavily
loaded with goods. There is now some hope of fresh food,
and my threatened *régime* of tinned provisions will be
averted. As the boat rounds a little spit of sand, we come

Hyphæne ventricosa.

upon a considerable concourse of people, who welcome us in a most friendly manner, with much clapping of hands and crying of "Mbote." Unfortunately, there is little to be had after all in the way of provisions. I buy some dried fish and a large jar of malafu, and am grossly cheated

HIGH-WOODED BANKS OF CONGO.

in both, for the fish is rotten, and the malafu has been filled up with muck and the refuse of the sugar-cane. However, this is not discovered until afterwards, and we part on the best of terms. These people are all coming from Bolobo, and are bringing ivory to sell to Ngaliéma at

Stanley Pool. I camped out rather late this evening, and fortunately hit upon a very pleasant spot in which to pass the night—a little clearing surrounded by the forest, with a pellucid stream of water running on one side of it to the Congo. Not a mosquito was to be seen. Thank Heaven! I dined comfortably and afterwards took a little walk along the river-shore by moonlight. The hippopotami, though not visible, were snorting loudly, the fishing-eagles were screaming at something that displeased them; goat-suckers and other night-birds were uttering their plaintive cries, and every now and then there was the sound of a splash and a swish in the water as some big crocodile had slid off the bank, startled at the crunching of my footsteps on the sandy beach.

Feb. 24*th.*—A delicious, dreamless night. Why should there be no mosquitoes here, and such incredible myriads a few miles lower down? The surroundings are apparently the same. The morning breaks lovely, and the day promises to pass without rain. We stopped about eleven o'clock to do some necessary washing and cooking. The spot chosen was a long stretch of sand, backed by thick forest. On the moist, smooth shore were hundreds of butterflies, many of most beautiful colours, azure blue and brilliant leaf-green. They collected in numbers round little patches of calcareous earth, where, in common with many bees, wasps, and dragon-flies, they seemed to find something so attractive that they never even moved at our approach, and one could catch them tranquilly by the thorax and pinch their life away before they could collect their airy faculties. The forest rising above the sand-bank was intersected with paths made by the buffaloes coming down to drink; and farther towards the interior was an open space trampled with their footmarks, the whole place having a strangely farm-yard look and smell. In the forest were many *cnestis* bushes with bright scarlet seed-vessels, and others with orange pods, so that the masses of green leaves were quite enlivened by these points of colour. We met some canoes this afternoon going down to Stanley Pool, filled with ivory, but with this exception there was no sign of man for some distance after leaving Kimpoko. The country, especially on the western bank, appears quite uninhabited,* and is a beautiful, uncultivated waste, with verdant slopes like natural meadows, clumps of shady forest and numberless rills of water. The vegetation overhanging the river is of a very rich character, and endlessly varying and ever-charming effects; above all, when it is mirrored in some tranquil bay, where the deep green of the foliage becomes enhanced by a brilliant shore-line of yellow-white sand, and the tender grace and the fanciful forms of the many parasitic creepers contrast with the whitened snags and fallen trees which rear their gnarled limbs out of the placid water. On these snags are perched many water birds. Little jewel-like kingfishers, smalt-blue and verditer, with scarlet beaks ; queer little bitterns, scarcely distinguishable by their modest grey coats and angular bearing from the branch on which they are posed, and an occasional black-and-white vulture or a sacred ibis. These spots offer a continual succession of little pictures with a never-ending natural charm, whether in diversity of composition or colouring. The sun has set and night has fallen ere we land at a village which as yet bears no name known to white men. It stands a little distance back from the river, but some natives fortunately come down and sell us fowls and bananas. I did not dine this evening until ten o'clock, but when Mafta at length announced the meal ready, I found it most enjoyable, for I had gained a great appetite and the dinner happened to be well cooked, one fowl being turned into soup and the other roasted. Moreover, Mafta has got into the way of making delicious " compôtes de bananes." He takes half-a-dozen of the small, sweet bananas, those that the French call " bananes d'argent," boils them in a little water to a pulp, puts in a spoonful of butter, the juice of a lemon, two or three drops of brandy (to replace sherry), stirs the whole vigorously, and turns out what seems to me an irreproach-

* Through recent internecine wars on the part of the natives.

able addition to our African cuisine. These little plump bananas are intensely sweet, so much so that no sugar is ever needed in cooking them. They, indeed, make up to me for the present want of saccharine matter which I am enduring. I have to drink my coffee without sugar, but the fried banana cakes quite atone for this want.

During my repast, I enjoyed the æsthetic delights of bright moonlight shining in softened radiance through the overarching forest, while numberless fireflies, like little points of electric light, whiz round the thick bushes. There are no mosquitoes here, and with the tranquil peace that pervades our little encampment, the perfect health that I enjoy, I feel that there are moments in Congo travel when a life of civilization is little to be envied.

February 25th.—This morning a number of people, men, women and children, flocked down to see us and to sell fowls and other articles of food. The chief, a decidedly good-looking man of about thirty, came also, and one of his attendant wives spread a leopard-skin for him to sit on. He had two little bells hung round his neck, with a multitude of teeth and beads; the teeth, which were of monkeys and leopards, being strung into fantastic neck-laces. He was pleasant and affable, and both he and his wives roared with laughter when, in order to ascertain the name of leopard in their dialect I leapt and snarled to imitate that animal. They call him here Ngui, a word which under slightly changing forms is common to many Bantu tongues. In Kiswahili it is Chui. A curious point about the Bantu languages is that the name for lion varies greatly, while that for leopard, and, above all, dog, is comparatively unchanging. The people at this village had ground-nuts (*Arachis hypogœa*) for sale, a thing I have not seen for some time on the Congo. In the river here, hippopotami are as abundant and impudent as usual. Shortly after we had set off this morning, I was startled considerably, and my breakfast went flying out of my lap at the sudden and unexpected bump which a big hippo-potamus gave to the bottom of the boat. If we had been in a canoe he would, of course, have wrecked us; as it was, although he did no great harm, yet, on afterwards examining the keel we found a decided dent in it where he had struck the iron. I felt so cross at having my nice breakfast scattered over the luggage, that I seized my Winchester, and fired it at his head as the great creature lifted it from the water a few yards off to see what damage he had done. I don't think I killed him, but his struggles in the water and the streaks of blood appearing round the spot showed that he had been sharply warned not to molest travellers again.

On a sand-bank where I stopped to bargain with some natives, there was an even greater number of butterflies collected than yesterday. They seemed to be drinking with intense pleasure from the wet shore, and I caught ten of them in no time by simply laying hold of them by the thorax.

The natives on this island were all seated in trees, perhaps for the sake of shade, but they looked terribly like gorillas. The commonest birds along the river, which hereabouts has an average breadth of 800 yards, are Egyptian geese, Gypohierax vultures, grey parrots, jaçanàs,* darters,† and the chocolate-brown Scopus um-bretta. I also saw, but failed to shoot, Lophotibis, a curious, dun-coloured species of ibis, with greenish wings, and a relatively short bill, very deep at the base, the general contour of the bird recalling the above-named *Scopus umbretta.*

February 26th.—The scenery is becoming really pic-turesque. Ordinarily the Congo is beautiful in detail, unimposing as a whole. Indeed for a river of its magni-tude it would need Alps to form suitable cliffs for such a breadth of water. In this portion, however, some of the general effects are strikingly impressive. A splendid expanse of stream reflects on its placid surface the blue sky and creamy-white clouds above it; on one side are green hills and purple woods, and on the other the inimitably graceful Hyphœne palms which in rows and

* *Parra Africana.*
† *Plotus levaillanti.*

groups rise on their slender trunks high above the low
green shrubs, and crown majestically the long spits of
white sand that launch themselves boldly into the shining,
all-reflecting river.

The Zanzibaris having found a fine fish just caught in
one of the native basket-work traps, ask permission to
stop at some sand-bank and cook it. This is accorded,
and we are soon alongside a long reach of sand, on which
some Ba-yansi are already seated. Of course our reception is cordial, and whilst the Zanzibaris are commencing their cooking I go off to see the native village
close by, called Mbila. It is a pretty, contented, quiet-
looking spot, embosomed in great groves of bananas, and
surrounded by plantations of manioc. At the time I
enter it, except a few women who are attending to their
household duties, every one is absent on the beach,
chaffering with the Zanzibaris, therefore I have it pretty
much to myself; but my arrival causes much excitement
among the fowls and dogs, who apparently are frightened
at my white face, and fly in all directions. The fowls
cackle and screech, but the dogs are too awestruck to
make any noise; indeed in this country they never seem
to have acquired the power of barking. In front of
several dwellings are the signs of domestic vocations
being actively carried on. Large jars and other vessels of
pottery are standing to dry in the sun, and basket-work
in all its stages is lying about. The houses are well
constructed and well kept, and the people, who are now
flocking back to the village, look well fed and prosperous.
Involuntarily the thought comes to me, "What a contented, peaceful sort of life this is!" Few wants, and
those easily supplied; no luxury, and no starvation; no
yearnings after the unknown, no vague, unsatisfied aspira-
tions, and no heart-breakings: everything thoroughly
positive, well-ordered, and material. How will this meet
the shock of advancing civilization—of the approaching
contact of black and white? The natives tell me I am
the first of my colour who has set foot in their village
and they seem proud and pleased at my visit. May they,

never look back to it with sorrow, as marking the advent
of a new and troublous change in their hitherto peaceful
annals! The chief of Mbila presented me ere leaving
with a fleeting souvenir of the village in the shape of the
biggest plantains I have ever seen. They measured twenty
inches in length and were very eatable.

Now the sky began to threaten. Fearful peals of
thunder resounded over the distant hills, and flashes of
lightning played against the sombre grey clouds. Yet we
escaped for a long time the threatened downpour, whilst
the storm rolled half round the horizon, but at last we
could hope no longer for immunity, and I strained my
eyes anxiously to see the station of Msuãta, which the
Zanzibaris were already able to descry with their practised
vision. Great drops began to fall, and when we at length
landed on the clayey shore a tremendous sheet of rain
was hissing through the air, hurrying the still lingering
twilight into darkness.

The chief of the station was absent at the time I
arrived, but his men showed me the most prompt attention, and I was soon installed in a comfortable bedroom,
able to wash, change my clothes, and ascertain the damage
my luggage had sustained—an almost daily occupation.

February 27th.—When I had risen this morning I
found that Lieutenant Janssen (the chief of Msuãta
Station) had arrived late the night before from a visit to a
great chief across the water, Mpumo Ntaba (the "goat"
chief), Makoko's successor. He was, however, already up,
and gave me a very kind welcome when I went to meet
him in the *salle à manger*, where an appetising breakfast
had been prepared. It consisted, if you are not tired of
continually perusing African *menus*—of mugs of goat's
milk flavoured with a little tea, roast chickens, and
"kikwanga" fried in ground-nut oil. ("Kikwanga" is,
as I have already mentioned, the root of the manioc or
cassava, pounded, soaked and fermented, somewhat sour
and "gluey" in taste. There is the ordinary article,
called here by the natives Bingolo, and a superior kind
more carefully prepared, with little air-holes in it like a

Gruyère cheese. This is Luku, and it faintly resembles muffins when hot and eaten with butter.)

M. Janssen is one of the most practical and sensible members of the Expedition.* His talent for making the best of limited resources is wonderful, and Msuāta, purely through his energetic and enterprising labours, has become one of the most comfortable stations on the route. He has constructed a swimming-bath by damming up a little river, he has made a large and a small gridiron out of the barrels of damaged guns, a table and benches from the planks of old canoes, and an oven of sun-dried bricks. He has planted a kitchen-garden which produces all manner of vegetables; has organised a well-stocked poultry-yard, containing over eighty fowls, with a house for their numerous eggs to be laid in; four or five of his goats are always in milk, and amongst other discoveries he has learnt to make native salads and sauces, and to extract an excellent oil from the ground-nuts, which at once serves for cooking purposes and for lighting up the lamps he has manufactured to use when his candles give out.

Around the station of Msuāta, the commonest birds are little "bishop" finches, or more properly, weaver-birds, with scarlet and black plumage; huge plantain-eaters,† blue-green in colour, with a violet crest; large bee-eaters, kites, egrets, and cuckoos. On the northern bank of the river the lion is said to be known, and the chief Makoko received De Brazza seated on the skin of one of these animals. If *Felis leo* is really found in this part of the Congo regions it is curious, as he is not a forest-loving animal, and moreover would not find in these countries the herds of big game which are and have been the *raisin d'être* of this great cat.

The natives on the northern bank opposite Msuāta profess to know the gorilla, and certainly describe it accurately, but say it is found far inland, and does not reach to the

* He is since unhappily dead; drowned by the upsetting of a canoe on the Congo, July, 1883.
† *Schizorhis gigantea.*

banks of the Congo. A curious roller-bird, *Eurystomus*, is found here, and in small numbers mobs and chases fiercely the hawks and fishing-eagles of the river.

The country in the neighbourhood of Msuâta is thickly populated, in fact we are beginning to enter the densely-peopled basin of the Upper Congo.

The villages hereabouts belong principally to the Ba-teke men, and the Ba-yansi people that one meets with are mostly traders and not as yet settled in any permanent colonies. Farther up the Congo, these two races are strangely intermixed, the villages being often alternately of either nationality. Still, while the Ba-teke seem to have their real home and origin to the N.W. and towards the Ogowé, the Ba-yansi come from farther up the river, and border on the (so-called) savage Ba-ngala of the Equator.

February 28th.—We started this morning for the mouth of the Kwa or Wabûma River, fifteen miles from Msuâta, where I intended to stop the night in a large village. On our way we passed the curious promonotory of Ganchu—a long spit of land advancing into the river, which seems to alternate between island and peninsula. Here is situated the village of Ganchu, ruled by an important and powerful chief of that name, who, like Lutete and other minor potentates on the Congo, gives his name to his residential town. The houses of this village are mostly built on piles, evidently, as the ground is low, to minimise the dangers and inconveniences of a flood. It was this village that Stanley, on his first and celebrated descent of the Congo, imagined to be inhabited by river pirates, mis-understanding the peaceful intention of the inhabitants, and it was for some time, I believe, marked "Piraten Dorf" on the German maps.

At the mouth of the Kwa River (which, parenthetically, I might mention flows from Lake Léopold II., joins the great Kwango from Angola, and enters the Congo about 3° 20' S. latitude *) is a large and populous Ba-yansi

* The Kwa River stream at its juncture with the Congo is about as broad as the Thames at Westminster. The landscapes and river-

village, the first fixed settlement of this enterprising tribe to be encountered on a journey up the Congo. It is exactly at the confluence of the Kwa and the Congo, and is very picturesque as seen from the water, a broad lane leading up to a grove of oil-palms and bananas, with compact and tidy-looking houses interspersed among them; but the favourable impression is rather spoilt on landing by the horrible black fetid mud, strewn with decaying offal, that one has to cross. The people, of course, are assembled to greet us, and the chief is there, clad in a rusty red garment, and looking not half such a fine fellow as many of his subjects. These people here are a finer-looking race than any I have yet seen on the Congo. Some of the men are perfect Greek statues as regards the splendid development and poise of their figures. They all have pleasing faces because of the good humour which enlivens their features. Another remarkable point about

---

scapes along the banks of this affluent are pretty, being mostly shadowy water and rich forest, but otherwise, considering the bulk of this mighty river, it is unimposing. The mouth of the Kwa is not very well adapted for navigation, there being a long sand-bank on one side, and a line of rocks on the other, only a tortuous passage laying between, while the force of the current through this channel is very strong. The upper course of the Kwa much resembles the Congo in appearance. Issuing from Lake Léopold II., an expansion of water about seventy miles in length, it broadens out greatly in a flat country of dense forest, and is covered with many islands. It narrows again where it receives the great Kwango, and the embouchure of these two great rivers united is somewhat insignificant. Their waters flow for some time side by side without mingling with those of the Congo.

NOTE.—Since this was written, the explorations of Wissmann, Grenfell, Wolff and others have resulted in the discovery that the Kwa is none other than the Great Kasai, the most important affluent of the Congo, to which are joined the Saukuru with all its affluents, the Kwango and its tributary streams, and the rivers from the Bakundi country. The Kasai or Kwa system, therefore, drains almost a third of the entire Congo basin. These rivers, also, are navigable for hundreds of miles by light-draught steamers. The extraordinary importance of these navigable routes into the heart of Africa is only just beginning to be realized, though Stanley appreciated it fully fifteen years ago. Manchester scoffed then, and is the loser now.

them is their comparatively great development of hair, on the head especially, but also at an early age, all over the body, although arrived at maturity their persons are quite hairless, for, like most negroes, they dislike extremely all growth of hair on the body, and pluck out every hair that makes its appearance, scarcely liking even the beard to grow. However, *en revanche*, the hair of the head is much encouraged, and really attains to an astonishing length, and though crisp and curly, is tortured and twisted by its possessors into all sorts of fantastic coiffures. The men wear it usually in horns, either on the top of the head, or in a pigtail, or depending on each side of their cheek; also in a sort of "chignon." The women sometimes just frizz it up round the head, or comb it out smoothly and strain it over pads in a manner much resembling a hideous style in vogue with us some fifteen years ago; or they will plait it into an infinitude of little rat's tails that, from their stiffness, stand up all round the head in a bristling manner.

A red dye, which is got from the bark of a certain tree, probably the "camwood" * is used to a great extent for colouring their nails, and often their bodies and clothes, with a warm tinge of red. They also further decorate themselves with white, yellow, and black patterns, made respectively with calcareous earth, yellow-ochre, and burnt wood. There is much diversity in these designs. Sometimes they will draw a white line round their eye-lids and down the bridge of their noses, with a line of yellow straight down the body from the throat to the navel, and black patches on the cheek-bones; but the variety of patterns and designs is too numerous to cata-logue. They also practise largely a curious mode of decoration by cicatrisation, scoring the cheeks with parallel lines, and forming eccentric designs, with raised weals or lumps of skin all over their bodies. The cloth they wear is nearly all of native manufacture (made of woven grass), and is largely dyed and tinged with the

* *Baphia nitida.*

favourite maroon dye. Did they know it, these home-made stuffs are far more tasteful than the staring Manchester cottons which they are just beginning to covet. The women are always more clothed than the men, from the time that they are nubile, but as children, and in adolescence they are generally without even a scrap of clothing, whereas the little boys never seem unprovided with a tiny apron. The women do not attempt, as in some tribes, to hide their breasts; perhaps for the reason that their busts are modelled and developed to a much more artistic degree than is usual among African races.

Some of the young girls are charming little creatures, with their tidily dressed hair, their small hands and feet, and their budding forms of womanhood. Until they reach a marriageable age, they run about gaily in all the beauty and innocence of perfect nudity, the sole attempt at—what shall I say?—clothing, or personal adornment, being a large brass collar round the neck, and copper anklets. There was one such child that I shall always remember with affection in this village at the mouth of the Kwa. We took a mutual fancy to one another, and she constituted herself my little guide, taking my hand with the greatest confidence and leading me through the village to show me the sights. Seeing me gather flowers to preserve, she afterwards presented me with an armful which she had laboriously plucked, and later on she pressed into my hand three new-laid eggs, warm from the nest, from which she had probably robbed them.

One word for the babies: they squall terribly, and are endowed with plentiful crops of hair, which is finer in quality and less curly than that of their grown-up parents.

The people here have a regular craving for salt, and the chief was enraptured with the bestowal of a handful; one gentleman brought his wife, or one of his wives, and wished to exchange her for a moderate quantity of the precious condiment.

There was a fine handsome tree in the centre of a broad square here, covered with large yellow blossoms of graceful shape and delicate vanilla-like perfume. It was evidently regarded by the natives with some veneration, for I could see they did not like me to gather the flowers, and after I had picked one or two sprays, they asked me to desist, offering me yellow pumpkin flowers as an equivalent.

I slept this night in a comfortable and cleanly house, divided into three rooms, which might be described as kitchen, parlour, and bedroom. The more we advance into the interior along the Congo, the higher in social science the natives seem to stand; the houses, their furniture, decoration and orderly comfort; the utensils, the pottery and the work in metal : all seem to undergo a material improvement and development in proportion as we leave the coast behind us.

March 1st.—We bid adieu to our friends this morning with many protestations of mutual regard, and they came down to the slimy shore and shouted, " Mbote ! " until we were out of sight. I was hardly in a state to reciprocate their boisterous friendship, for an insidious attack of fever was creeping over me. It began, as usual, with a great increase of mental activity. One is too excited to stop and write down one's thoughts, although you feel that had you done so, some very brilliant things might have been preserved. But all exertion is disagreeable to the fever's victim, and he feels content to sit and compose chapters of novels and disquisitions on Natural History problems in his whirling brain, without attempting to commit the fleeting kaleidoscope images to paper. This first stage of the fever is by no means disagreeable. One enjoys the same sensations as those produced by a sufficiency of good champagne ; but, unfortunately, the phase of utter weariness and melancholy that follows is a bitter contrast to the preceding elevation and excitement, and the brilliant images of heretofore now seem trite stupidities.*

---

* However, I was singularly lucky in Africa. These fleeting touches of fever, rarely lasting more than a few hours, and scarcely worthy to be chronicled, were the only form of indisposition I ever had during my sixteen months passed in the Dark Continent.

We advanced but little to-day beyond the Kwa for continuing to feel poorly, I stopped the boat at noon and had my tent put up on the eastern shore, so that I might go to bed and get rid of the fever. We were here nearly opposite to the embouchure of some large river flowing in on the western bank of the Congo.*   The country is so populous hereabouts that it is impossible to camp anywhere without being near a village, consequently we were soon surrounded by crowds of noisy though good-tempered natives.   I noticed this afternoon among the people that came to look at me a curious type, quite different from the rest, a small youth (or a young man?) with rather long, curly, and yellowish hair, arranged on his scalp in separate tufts, *floconné*, as the French would call it, having, moreover, a savage and wild expression on his features and a general *tournure* of body recalling the bushmen whom I have seen in South-Western Africa. Curiously enough, there was an old woman, also with yellowish hair, and stunted in form, in the last village we passed. "Yellowish" is perhaps not quite accurate enough. I might rather say a dirty dun-colour like the skins of these queer beings. I made inquiries through the Zanzibaris as to who they were in each village, but beyond learning that they were slaves and came from the East, I ascertained nothing further, nor could I find out whether they belonged to a tribe of dwarfs or not. The little boy with his bow and arrows and his savage face and gestures was a strange and striking type, utterly different to the grinning, good-tempered children round him, who, by contrast, appeared quite black, so pale in colour was his skin.

* De Brazza's *Alima*.   The "Lawson" River of Stanley.

CHAPTER IX.

TO BOLOBO.

Mbongo—French Flags at Mbamo—Embe—Value of Salt—
Footprints of Hippopotami—Sand-banks and Islands—
Bolobo—The Great Chief Ibaka—The Mosquitoes—A Royal
Visit—A Drinking Ceremony—Ibaka's peculiar Hat—Houses
at Bolobo—A Sketching Adventure—The Fetish Man—
His Duties and Occupations—Herds of Elephants and
Buffaloes—Animals of the District—Metals—Monkoli
Topaz.

March 2nd.—The forest scenery is becoming richer and
more "tropical looking" the farther we advance towards
the Equator, that is, I mean, that the vegetation is assuming the same luxuriant character, the wild exuberant
growth which are usually associated with aspects of nature
under an equatorial sun and a zone of constant rain.
The stream of the Congo is at the present time thronged
with masses of a brilliantly green water-plant, *Pistia
stratiotes*, common to most tropical rivers. The recent
floods have detached it from the little inlets and quiet
reaches, where it ordinarily grows, and have brought it
down in great quantities with the stream, and are also the
cause of the many floating logs and torn-up trees which
frequently block the navigation.

There are many rocks along the river's bank and
stretching out some distance into the current, suggesting
the idea of their being the remains of ancient cataracts.
Indeed when one says that the falls of the Congo do not
begin until below Stanley Pool, it is hardly correct. The
only difference between the upper and lower river is this,
that above Stanley Pool the rapids are never sufficiently
serious to hinder navigation.

About four o'clock, the men wanted to stop at a large
and populous village, the natives of which, to the number
of nearly a hundred, were assembled along the sandy
beach imploring us to land and pass the night in their
town.   They vaunted the abundance of fowls, kikwanga,
and other victuals, but I would not yield, for we had yet
two hours of daylight which it was imperative not to

Piotia otratiotes.

waste, and I felt sure, as all this eastern side of the river
is thickly populated, that we should be likely to find
another village farther on.   We did so an hour and a half
later, but there was a furious rapid to cross before we
could reach it—one that had to be attempted twice before
we could struggle past the rocks.   Unfortunately, the
men broke two oars here, and, therefore, for the rest of the

journey we shall have lost two rowers. Once we had
landed, I felt pleased at having opposed the wishes of the
Zanzibaris, because I had gained two hours of daylight,
passed the formidable rapids, and chosen for our night's
sojourn the nicest little village I have met with on the
Congo. Its name is Mbongo. The people were very kind
and courteous. They spread grass mats for me to sit on,
brought me fresh malafu to drink, and seeing I had a

Pistia stratiotes.

feverish attack, left me in peace in my tent with many
expressions of sympathy. Later on in the evening, the
chief arrived with a present of four fowls, a calabash of
malafu, and, most welcome of all, some new-laid eggs.
The malafu here is made exclusively from the juice of the
sugar-cane. The fermented drink made from the wine
palm (*Raphia vinifera*) or the oil-palm (*Elaïs guineënsis*)
is unknown, though in each village many of these trees

are growing.   Strange that the sugar-cane, another of the
many gifts from rich America to needy Africa, should
have spread so quickly and so far inland, and have become
so identified with the habits and customs of its new cultivators.   Though this cane was originally an inhabitant of
Eastern Asia, and was introduced by the Arabs to Europe,
and by the Europeans to America, still Western Africa
received it from the latter continent in the seventeenth
century through the hands of the Portuguese.*

March 3rd.—I obtained this morning a basket-work
fish-trap from a boy, with a few curious fish in it.   Most
of them were too damaged to be of any use, but one,
fortunately just caught and still alive, was in excellent
preservation ; so I set to work and drew it as we went
along in the boat.   Just as I was finishing the sketch we
approached a village called Mbãmo, where two or three
tattered French flags were flying.   At first the natives
answered civilly our questions, and told us that Malamine
(Malamine was a Senegalese sergeant of De Brazza's) had
given them the tricoloured banners of France ; but afterwards, when we proposed landing to cook the lunch, they
began to grow very insolent and menacing—they yelled
and shrieked at us in gradually increasing wrath, and,
whilst the women and children fled into the village, the
men got their guns and began cramming stones into the
muzzles.   They were very near firing, but the Zanzibaris
showed their Sniders opportunely, and at the same time
rowed out into the stream, and we passed the place
without breaking the peace.   Curiously enough, on
rounding a little point of rocks, and arriving at another
village, we found the people there perfectly friendly and
pleasant.   They waded out to the boat and shook hands,
and looked at my sketch-book with screams of delight.

---

* Since writing this, I find on examining the subject by means of
Cameron's and Stanley's books, together with other authorities, that
the sugar-cane seems to be cultivated right across Africa from east to
west.   Possibly, therefore, the West Africans owe it to the Arabs, who
brought it to the east coast a thousand years ago, whence it has spread
all over the continent.

The chief here, at this village of Embe, had a most unusual crop of hair. These Ba-yansi are, indeed, remarkable for the abundance and glossiness of their "chevelure." In the next village (the eastern bank of the river has become a continuous series of hamlets) I saw a woman with an even more magnificent head of hair. Her locks were combed out in a sort of "aureola" round her well-shaped head. This race of the Ba-yansi, and, indeed, all

THE CHIEF OF EMBE.

other highly developed types of Bantu peoples, remind me so much, with their high-bridged noses and bushy hair, of the Papuans, as one may judge of them from the descriptions and photographs of Wallace and other travellers. The banks of the Congo are here and for some distance further back strewn with great masses of rock, seemingly of igneous origin. Interspersed among these craggy blocks are patches of silvery sand, and the natives run along the banks, jumping from rock to rock to try and keep up with the boat. Some of them, generally women

M

carrying babies, will get far ahead, and station themselves
on some little promontory, thence hailing our approach
with deafening screams and laughter. The villages are
very prettily situated amid majestic groves of oil-palms
and bright green bananas, with a background of deep
purple forest.

The neatly-made houses, often quite yellow in colour
from the sun-burnt grass with which they are thatched,
overhang the river on the edge of a slight plateau, and
form a pretty contrast against the dark-green vegetation.
Numbers of grey parrots are here, and they seem to rather
seek than avoid the society of man, for in every village
they flock to the oil-palms, where they squawk and whistle
all day long.

Now the Congo begins to open out into truly splendid
breadth. Right before us is a clear horizon of water and
sky, only broken by one wooded islet that stands right in
the middle of the stream. The river is as broad or broader
here than Stanley Pool. A traveller viewing the Congo
from this direction, and knowing nothing of what was
before him, might well believe he was entering upon some
great lake or inland sea.

The day is magnificent; and towards the close of a
tranquil afternoon, when the sky assumes a faint golden
tone, the great smooth sheet of water of the same rich
colour, stretches away towards the horizon, where it melts
indistinguishably into the warm sky. Save one or two
ripples that look like blue scratches on its surface, there
is nothing to disturb its glowing calm, and the very
hippopotami, who but a short while before were playing,
splashing and snorting so obstreperously, seem awed
into quietude by the perfect air of peace that envelopes
everything. The foliage of the great forest trees that
tower above the shore, where the tiniest of wavelets are
lapping the golden sand, is unmoved by the slightest
breeze, and the few salmon-coloured clouds that have
mounted the horizon are arrested in their flight, and hang
motionless in the mellow sky. It is a harmony in the
palest pink and the palest gold, to which the Zanzibaris

are quite insensible, for they interrupt my musings by asking if they may stop for the night at a large and populous village which we have just reached, and their request is seconded by the natives on the shore, who offer us the most vociferous greetings and entreaties to honour their village with our presence. However, it is only four o'clock and we have two hours more daylight, so I will not yield, and the Zanzibaris with a very bad grace put their oars into the water again. They rowed for about an hour, but did not make much progress, for there were several rapids to cross, and the men were, or affected to be, tired, and patted their stomachs lugubriously, predicting "no chop and natives plenty bad" at the next village we meet. They are fairly right, for when we direct our course towards some huts embosomed in palm trees at the end of a pretty little creek, the inhabitants rush down to the beach and ask us in African phraseology *just* to wait until they can get their guns, and then they will give us a warm reception. Even the little boys imitate the action of putting a gun to the shoulder with their tiny lances, and the women shriek, and laugh, and utter all sorts of derisive things. I suspect it was more than half of it "show off," as, had there been any prospect of a real conflict, the women and children would have been sent away to the bush. However, as it was only five o'clock, and there was sure to be another village round the distant point of rocks (we could already distinguish its bananas and palm-trees), it was decided that we should leave these inhospitable savages to themselves. We were soon in front of the next hamlet, whence a friendly greeting reached us over the water, but between us and them stretched a terrible line of rocks and breakers that took us a whole hour to cross, the men having to get into the water and drag the boat along by main force. Our landing was momentarily delayed by the arrival of a deputation from the preceding village, which had followed us quickly along the shore. They met the friendly natives and entreated them not to let us land, but the timely waving of some bright coloured pocket-handkerchiefs and the

jingling of brass rods decided all hesitation as to our
reception, and the hostile natives beat a swift and
ignominious retreat, followed by the taunts of the friendly
ones.   We landed at dusk, and were met with a clamour
of greetings that was perfectly deafening.   Fowls and

THE FRIENDLY VILLAGE.

eggs were brought for sale, and, though rather dear, I
bought them to strengthen our mutual friendship, for
there is nothing like commerce to inspire confidence and
lull suspicion.   When I gave one man a handful of salt,
which they call "Mpongwe," his yells of delight were

quite painful, whilst each of his comrades repeated after him, with an hysterical, and a falsetto voice, "Mpongwe, mpongwe!" Therefore, being on terms of such cordiality, I took the liberty of asking them to go away and let me eat and sleep in peace, which, to my relief, they promptly did, telling the Zanzibaris before leaving that I must indeed be a great chief to possess two whole bottles of salt.

March 4th.—What a miserable morning! One can hardly believe oneself in the same world as yesterday— a sky filled with fearful storm-clouds and a thick rain falling. It required some resolution to start, and the Zanzibaris suggested our remaining till noon where we were, but right or wrong I insisted on going on. I don't think I stood very well in the men's graces this morning. Yesterday I gave them two hours' more work than they wanted, and to-day I made them start in the rain. Two or three smart showers followed up the storm, then a burst of furious wind which lashed the Congo into waves and rocked our boat as if we were on the sea; then a dead calm and, at last, our faithless friend, the sun, veiling himself with white clouds, appeared in a half-hearted, shame-stricken manner. About noon, the orb now shining brightly, we stopped at a little island, one of the many that dot the surface of the vast river, to give the men time to cook their bananas. It was not remarkable for much beyond footprints in the moist soil. I drew several of these impressions in my sketch-book, as they gave an excellent idea of the "artiodactyle" foot in an incipient stage. Here too, and on other neighbouring islands, was growing a papilionaceous plant new to me, having leaves and a thorny stem like the mimosas, with flowers of a gaudy orange.

Towards sunset we halted at a sand-bank, or sandy island, in the middle of the Congo, half a mile in width and perhaps a mile long. On arriving, a multitude of water birds were in possession, but at our approach they flew off to other haunts. There only remained large flocks of red-billed terns, which circled and screamed round our heads as if demanding compensation for being turned out of their own property.

Here, on this island, it seemed like the land of a visionary. A gorgeous sunset, with glowing masses of golden-red clouds irradiated the west, and repeated its glories with almost undiminished brilliancy in the vast sheet of tranquil water. On one side of us fantastically wooded, palm-crested islets floated in reflected gold, with every branch and frond of their tree-tops telling out against the shining sky. Long lines of weary birds flew low over the water, with faint cries of greeting to each other as they neared their shelter for the night. On the other side of the island, and so close as almost to overshadow us, great masses of waterside forest rose into the sky, tinged with the warm yellow light of the opposite sunset, and filling with their long and clear reflections the strait of water that lay between them and our sandy shore.

The grey parrots were in high spirits to-night, as they flew home across the river. They seemed to be telling each other "good things" as they passed over our heads in little bands, for their exulting screams and chuckling whistles were full of wild merriment. Whenever the grey parrot appears to be in a good temper flying home it is a sign, according to my observation, that the morrow is going to be a fine day, as also when he is out on his travels early in the morning.

At length the glowing sunset died away, and I had, half reluctantly, to turn from this dreamland, where somehow thoughts of home seemed insensibly mingled with the clouds, the birds and the shimmering water, and attend to the necessities of the moment. Without my personal superintendence dinner would be an uncertain result, so the chest of provisions had to be unpacked and its contents distributed; and whilst Mafta, the Zanzibari cook, my pupil in the culinary art, was killing a lean fowl, first reverently saying, "In the name of Allah" as he cut its throat, I sat on a camp-stool dealing out the preserved vegetables, the lemon-juice, the flour, butter, rice, bananas, salt and pepper, that were to go, together with the fowl bouillon, to make a perfect soup. The flesh has to be cut off from the fowl bones, and is put with them into the pot to simmer slowly. Then the liver and gizzard are chopped up fine and thrown into the savoury bubbling broth, and the result is an appetising and soothing soup, in which a great amount of nourishment may be commodiously swallowed. The preparation of this meal, however, is somewhat lengthy, and ere it is served to me on my impromptu table of chests and boxes, the dusky drowsy night has swallowed up the beauties of the twilight. How utter is the feeling of isolation here! There is nothing to alarm or sadden; on the contrary, the girdle of darkness round our little island gives it a cosy feeling of security and peace, but we seem here so remote from everything but the stars.

March 5th.—We started by the early dawn in order to reach Bolobo by the evening if possible. The river, in this part of its course, owing no doubt to its great breadth, appears to be very shallow, and the boat is constantly running aground on sand-banks: nor do the natives' canoes that are round us escape entirely this contrariety, however slight their draught of water may be. It has a very extraordinary effect to see men walking halfway over a great branch of the river, with water only up to their ankles, tracing the course of some hidden sand-bank.

The high hills and downs that have hitherto bordered the Congo begin to grow more and more distant, and finally disappear into blue obscurity. One last range comes into view and terminates abruptly in a solitary peak, somewhat picturesquely jagged, and then the great basin of central Africa begins, and splendid forests take possession of the banks of the river, woods of such a magnificent character that I think I have never seen richer growth of vegetation in Africa.

There are here so many islands that it is difficult to see the mainland, except at rare intervals. One of them alone is ten miles long.

A great concourse of people, and an almost continuous series of villages on the east bank, show that we are entering the very populous district of Bolobo. At the principal assemblage of houses, in a picturesque and leafy spot, the Zanzibaris stop rowing, for the great chief of all this district, Ibaka, " Roi de Bolobo," as he is called in the Expedition, is seen wending his way down to the beach, accompanied by many women, to greet the white man who has entered his territory. He wears a hat as famous as that of Chumbiri in Stanley's 'Dark Continent.' Ibaka comes down to the water-side, leans over the boat and shakes hands cordially, after which, with many "Mbotes"—magic word!—we continue our route on towards the station, while Ibaka shouts out an equivalent to " au revoir." We can now descry our destination on a distant headland, but, in spite of the utmost efforts on the part of the Zanzibaris, we do not arrive until nightfall, for we are constantly sticking on sand-banks and running upon sunken trees.

Bólóbó station * is situated on the summit of a bluff rising directly from the river. The place consists of one large stockaded building, at once a residence for the white man, and a citadel of resistance in case of attack, and a series of little habitations clustered round the centre, where the Zanzibaris and the Krumanos † live. This little station and its tiny garrison were very nearly having to fight for their lives a short time before my arrival. Some relative of King Ibaka's wishing to get up a little diversion which would redound to his glory, proposed to his followers to loot the station and massacre the whites. Fortunately, when all were preparing for the struggle, King Ibaka intervened, and matters now looked very smooth, the

---

* This establishment was the farthest settlement of white men on the Congo at the time of my visit, though, now there are many other stations founded far beyond it.

† " Krumanos," a Portuguese corruption of Kru man or Kru boy, is conventionally used on the upper river to indicate the indigenous carriers and servants who work for hire. On the lower river it means " slaves."

fortifications, however, remained to show through what a time of anxiety the station had passed.*

There are three Europeans here, Lieut. Orban, the chief of the station, and two commercial agents, a Frenchman and a Belgian.

Bolobo has one terrible disadvantage. Mosquitoes abound to such an incredible degree that after dark it is torture to have to sit at dinner, for they bite through your trousers and socks—your hands, too, are soon swollen and poisoned. Consequently all pleasant conversation at Bolobo is impossible after the cloth has been withdrawn; and you hasten off to bed to put a mosquito-curtain between yourself and your enemies. There was one great and unaccustomed treat I enjoyed at Bolobo, which, after my long deprivation, seemed to compensate for all other things lacking—plenty of coffee and good goat's milk. Food generally is scarce, and what there is consists of the same unchanging fowls, goats, and kikwanga.

March 6th.—This morning early, King Ibaka, attended by a numerous and distingushed suite, arrived to pay us a visit. After the palaver of ceremony was over I asked permission to take his portrait, which was accorded, but he had not the slightest intention of sitting for it, and moved about at will. At length Orban hit on an excellent expedient for inducing the King to give me a chance of successfully portraying his features, and at the same time of exhibiting to me a curious native custom. So he proposed to Ibaka a solemn drinking bout of malafu. "Le Roi de Bolobo" willingly assented, and certain hirelings were told off to go and fetch some large jars of freshly-drawn palm-wine.

Long, long ago, in the legends of the Ba-yansi,† a King of Bolobo was drinking malafu at his ease one day when

---

* Since I left Bolobo, war actually took place, and the besieged garrison were only relieved by the opportune arrival of Mr. Stanley, who quelled the disturbances without firing a shot.

† This is one of the many local explanations of these curious drinking customs, but it will not suffice to explain them all, nor to account for their wide-spread existence in Western Africa.

a leopard stole up behind him unawares, jumped on his back, and strangled him before the King could cry for help.   To avoid such a catastrophe in future, the following ceremony was instituted by his successor.   Before the King is about to drink, he imposes silence on the people assembled by snapping his fingers towards them and crying "Mà" ("mà" is an exclamation to call attention to anything: it is used to dogs).   A wife is crouched behind him, a little boy on his left hand.   The wife then also calls "Mà," and clasps her lord tightly round the stomach with both hands.   The little boy covers his face with one hand, and claps the other continually on his extended leg.   Then the King, sticking the first finger of his left hand into his throat, below the ear, with the right hand raises the glass and drinks.   After he has quenched his thirst he passes his hand across his mouth, and then points with his first finger in the direction where he next intends to levy war.   When he has not any quarrel immediately on hand, he simply points his finger upwards ; then snaps his finger, says "Mà" again, and the ceremony is at an end and talking is resumed.   All the details of this tiring performance were carefully gone through whilst Ibaka drank the malafu in our presence ; but I should think the constant repetition of this ritual every time he drinks must be very wearying to the flesh.   Orban tells me, however, that on occasions of hurry or emergency there is a sort of shorter service, when it suffices the King to be in absolute darkness, like a sensitive "negative," to quench his thirst without going through the more elaborate ceremonies observed on other occasions.   Ibaka's hat is a very remarkable one.   There is literally more in it than meets the eye, for within this capacious receptacle much "cloth" and all his most special and private valuables are stored.   This extraordinary structure, which is made out of plaited grass, never leaves Ibaka's head more than once a twelvemonth, "for our annual cleaning," and he wears it day and night.   "Uneasy lies the head that wears a crown."   The decorations of Ibaka's hat are of exotic origin.   The lizards are cut out of tinfoil, and manufactured, possibly in Birmingham, and that curious plaque in the centre is the label of the first and only champagne bottle which ever reached Bolobo, and which was drunk on the birthday of the King of the Belgians. Ibaka attended the banquet, but declined any champagne, asking, however, for its glittering label.

These curious wicker-work, or plaited-grass hats, are common to all the great chiefs in this part of the Upper Congo.

The civilization of the natives of Bolobo, who are Ba-yansi people, is of a higher order than is usually met with in savage Africa, and it is certainly purely indigenous. Their houses, arms, and household implements are constructed with skill and taste, and the people generally exhibit a considerable amount of *savoir faire et vivre.* They are great traders, and travel many hundred miles up and down the river, engaged in trafficking their ivory, slaves, and smoked fish.

In the afternoon, to-day, I went into one of the neighbouring towns, some two miles distant, where I wished to draw a house, for the dwellings here differ considerably in design and construction from those farther down the river, and to study the way of living of its inhabitants. The natives received me very well, and took great interest in my work; too much interest, in fact, for certain officious friends, in their anxiety to keep the course clear, showed an ill-judged severity towards the unwitting persons who came between me and my object. They beat a woman, who beat a boy, who threw a stone at somebody else, and soon there was a general row, in the middle of which I thought it best to retire, in case the excitement which was surging amongst them should be turned against the white man who had unwittingly brought discord into their peaceful village with his sorcerish practices of "scratching images on white cloth with a piece of stick." Indeed, had I doubted as to the propriety of retiring to fresh fields and pastures new, my hesitation would not have lasted long, for a friendly young man, who had in a measure constituted himself my guide, took my sketch-

book with an apologetic " Mbote," closed it gently, and
taking me by the hand led me out of the crowd.   Fortunately my sketch of the house itself was finished, and I
was only obliged to leave incomplete a group of natives in
the foreground.   I tried to make my retreat seem as little
like one as possible, and stopped frequently to play with
children and admire the arms and spears of the natives
who were closing up behind me.   All the same, I felt
myself being as politely as possible ejected from the
village, and the smiling natives insisted on accompanying

HOUSE IN BOLOĽO.

me until I was well out of the precincts of their place,
and on the road to the station.   After all, I think they
behaved very well in not assaulting me.   I was alone,
unarmed, and completely in their power.   It was the first
time a white man had ever visited that spot, and then he
must needs signalise his visit by doing such uncanny
things as making sketches and collecting plants, from
either of which mal-practices any sensitive negro might
have been justified in accusing him of witchcraft, and
excused for wishing to break the spell by shedding his
blood.

However, shortly after my return to the station King Ibaka arrived, with the most profuse apologies for my ejectment by his subjects; in fact, he said he felt so bitterly the slight which had been offered to one of his friends, that he could only be assured of the restoration of our former good relations if, just as a form, I would give him a present of some blue cloth. I paid this debt to friendship, but King Ibaka received evasively my request to come and visit him *chez lui*, although I did afterwards make a sort of formal tour of a little village, being walked round the place by the King himself, but not allowed to stop anywhere and sketch.

A few pine-apples are found at Bolobo between the station and the native towns, but the fruit appears to be rare elsewhere in the vicinity, and we are evidently here on the confines of the district over which "Ananassa sativa" has spread with such wonderful vigour and rapidity. Another American introduction of a much later date, and of decidedly different bearing towards mankind—the horrible little "jigger" or burrowing flea—has just reached Bolobo from the coast, though so recently that the natives are only just beginning to be conscious of its presence, and have not yet given it a name.

This evening was passed like most others at Bolobo. We held out against the mosquitoes just long enough to eat our dinner, and then hurried off to bed and the relief from these tortures that is only to be found within.

SUPPLEMENTARY NOTES ON BOLOBO.

The people inhabiting the banks of the Congo in this district are, as has already been stated, Ba-yansi, but this race seems limited to little more than a strip of land bordering the river, and does not extend its settlements far from the banks. On the eastern side of the Congo the race of the interior is the Ba-nūnū, who seem to live on friendly terms with the Ba-yansi. At Bolobo there is no local fetish-man or doctor, and the people there have to depend on the Ba-nūnū to supply one when necessary. This personage is required for many purposes—to perform certain rites and ceremonies such as circumcision, to heal sicknesses, and to decide legal disputes or judge criminals. The fetish-man's decisions on all knotty points of law, and his general perspicacity in judicial investigations, are much thought of among the Ba-yansi. When the Mu-nūnū is called upon to examine into some case of theft or crime, he subjects the implicated persons to a most rigorous questioning before arriving at a decision. The "costs" exacted by this gentleman are tremendous, and act effectively as a prevention against undue litigiousness on the part of natives.

Ibaka, the paramount chief of Bolobo, is one of the few potentates of the Western Congo that can be said in any way to be a ruler or kinglet of importance. His sovereignty is hereditary, and his family is considered royal even in its collateral branches. He rules over a thickly inhabited strip of the river about seventy miles in length, of uncertain width, and with a population of from forty to fifty thousand. Beyond his own subjects, however, his influence is widely felt throughout the Ba-yansi tribes, and he occupies perhaps the same position towards that people as Mpūmo Ntaba, the successor of Makoko, does towards the Ba-teke.

The country in the vicinity of Bolobo is a low table-land covered with dense forest. We are here in the central basin of Africa, through which the course of the Upper Congo lies, and the forests owe much of their luxuriance to the abundant rain-fall and to the short duration of the dry season.

Owing to the dense population and the prevalence of cultivated districts even in the forest, many wild animals seem to shun this country; still there are large herds of elephants and buffaloes which are little interfered with by the natives, whose sporting proclivities are not very strong, and whose ivory is all received from tribes further up the river, and not procured from the herds of proboscideans which range these forests. In the same way, although the red buffalo's skulls and horns may be constantly seen in the villages, I never heard of the people taking the trouble to hunt it; they seem rather to content themselves with gathering these relics whenever they meet with them, doubtless after the feast of some lion or leopard, and depositing them among the half-sacred curiosities of their villages.*

The lion, leopard, striped hyæna, black-backed jackal, and civet cat are known here, and the gorilla, or some kindred anthropoid ape, is described by the natives as inhabiting the northern or western bank of the Congo. The red river-hog,† which the natives call by the same name as their domestic pig—Ngulu—is very common, and although often killed and eaten by the natives, does not seem to shun their villages. I even have reason to believe that in parts it lives in the same half-domesticated state as noticed by Schweinfurth among the Nyam-nyams.

Iron seems to be largely worked in the interior, and the Ba-yansi of Bolobo shape it into many beautiful knives, axes, and spear heads. Copper they also possess, largely, but I cannot say whether it is locally found and melted.

The natives speak of a kind of topaz which they call "Monkoli." It is described as either pale blue or yellow in colour, and abundantly found in the interior of the country.

---

* In Ki-yansi, the name for buffalo is *ng'ombu*, a classic term in most Bantu tongues for "ox." The Ba-yansi have no domestic cattle.

† *Sus poreus.*

CHAPTER X.

MSUĀTA.

RETURN FROM BOLOBO—ITIMBA—A BURIAL SCENE—A VILLAGE
DECORATED WITH SKULLS — EUPHORBIAS — MBONGO AGAIN—
MUKEMO—THE OUTLET OF THE LAWSON—JOIN LIEUTENANT
JANSSEN—LIFE AT MSUĀTA—THE HAUNT OF THE ELEPHANT—
THE BLUE PLANTAIN EATER—BIRDS AND CROCODILES—THE
CLOUDS—THE STORM—A VISIT TO GOBILA—MAKÓLÉ UNDER
TREATMENT—A TRAP FOR THE LEOPARD—HIS DEATH.

I LEFT Bolobo, after a few days' stay, to return to Msuāta,
the station near the confluence of the Kwa river.   I had
hoped to pursue my journey farther up the Congo, but
with the paucity of men at my disposal, and the somewhat
turbulent character of the natives, I thought it better not
to do so, just at that time, fearing to throw difficulties
in Mr. Stanley's path, should I involve myself in an
altercation with the natives, when he was trusting that
everything would go smoothly, with time, patience, and
a pacific bearing towards these impulsive Congo tribes.

I had intended, however, to spend some two months at
Bolobo, and use it as a centre for collecting and making
observations on anthropology; but various considerations
impelled me to prefer Msuāta for these ends, especially as
that spot, from its position, is just at the meeting-place
of three interesting races, the Ba-yansi, the Ba-teke, and
the Wa-būma, while at Bolobo you have merely Ba-yansi.
Then also, at Bolobo the food supply was scanty and
variable, whereas at Msuāta the commissariat was more
skilfully managed; and finally—and perhaps this was the
reason that most affected my choice—the mosquitoes at
Bolobo rendered life unbearable, and Msuāta, happy place,

was exempt from this plague. So I finally decided to return in the boat which had brought me, and which was

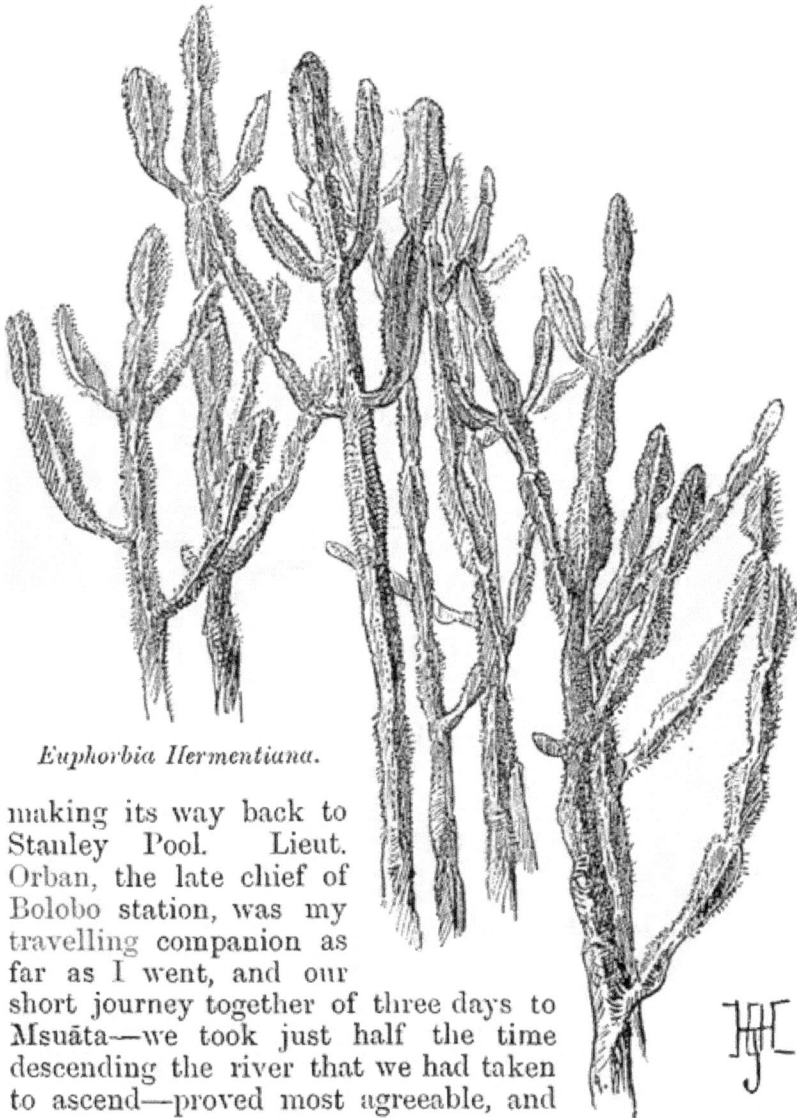

Euphorbia Hermentiana.

making its way back to Stanley Pool. Lieut. Orban, the late chief of Bolobo station, was my travelling companion as far as I went, and our short journey together of three days to Msuāta—we took just half the time descending the river that we had taken to ascend—proved most agreeable, and amusing.

On the first evening after leaving Bolobo we stopped at

a village called Itimba, a little below Chumbiri's town,
near the point where the Congo begins to narrow down
from a breadth of nine or ten miles to a few hundred
yards. Here, at Itimba, we found the people just about
to proceed to the obsequies of a dead fellow-townsman, an
old man, apparently of some standing. The chief and his
subjects were in great perplexity. Of late years it has
become "de rigueur," since guns were introduced into the
Upper Congo regions, to fire a salute over the body of a
defunct person, especially if he be of any distinction ; and
the inhabitants of this village, possessing only one pitiful
old flintlock amongst them, and that terribly out of repair,
were hesitating, when we arrived, as to what course they
should pursue—whether they should charge and fire this
one dilapidated gun and risk its bursting, or whether the
deceased should be allowed to wend his way to the land
of spirits unhonoured and unsaluted. Seeing their perplexity, Lieutenant Orban volunteered to fire a round of
twenty cartridges from his "Winchester." The chief and
people were delighted. Could there be greater honour for
the deceased than to receive his farewell salute at the
hands of a white man, with his wonderful gun from
Mpūto—the mysterious region beyond the sea—the unknown—perhaps heaven itself? ("for are not these white
men sons of heaven?") So thought the old chief, as he
led us to see the corpse, with an earnest, pleading tone, he
took our hands in his, and said, "Oh you, who are going
home!"—and he pointed to the pale and peaceful evening
sky—"you will send him back to us, will you not? you
will tell him his hut is waiting for him, his wives will
prepare his manioc white as cotton-cloth, and there shall
be malafu in plenty, and a goat killed. You will send
him back will you not?" This expression of feeling
quite took us by surprise. Ordinarily the African chief
is so stolid, so thoroughly material, that one never expects
from him anything like sentiment or poetical ideas. We
tried as gently as possible—for he appealed to both of us
in his distress—to explain at once our utter inability to
reanimate this hideous corpse with the breath of life, and

to encourage him with vague hopes that all was not in vain, but he shook his grizzled head sadly at the confession of our powerlessness face to face with death.

The body of the dead man had been previously smoked and dried over a slow fire, so that the flesh, except upon the hands, was shrunken and reduced to a leathery covering round the gaunt bones. The face had been gaudily painted with scarlet, yellow and white pigments, and the whole body was encrusted with the red dye of the camwood tree. Round the nose and mouth was wrapped a band of cloth, and gay-patterned cottons swathed the body. For some reason the hands were quite plump and well covered with flesh, as if in life. The dead man had been placed in his grave in a sitting posture, many layers of native cloth lying under him, and ready to cover him up on the top were piles of cotton stuffs received in trade from the far-off coast, and representing to these natives a considerable amount of wealth. In the vague, half-determined notions which the people here have conceived as to a future existence, everything in the Spirit World is supposed to be a pale copy of things existing on the earth, so that for this reason they put cloth, vessels of pottery, and, in the case of a chief, dead slaves into the graves, in order that the deceased, on arriving in the land of shades, may not appear unprovided with the necessary means of making a fresh start in a new life.

The grave in which this man was buried had been dug in a hut, and the head of the corpse was not more than two feet below the surface. We could not ascertain whether the hut, or rather house—for it was a substantial building of poles and thatch—would be abandoned or not. I fancy not, as it is only in the case of a chief that this is done ; and the man that was dead, although he died rich and influential, was, after all, only the favourite slave of the chief.

In this village many skulls were stuck on the top of the houses. They were those of mis-doers, we were told, who had been slain by the fetish-man for their crimes, and their skulls were thus exposed for the admonition of others. If this was the sole explanation of an epidemic of cranial adornment which seemed to have broken out all over the village, on every house, then there must have been a corresponding epidemic of crime amongst the inhabitants; but I think there were other causes, such as recent wars, which would help to account for these grim appurtenances to house decoration. One man, indeed, admitted to me that the two skulls he possessed were those of two slaves whose throats he had cut for some grievous offence on their part.

Out of mere fun, we asked if they would sell us some of these crania, knowing the horror that these people have of parting with any human remains, and expecting a decided refusal. To our surprise, however, they immediately asked a certain price, which was afterwards reduced to three brass rods for each skull, at which rate two were soon bought, and more might probably have been procured if we had cared to stop and bargain, for now that the people found their osteological collections of any value they hastened to realize them, and brought us, besides skulls, all manner of odds and ends of bones, few of which, however, were of any value. Many would have jumped to the conclusion that we were here in some cannibal country, merely because of the abundance of human remains in this village, but I do not think there is the slightest foundation for such an accusation. In many villages—in fact in nearly all the villages hereabouts—there are bones of animals or men stuck about under the trees or in the fetish huts for various complicated reasons of religion, of boastfulness, and perhaps also fear—fear of the avenging manes of the departed who might wreak vengeance on his slayers, did they not hold his bones as a security for good behaviour. When we got on terms of intimacy with the natives of Itimba—it takes a very short time to win the confidence of these simple people—I asked some of them confidentially if they ever eat man, proffering the inquiry with assumed carelessness, so that if they might feel any false shame in admitting this addition to their diet, they would be reassured by my freedom from prejudice, and confess. At first, however, they did not clearly understand me, but when, by more vigorous pantomime and better chosen terms, I had made my meaning plainer, they repelled the suggestion with the utmost horror, replying to my interrogation an emphatic " *Vé, vê, vê,*" ("*No, no, no,*"), and then adding a timid inquiry, " Na Baïo ? " ("And you ? do you ?")

Ere this excitement about the skulls was over, fresh objects of interest arrived in the shape of some splendid fish that had just been caught. We bought the lot, and I sat down by candlelight to make a drawing of the biggest. He measured 3 ft. 7 in. in length, and a fuller description of him will be found in Chapter XIII.

Round this village, Itimba, there were many fine clumps of Euphorbia growing, probably *Euphorbia Hermentiana,* apparently protected and encouraged by the inhabitants, who appear to have some superstitious, or perhaps practical, liking for these curious prickly plants. It is strange that although these Euphorbias are found in nearly all West African villages, they should yet, as far as I have noticed, be absent from the wild uncultivated country. Can they be a semi-domesticated species that is carried from village to village, either from some superstitious preference, or to form protective hedges, or because they furnish some useful product, such as a poisonous juice, or a fibrous matter ?

The next morning we stopped at that pleasant little village called Mbongo, where I had been before so well received. The people greeted me quite enthusiastically ; and although there was no malafu, they brought sugarcane in abundance. I obtained here a curious little river tortoise, a species of *Trionyx* provided with a soft and flexible shell and a quaint little proboscis.

We camped out for the night at a village of Ba-yansi, called Mukemo, or "the Little," though it must have evidently changed since its name was first given, for it was large, spacious and populous. The houses were well built, and the open squares clean and swept, and garnished with handsome trees. The people were in the best of tempers, for a drinking-bout of malafu had just taken place; and though the chief was nearly dead drunk, his subjects had merely taken sufficient to raise their spirits and set their tongues going. They led us up to the place where the chief and his principal men were sitting on mats, with jars of palm wine round them, and slaves serving it out into a cracked tumbler and a battered tin. We were obliged to drink two glasses each as a testimony of good-will. I say "obliged," though the obligation was by no means unpleasant, for the malafu, made from the

THE SHORE AT MUKEMO.

sap of the Hyphœne palm, was most delicious and re-freshing, and, moreover, as strong as good beer. The chief here possessed a cat, which was regarded somewhat as a curiosity by the natives. It was the first I had ever seen in a Ba-yansi village, although I believe this local scarcity was merely accidental, for the domestic cat is fairly abundant in West Africa.

Many of the children in this place were suffering from whooping-cough, and during the night made much disturbance with their screaming coughs and fretful cries.

The next day we passed the tortuous outlet—much

blocked by sand-banks—of the Lawson or Alima * river, on the western bank of the Congo, and then came in view of the great Kwa River, finally passing the point of Ganchu, and its dangerous current, and arriving at Msuāta towards noon. Here Janssen gave us his usual hearty welcome and good cheer, and here I proceeded to settle down with my three Zanzibaris into comfortable quarters, looking forward to a long rest after my tiring journeys. Orban bade us farewell at Msuāta. He was going on in the boat to Stanley Pool, and intended to regain the coast in order to recruit his health. Msuāta has many advantages as a centre of study, as a place to spend a few months of research in Natural History subjects. It is fairly healthy, well provided with good native food— eighty fowls can, if necessary, be bought in one day from the surrounding villages—the scenery in the environs is pretty and accessible, while the kindly natives leave nothing to desire either for amiability or gentle demeanour.

Life was pleasantly monotonous, but although the programme of my day was almost unvarying in its arrangement, the details of each branch of study offered continual novelty and change, and, in the same sense that "happy are the people who have no history," so, although no wonderful adventures or marvellous occurrences happened to me here, I yet look back on these six weeks passed at Msuāta as the happiest time I have known in Africa.

"*Les jours s'écoulent et se ressemblent*," and the detailed description of the way one day was spent at this station will serve as a history of the remaining forty-one, with the few rare or exceptional incidents inserted.

My daily life begins at about half-past five, when I become dimly conscious that the curtain covering the doorway of my room is no longer opaque, but that a cold bright light is filtering through. Then I notice the strange silence: the crickets have suddenly ceased their exasperating "creek, creek creek," which has been going on all night, and there is a slight pause in nature between

* It was down this river that De Brazza came when he journeyed from the Upper Ogowé to the Congo.

the noises of darkness and light. The silence does not last long, for the turtle-doves begin to coo in the adjoining woods, and a flock of grey parrots passes over my roof with loud whistles and gay chuckles of merriment. A shrill chorus of twittering weaver-birds and wax-bills arises from the grass fields, the cuckoos laugh from tree to tree, and up from the river comes the metallic cry of the spur-winged plovers. It is day, and a thin streak of sunshine steals in through the gap between the curtain and the door-post, and cuts right across my mosquito curtain like a golden sword. I hesitate no longer ; the sloth of night has passed, and I impatiently long for freshness and eager work. Lifting off the muslin which has secured me immunity all night from mosquito bites, I somewhat ungratefully fling it into a corner, and pulling aside the curtain which has veiled my doorless doorway, I step out into the fresh, even chilly morning air, and call loudly " Faraji we ! " Faraji, who is just winding his turban round his head and putting on his slight raiment after the river bath which has left him glistening, comes with docile haste to my room, and helps me to perform my hasty toilet. Then the curtain is looped up over the wide doorway, and the yellow sunlight fills the room, and shows up all sorts of queer creatures that have been my near companions in the night. Large blue-black velvety spiders are revealed on the clay wall, a pretty lizard darts under the bed, while all around on the matted floor, on the walls, on the boxes are seated the odious *grylli*, the crickets whose chirping has so wearied and annoyed me in the hours of wakefulness. However, I leave Faraji to disperse and slay these creatures—always excepting the lizard, who is quite unobjectionable, and the spider, who eats so many flies—and I go to the breakfast-table in the next room—our *salle à manger*—to await the arrival of my host, Janssen. Suddenly he comes in, not from his bedroom, but from the outer piazza. There is rage in his face mingled with a fierce longing for vengeance. I divine the truth—*Another* leopard has been whilst we slumbered, and *another* milch goat is robbed from the

fold—No, it is worse, three of our four milk-providers
have been strangled, and the fourth is going about
bleeding at the neck and baaing piteously. This is
indeed a disaster, but after all it has occurred several
times before, so we sit down to our breakfast and discuss
with resignation the best mode of setting a trap for the
depredator. When the meal is finished, Janssen goes to
review the men and settle the routine of work for the day,
and I, with Faraji, Mafta, and Imbono, start for a morning's ramble in the river-side forest. Perhaps for that
end I cross the Congo, for on the northern bank the
country is almost an uninhabited wilderness, wholly
given up to nature in parts. We go, then, to the clayey
shore, below the station, and loose from its moorings a
native canoe, a "dug-out," perhaps fifteen feet in length
and three feet in its greatest width. But before embarking the sky is carefully scanned to ascertain the probable
state of the weather for the next few hours, for should a
storm be threatening it would be madness to adventure
ourselves on the river. If the verdict be "set fair," we
enter the canoe, the men take the paddles, and the wobbly
craft, with a disagreeable rocking motion from side to
side, that brings either edge in turn on a level with
the water, proceeds to make way laboriously up-stream.
We coast along past the landing-place of the village of
Msuāta, or Gobila as it is sometimes called, after its chief,
where all the natives' canoes are drawn up on the beach
or fastened to piles rising out of the water, and where
many little children are playing the innocent, imaginative
games common to all childkind, while a few of their
elders are fishing or making ready to set out on a journey;
past the banana groves skirting the groups of yellow-
thatched houses, then along the great river-fronting wall
of forest, where the sprawling, untidy calamus palms
clamber up over the noble eriodendron trees, untidy and
irregular in their means of ascent, but endowed with an
indefatigable ambition to be at the top of everything.
Then we reach a certain dead tree lying prone on the
shore, with its leafless branches stretching upwards almost

pathetically, crowned with small water-birds, and here, turning at this land-mark, we proceed to strike away across the Congo for a little cove or inlet nearly opposite Msuāta. Owing to the force of the current we have to row a mile and a half up-stream to be able to land at the place desired, and allow for the inevitable descent of the canoe. When we leave the shore to cross as rapidly as may be the broad Congo, it is always a time of some anxiety. Before we are out of the shallows a hippopotamus may come and wreck us, or once in the terrible mid-current, where the waves are leaping over each other, a wind storm may suddenly capsize our unstable bark. However, the further shore comes nearer and nearer, and we at length enter the quiet little bay for which we have steered, where there is a placid backwater shielded by a spit of forest. Here the canoe is tied to a fallen tree, and the tent is put up on the beach to protect the heavier baggage, and our *batterie de cuisine* from the sun, whilst we, leaving Mafta behind to commence preparations for the mid-day meal, with eager haste on my part leave the open beach of white sand, and following an elephant path, plunge into the cool forest.

In England I am a fire-worshipper; in the tropics I adore the trees. My heart goes out to the erring (?) Jews of old who " built them high places and images and groves, on every high hill and under every green tree," and who, in spite of occasional iconoclastic or " dendroclastic " rulers who arose and cut down the groves, relapsed repeatedly from their harsher, sterner, *desert* faith —the faith of Job and the modern Bedouin—into the softer cult of towering, shade-giving trees. The Forest is most to be appreciated in the Lands of the Sun, where its cool green gloom contrasts so soothingly with the hard, white heat in the open. So we follow the elephant's track with careful steps and slow, avoiding crackling twigs and thorny branches and ant-infested shrubs. The less noise we make in this arcana of wild things, the more shall we see of its higher life. Sh !—listen, what was that ? A series of crashes in the forest follow my query, then a rustling of leaves. Faraji pulls me by the sleeve and whispers, "Tembo, bwana, tembo." Then in the direction in which he points I see through the stems and the creeper-stalks a grey mass. It is an elephant, who, whether he hears us or no, calmly goes on feeding. We somewhat tremblingly continue on our road amid the noise of creaking, breaking boughs and swishing leaves, quite resolved to leave the elephant alone; for of what avail would my little bird-gun be against his hide or bony skull? Here the path becomes pitted with great round water-holes where the elephant's feet have sunk into the soft soil and the rain has filled the depressions. Already these pools of a day swarm with life. Little striped toads squat on their margins, myriads of glancing water-beetles and water-spiders skim the surface, and in the muddy depths there seem to be many wriggling indefinite creatures. Another warning pull from Faraji. I look up above my head and see a dark blot in the maze of twigs. It is some big bird, so I fire my little "collector's" gun and down it comes with many a flop and a temporary stoppage in the forks of branches, until it falls an inanimate lump in the herbage at my feet. It is a great prize—the beautiful Blue Plantain-eater,* a bird remarkable for lovely plumage and high comestible qualities. Following the report of the gun, is a momentary panic among the denizens of the woods. The elephant is heard retreating through the forest alleys, many birds call loudly and indignantly from their unseen posts of vantage—the fishing-eagles giving vent to almost hysterical screams and the cuckoos cynically laughing—and for a while the spell of peace is rudely broken. But crimes are soon buried and forgotten in the forest, and everything after the momentary pause of surprised attention goes on feeding, fighting, or making love.

Slowly we traverse this belt of woodland until we have crossed the little peninsula that divides us from our landing place. Now we emerge quietly on a tiny bay or sound between two promontories that end in a green, grassy headland. Here is a study to make which repeats

* *Schizorhis gigantea;* for illustration of head and crest, see chapter xiv.

itself throughout the Congo scenery. A line of forest reflected in the still water, an old, gnarled, and withered tree-trunk in the foreground, half in the ooze, half high and dry above, on the white sand. If you do not approach too near, you may see the crocodiles lying under the boughs of the fallen tree, their mouths gaping open from sheer listlessness, ⌐and their bodies motionless in the warm shallow water, or basking and baking in the open sunlight, the whole creature revelling in the pleasure of *dolce far niente.* Then above, about, and around them, a multitude of lovely forms, water-birds and waders standing fearlessly pluming themselves regardless of the crocodiles, with whom they must make a compact, a mutual alliance. The crocodiles agree not to eat the birds, and the birds keep a good look out to warn the crocodiles by loud cries when their only enemy, man, is coming. I have observed this strange intimacy between these very dissimilar creatures on all African rivers. How the advent of man must have re-acted on the relations between many of the higher forms of vertebrate life, compelling them almost to subordinate their own pre-existing fears, quarrels and rapacities to the common dread of the universal enemy ! Whom could the crocodiles have feared before this abnormal ape took to slaying instead of being slain ? From the day that the first *Protanthropos* flung a stone at, or jabbed a sharp reed into a crocodile's eye, this strange intimacy for mutual defence must have sprung up between the crocodile and the shore-frequenting birds. So, on the withered tree-trunk, and on the many twisted snaggs that rise above the water, perch the egrets, the bitterns, the herons, and the darters. Fat pelicans lounge on the oozy margin of the river's wavelets, spur-winged and Egyptian geese stand in little groups on the sand, and Zikzak plovers, with yellow wattle and spurs to their wings, hop on the crocodiles' bodies, and, if they do not, as some suppose, pick the teeth, they at any rate linger strangely, and, as one would think, rashly, round the jaws of the grim saurians.

Ah ! Faraji, you have broken the spell ! Startled by a sudden inroad of black ants over his unprotected skin, he

A LANDSCAPE ON THE UPPER CONGO.

has loudly smacked a limb that has been smartly bitten by the great mandibles of these headstrong insects. The charm has vanished, the picture is dispersed. The egrets and the herons are flying to far-off shores, the pelicans flop into the water, and thence scutter away, half swimming, half flying, till they are out of sight, while the outraged plovers, with their loud, almost human cry, wake up the crocodiles, and, having seen their friends glide smoothly into the deep, they address a few more invectives to our party, and then flap their black-and-white wings over the water to a point further along the shore, where they fold their attractive pinions under modest grey wing-coverts, and strut about the beach in self-satisfied conceit at having baulked the slaughterous propensities of those odious men. However, the surroundings of this bird and crocodile grouping still remain, and are worth studying in themselves. There is the fallen tree in the foreground, in sharply contrasted light and dark, and beneath it the yellow sand and green ooze. Then the stretch of tranquil water, reflecting first the variegated sky with its cloud effects of iron-grey and snowy white dappled with patches of bright blue—the tone of the red sandy bottom shining warmly through this reflection in the shallows—and beyond, the glassy reproduction of the wall of forest in the middle distance, which but for the occasional scratches of silvery white where the light breeze ruffles the water, would seem as real as the reality above it. In the actual forest, although it is separated from you by a few hundred yards of river, much detail may be observed in the clear noon-day sunlight. There are the purple depths of shade and the glowing masses of yellow-green foliage; there are the white skeletons of dead and leafless trees and the fanciful trellis-work of emerald-green calamus palms, trailing their disorderly fronds over the water's edge and curving their prying, impertinent heads into every gulf of vegetation, and peeping over the tops of the highest trees. Beyond the forest, the background is the sky, and what a heaven it is to gaze at! In Africa, during the rainy season, the cloudscapes are pictures in themselves. Those noble masses of vapour which begin in tiny shapes of blue-grey over the sharp horizon of the Congo, gradually lift themselves up, throw out wings and limbs, and while their dark bellies stretch away in exaggerated perspective till they vanish into haze, their great snowy heads and shining arms expand over the heavens as if they would, in their rapacity, conquer and swallow all the cerulean blue. Then in their moments of proudest development they break up like unwieldy empires. One province after another deserts and floats away into independence, and the one great cloud that erewhile occupied three-quarters of the sky gives birth to many cloudlets, each with a dark grey body and a white border, and these in their divisions and separations let the sunlight pierce their ranks through and through with many darts and broad-swords of gold, and thus, thoroughly disorganised and disunited, the cloud titans are swept from off the blue heavens by their fickle friend, the wind, and for a while the sky is empty and serene. But not for long: as I am eating my lunch under the shade of the palm groves, the air becomes stifling ; over the water is a shimmering reverberation of heat, the crocodiles on the distant banks positively gasp for breath with expanded jaws, the flies forget to bite, the birds and the insects cease their chirping—there is an awful silence. Something is going to happen, and every-thing animate is conscious of the suspense and the impending struggle. Faraji comes to my retreat, and, pointing to the line of open water where the Congo meets the sky, his finger indicates a faint purplish nebula or haze which is shapeless and yet has limits to its small extent. It is the *avant garde* of an awful army, the real trained hosts of the storm-fiend, who in his struggle for the empire of the sky now puts forth his utmost strength. The former clouds were but a slight skirmishing force in comparison, and the Zanzibaris, my weather guides, paid no attention to their movements, but now they all come to me, although the sky is a hard, unsullied blue, save for the purplish stain near the eastern horizon, and say with emphasis, " Rain is coming."

Fearing to be cut off from Msuáta by the approaching storm for the remaining hours of daylight, and perhaps have to pass a night in the damp and dripping woods, our one thought is to take advantage of a brief spell of immunity and cross the Congo before the elements can hinder our progress. So the sketching materials are hastily put together, the tent is taken down and rolled up, the remainder of the lunch is left to the ants and birds, and rapidly unmooring the canoe, we paddle out from our little tranquil harbour into the open Congo. How the storm grows! In five minutes the haze has become a black, densely-packed ridge of clouds along the horizon. The extreme edge of the water tells out against the dark cloud-bank in ominous white: still there is time. We paddle with feverish energy—yes, *we*, for I, too, strive to increase the speed with measured strokes. Shall we never cross the mile-wide stream?

See, the artillery is beginning. It flashes and blazes fitfully in the far distance. As yet all is still. We see the lightning but do not hear the thunder. The water is like solid glass; to our right it is still smilingly, vacuously blue, but storm-wards it has become a sullen grey, ever deepening in tint. Ah, there is the thunder, beginning in a low muttering with occasional isolated pops and reports like single shots. A third of the sky is now filled with a pall of uniformly black-grey cloud, quite unbroken save by one small, whitish fleck that to a fanciful eye might seem a general on a white horse directing the movements of the vast compact hosts. The edge of the storm-cloud is torn, irregular, harried, and is fast stretching with disordered outline over our heads. Now comes a splendid coruscation, a dazzling blaze of lightning over the face of the cloud, followed by a perfect roar of thunder that makes us unconsciously tremble.

The hour of danger is fast approaching, but, save for the steady advance of the storm, nothing moves in nature. The water is unruffled, the foliage of the nearer shore is unstirred by any breath of air. We have done three-quarters of the journey, can we accomplish the rest unharmed? Ah, no! too late—the *Wind* is coming, and Faraji, catching sight of the distant waves, says under his breath, "Oh Muhammad, Oh Prophet of God, save us."

It is on us, it is here! The men lie down cowering in the
boat that they may offer no resistance to the fearful blast
which all but overturns the canoe, and hurls on to us the
white-capped waves which leap one over the other in their
anxiety to swamp us. Still, from their crouching posture
the men dig the paddles into the water, and seem to carve
a way to the fast-approaching shore, aided somewhat by
the wind which is sweeping us thither. Shall we escape?
It seems unlikely. A great hissing wall of rain advances
towards us over the river, envelops, surrounds, and well-
nigh overwhelms us. I feel crushed by the mass of water,
my breath is gone, I am beaten into the trough of the
canoe where the men lie exhausted, without other feelings
than stolid resignation.

I can distinguish nothing in the blinding rain, but I
think I hear a despairing voice quite close. Suddenly we
bump on a log and find ourselves stranded on the shore,
driven thither by the wind, and at last in safety. The
men jump out with expressions of devout thankfulness to
their prophet, and Janssen is clutching me by the hand to
drag me up the slimy bank, full of congratulations at our
escape. All is well that ends well. In Africa dangers
incurred are soon forgotten. When I have changed my
clothes and had some hot coffee, I feel nothing more disagreeable than a glow from the dousing of cold rain, and
almost forget that half an hour ago I thought myself
doomed to feed the crocodiles of the Congo. As I am
sipping my coffee, too, and chatting with Janssen about
the leopard of last night and the means of shooting him,
I notice in the glimpses of sky that are framed by the
windows indications of approaching peace. The storm-
fiend, raised by the sun, is conquered by that luminary,
and his ragged battalions, torn and rent, are being driven
off by the changeable wind, a fickle coadjutor that ever
turns against you in the hour of defeat. Soon there is
calm. The sun glancing radiantly in the rain-pools, lights
up a somewhat tearful scene, and the ground is strewn
with leaves, branches, *débris* of the forest carried hither
and thither by the wind.

The later afternoon is mellow and fine. There is a

delicious freshness in the air, the sky is a pale washed-out blue, and the descending sun brings out all the forest background in exaggerated relief.

We put on our thick boots and set off on a walk to the village. The path is not only marshy in parts, but even crosses positive lagoons, through which the Zanzibaris carry us on their backs. This watery condition of the route is owing to the recent heavy rainfall. As we enter the village and the first few people catch sight of us, the whole population is soon around us, shrieking out a welcome. "Susu Mpembe wa Buï!"* they scream, announcing us to their chief, Gobila, who is seated in front of his house, in a little private square, picking over the remains of an old flint-lock gun. Gobila greets us with many grins and Mbotes, and extends a fat paw to be shaken. He is a man of about forty, but looks older. His figure was once fine and stalwart, but latterly, owing to a more slothful existence and good living, he has become too fat. His face is not unhandsome. He has good clear eyes, a straightish nose, perfect teeth, save for the artificial chipping of the two middle incisors, a slight moustache and a peaked beard. His bull-neck is a column of strength, but there are wrinkles of fat in the nape. His arms are immense and tempt you to pinch them, a pleasantry which makes him—for he is of a sunny nature —roar with laughter. Gobila has almost pendant breasts like a woman, a thing constantly seen in these middle-aged men, and his thighs are somewhat misshapen with obesity. But for this full habit of body he appears a stately man, and in spite of his love of joking has a certain dignity of manner. Gobila does not like me *very* much— not half as much as Janssen. He cannot understand why I am always asking questions, why my black "stick" is always making marks on pieces of "cloth" (writing), why I gather herbs (unless for magic), and why I am anxious to take his portrait. This latter attempt has been a great

---

* The "white fowl" and the "spider," the native names of Janssen and myself. Janssen was called the "white fowl," for some obscure reason, and I was nicknamed the "spider," "because I was always catching insects."

source of contention between us. When I first visited the chief of Msuäta, I took advantage of the impression produced by my "present" to extract from him an un-willing promise to sit to me as a model. I arrived on the succeeding day with all my implements of magic, and poor, fat, trembling Gobila had to sit in immobility before me on a square of matting. The constant lifting of my eye from the paper and the way I scanned his features so disconcerted him, that after the first few minutes of the sitting he became quite miserable and implored a momentary release. Then he got two of his wives to sit on either side of him and mitigate by absorption the effect of my evil eye. Thus flanked he sat out bravely a whole half-hour but ever averted his head from my gaze, in such fashion that after many futile attempts to reproduce his features, I gave up the attempt in despair. Gobila was radiant at my defeat. His fetish was stronger than the white man's. Nevertheless he shirked any other contest of our psychic forces, and I never persuaded him to give me another chance. However, on this occasion we avoid any such disagreeable subject. The note-book is kept in hiding, and we attempt to draw Gobila out in a most innocent manner. Lest my queries should arouse his suspicions, Janssen is primed with the necessary questions to be put. Gobila is asking about guns—a good idea— Janssen carelessly inquires how long is it since the Ba-teke have known this weapon. The chief replies, after stopping a moment to think, that his father fought with bows and arrows and spears, and knew not guns, which were only introduced towards the close of his life, when Gobila was a little boy.*

"Can he ever remember to have heard speak of the time when there were no pine-apples, oranges, maize, manioc or sugar-cane?" "No; were not those things

---

* Gobila is not the real name of the present chief of Msuäta. It is the name of an elder brother who was formerly chief, but who suffered from occasional fits of madness, or melancholia, in which he cut off too many of his lieges' heads. Consequently he was quitted by almost the entirety of his people and slaves, who crossed the Congo under the leadership of Gampama (the present Gobila) and established themselves

always with us?" he replies inquiringly. Gobila answers several more questions and then begins to yawn, so we take the hint and leave him, going off to make a round of visits in the village.

A friend of ours, Makôlé, whose name is phonetically the same as our great English historian's, sends word to say he is ill, will we come and see him? Approaching his residence, we see that something very special is taking place. The palisaded compound round Makôlé's huts is festooned with great palm branches, interlaced at times so as to form arches of greenery across the pathway. The entrance to the principal house, where the ceremony we have been invited to see is going on, is a veritable bower, so thickly do the upright palm fronds cluster about it. Thirty-nine people are crammed into the interior, which is about twenty feet by ten. They are all playing on drums, "marimbas," and a rude sort of lyre, and singing at the top of their voices, their nearly naked bodies streaming with sweat, for in addition to the exhausting nature of their occupation there is a roasting fire burning in the centre of the hut, and its smoke mixes with the steam from the human bodies and produces a thick mist through which various details of the interior can but dimly be discerned. At one end of the hut, however, we can see Makôlé, who is sick, seated under an overarching canopy of palm branches, with the soles of his feet turned towards the blaze. On one side of him a wife crouches over a dish of food that she is preparing. All this time her husband, a stout, well-made man in the prime of life, remains perfectly motionless and silent, the perspiration streaming down his body, and we are informed that it is an important condition of the cure that he should not give utterance to a sound while the charm is working.

At length there is a pause for refreshments, and all the

---

at Msuāta. **Gampama-Gobila** is also called "Mbuma" by the Ba-yansi, either because he lives near the Wa-būma people, or because he is originally of that race. "Gampama is Ki-buma for *cat*. The real original Gobila still lives on in his ancient seat, "thinning" the few subjects that remain, and becoming a by-word for ferocity, and a bogey to frighten naughty black children.

occupiers of the hut, musicians, wives, and patient, turn out into the open, panting, laughing, and wiping the sweat from their glistening bodies. Jars of sweet and pleasant-tasting palm wine from the Malebu, or Hyphœne palms, is brought in by slaves, and all present, including ourselves, take a drink, Makôlé participating freely. Although he is bound to keep silent, he makes up for want of verbal welcome by the most effusive grins: in fact his face is wreathed in fatuous smiles, for he is evidently highly self-conscious, and imagines himself to be an interesting figure to the white men who have come to witness his "cure." His friends tell us he is suffering from headache, and to corroborate this, he himself points to his temples and forehead, which are painted with white pigment. But probably the whole affair is got up to serve as an excuse for a bout of malafu drinking and a grand function.

We return to the station by canoe, going down stream merrily and at a great rate.

The sun is very near setting as we arrive, so Janssen goes off to the goat's paddock to set a trap for the leopard in the little time of remaining daylight. He arranges a sort of narrow "boma," or three-sided structure of high stakes, at the end of which a bleating kid is tied to the triggers of three loaded guns, which are so placed that they command the only exit from the trap. The leopard, in the act of seizing the kid, will discharge the contents of the muskets into his body, and *ought* to die then and there from the effect.* Whilst Janssen is doing this, I am watching the sunset from the verandah. It is a beautiful scene, and one that makes me indignantly con-tradict certain writers who maintain that the tropics, both in flower-shows and fine sunsets, are inferior to the temperate zones.

To day the sun's career has been somewhat troubled, like that of many an earthly monarch. His rule at first was tranquil and undisputed. Then came the fearful

---

* On this occasion the creature *did* receive the whole charge of the three guns, but nevertheless afterwards managed, though riddled with bullets, to leap the ten-foot-high fence with kid, guns, and all, and drag itself to die in an adjoining field.

mid-day battles and convulsions, terminating in victory for the luminary, who throughout the afternoon of his reign ruled in peace. Now, as he declines, his enemies revive, and his sinking is marked with bloody, troublous signs in the west. The twilight that succeeds his immolation is some half-hour in length,* and the sky slowly changes from fiery red to orange and pale green. The expanse of river sympathetically follows these dying changes, and the whole scene is vast and mystic, and one to sit and dream over until dusky night sets in with its dismal obscurity. Then it is pleasant to turn one's head away from the riverward aspect and greet the glow of cheery lamplight which shines out from the open door of our dining-room. The sun is dead; long live the lamp! Let us to our dinner. The cook comes in with the great tureen of soup, staggering under its weight; and having changed our outgoing clothes, and brightened up our somewhat dowdy persons, we sit down to assist at that almost religious ceremony of the white man. One of the courses deserves notice—the plantain-eater I shot this morning is roasted on a spit and served up with fried kikwanga. It is delicious, and its large breast rivals a woodcock's in delicacy.

When the meal is over, we sit and discuss the events of the day and form plans for the morrow. About ten we retire to our respective rooms, and soon, tucked up within mosquito curtains, dreams of the coming night begin to interweave themselves with the occurrences of the day. . . . Bang, bang, bang!—I start up—am I still dreaming, or did I really hear the guns go off? Whilst I am still in doubt, Faraji comes in to say the leopard is shot. *Tant mieux!* we will skin him in the morning; and, sinking once more into my little bed, I fall into a sleep which terminates another day at Msuāta.

* The shortness of equatorial twilights is much exaggerated; night never sets in until half-an-hour after sunset.

CHAPTER XI.

HOMEWARDS.

The Start for Stanley Pool—A Floating Cassia Branch—A Troop of Elephants—Ba-yansi on the March—A Blood-brother—Chased by Hippopotami—Juma brings News from Home—The Hills of Stanley Pool—Their Trees and Flowers—Coquilhat's Welcome at Kimpoko—Arrive at Kinshasha—A Palaver—Dualla, Stanley's Prime Minister—Bankwa's Speech—My Stay at Léopoldville—Manyanga again—Boat-voyage to the Sea—Welcome at Boma—Arrival at Banana—Parting with my Zanzibaris—Back to Civilization.

IT was with considerable reluctance that I left Msuăta to return once more to Stanley Pool. But the thought that I was now on my homeward route somewhat alleviated the regret with which I bade good-bye to the Upper Congo. On a bright Sunday morning towards the end of April, I set out on my journey down the river with two good-sized native canoes, paddled by my three Zanzibaris and some Krumanos that Janssen had lent me. The first canoe was fitted up with an awning for the sun, and grass cushions to repose on, and the second contained my heavy baggage and the things I could best afford to lose in case of untoward accidents. In my own canoe I had a few small cases containing such remains of my natural history collections as were spared me by the ants and the rainy season; also my note-books and sketches, which I always carried in a box by my side, fearing to lose these results of my observations if I entrusted them to the care of the men.

Janssen stood on the fast-retreating shore of Msuăta, as

our canoes went six miles an hour down the stream. We
shouted *au-revoir* to one another without any presentiment that it was never " to the seeing again." Three
months later my kind host of Msuāta was drowned
opposite his station. But I did not foresee this sad end
to a bright career, so my parting was blithe and lighthearted. Everything seemed propitious to my journey.
The sun shone brightly out of a pale-blue sky, unspotted
by the slightest cloud, and his heat was tempered with
the tenderest breeze blowing from the west, seeming to
me like a message from the sea I was longing to greet.
There was a general sense of bright activity in all things.
The kingfishers and the bitterns had never sported with
such activity, nor squeaked so lustily at every capture.
The grey parrots were starting for their day's excursion,
and whistled melodiously as they whirred over our heads.
Even the very fish leapt in glad silvery shoals round
the prow of the advancing canoe. The men sang and
the paddles clove the water so energetically under their
vigorous strokes, that my contentment was at times
disturbed by the occasional showers of spray they flung
over me and my goods. But I could not check their
exuberance. It was too consistent with my own joy at
being homeward-bound. Sometimes we raced the floating
islands of arums and reeds, and beat them; but they
were resigned to that, seeing they would easily catch us
up in the night; sometimes we passed triumphantly
poor staggering trees, torn up by their roots, with whole
retinues of ferns, grasses, and parasitic plants attached,
which were quite bewildered by the impetuous current
that whirled them round and round, tossed them from
side to side, rolled them over, and hurried them along,
like miserable captives that they were, in its cruel clutch.
One of these torn-up trunks was a species of *Cassia*,
and its boughs were still in rich leaf and decked with
beautiful yellow blossoms. Moreover, it carried quite a
little population with it along its course. I noticed three
lizards running up and down the branches, some butterflies settled on the fragrant blossoms, and two water

wagtails sunning and pluming themselves, as if they had chosen the floating tree-stem as a temporary home.* I began to think my day's journey was to be deliciously tranquil, forgetting that in 'Africa agreeable anticipations are rarely realized. Towards noon, clouds began to collect in the east, from which quarter the rain always seems to come in this part of the Congo region. The wind was certainly blowing from the opposite direction, but this had little effect on the approaching storm, now fast covering the heavens with a blue-black pall, for storms in Africa are too imperious to care for the direction of the prevailing wind. They carry with them in their black bosoms a hurricane of their own, which goes before them in awful gusts and bellowings, and utterly silences the timid breeze that was feebly keeping back the rain. So, when the eye of the storm, a whirling mass of grey cloud round a purple centre, rose before us, we prudently put into the bank, tied the canoes to some stout trees, and then resignedly bent our heads to the tempest that roared over us. The storm was finished in a brief half-hour, but not so the rain, which dripped and dripped incessantly: yet I was too impatient to delay any further for this, and made the men take to their paddles once more. In spite of the wet weather, we achieved considerable progress. At about half-past five, we were coasting beside a very long and narrow island, in search of a camping-place, when I saw, not ten yards off, a large elephant, with moderate-sized tusks, standing amongst the high grass at the water's edge. He looked superb against the graceful glaucous-green Hyphœne palms which afforded such an artistic background. I did not shoot at him; firstly, because it would have spoiled the picture, and secondly because a bullet from a Winchester rifle could do him but little harm. We stayed and watched the mighty beast some five minutes, he not taking the least notice. His colour told out quite greyish-white (the ridge of his back-bone was particularly light

---

* On many rivers these floating trees must serve as a great means for the diffusion of species.

in tone) against the foliage, and the whole effect of the grouping made a very pretty composition. We heard other elephants in the interior of the island, breaking down trees and branches, and, curiously enough, round this solitary creature on the beach were several Hyphœne palms laid low, torn down by the voracious elephant for the sake of their round, yellow fruit, of which he is so ravenously fond. That troop of elephants must have reached the island by swimming, as even in the dry season there is water between it and the mainland—a broad channel, in fact. The island is of some magnitude, and is covered with over a thousand palm-trees.

We landed a short distance from the place where I had seen the elephant, and camped out for the night on a very small space of sand, which was unfortunately all on a slant, so that during the night I was constantly gliding, feet foremost, off my bed. Add to this myriads of mosquitoes, and it will seem as if the prospect appeared dismal; nevertheless I passed a fairly agreeable evening. The soup was an immense success, and then Janssen had given me some delicious wild honey, which very pleasantly varied the repast.

On the morning succeeding the storm, rain-clouds still sullied the sky, but the sun soon overmastered them, and the day became fine and hot. Towards noon, the men asked to stop a little while at a large village on the south bank of the Congo to buy provisions. I gave them a quarter of an hour to effect their purchases, and disembarked myself to go and visit some travelling Ba-yansi who were encamped on the shore. They were the same party that had visited Msuāta a few days ago to trade, and when I landed they rushed forward with loud cries of recognition. Indeed their greeting was quite affectionate. They patted my back, shook hands with me vigorously, and led me to look at their encampment. These people certainly understand how to journey comfortably according to the best of their means. A number of little—what shall I call them?—tents, hovels, huts, were constructed out of matting, impenetrable to the rain, and in shape something like a small archway, or a somewhat flattened half-circle. The ground underneath this shelter was also neatly covered with matting, and inside the hut was the owner's "fetish" or little house-idol, his pipe, his head-rest or pillow, his gun—if he had one—and various little odds and ends, all neatly done up in skins of animals or native cloth. I bought a head-rest of one man for a tattered old shawl which I had meditated tossing into the Congo as worthless just before.

The people here were handing round salt to each other in a large leaf. They eat it alone and with extraordinary gusto. One of these Ba-yansi men that I had previously met at Msuáta became so affectionate after I had given him a few pinches of table-salt—to them an indescribable delicacy—that he implored me to become his "blood brother." I half laughingly consented, and he took his knife and, with the point of it, gently scratched my skin (on my fore-arm) as if he were going to vaccinate me. When a few drops of blood had appeared on the scarified flesh, he greedily sucked them, and then, repeating the same process on his own arm, invited me to apply my lips to the wound. I made a show of doing so, and the ceremony was then concluded by our exchanging presents and mutual protestations of eternal friendship. I have never seen this blood-brother of mine from that day when I left him smiling at me as our canoes glided off from the shore, and I confess I should be curious to know whether he would remember me, should we ever meet again.

Shortly after we had quitted this place, and rounded a little promontory, we came very abruptly on a group of hippopotami, sunning themselves on a sand-bank. Three of them deliberately gave chase to us in the first canoe, but we merrily out-distanced them; then they turned about, and, seeing the baggage canoe coming on behind, swam towards it. For a moment I was anxious for my baggage, but the men put out into the open, and the hippopotami, finding a stern chase beyond their powers or inclinations, desisted and returned to sun themselves. It is true that in taking to the middle of the river the men ran a risk of encountering whirpools, but by a little skilful steering these were easily avoided, and it was fun to see one of the pursuing hippopotami caught in a foam-flecked vortex, wherein he went whirling round until he was thoroughly giddy, no doubt. Hippopotami are so bold and undisturbed on the Congo that they are a real source of danger to the canoes. One never knows whether to shoot or not. If you hit and do not kill the beast outright, he will come for you with a vengeance; but, at the same time, if you do not shoot, he may wreck you from a spirit of pure mischievousness.

We rowed long and far to-day. The weather was so fine, the water so smooth, and the scenery so lovely, that as I lay back on my grass cushion in the prow of the canoe, and watched the groups of Hyphœne palms and the hanging woods deploy before me, a beautiful, if somewhat monotonous panorama, the disquietudes and risks of canoe travelling seemed very trifling and the pleasure great. I was also able to observe no less than three separate storms, north, east, and south, going on at once, and to watch their great curtains of rain deluging the sky and literally streaming themselves out, becoming at last a thin veil, through which the distant landscapes might be observed as a picture that is seen through a veil of double gauze. We fortunately escaped without a wetting, which was exceptionally lucky.

Towards five o'clock that afternoon we stopped and disembarked on a strip of sandy beach, surrounded by high grass and stunted trees, with the fine hills on the opposite shore rising above the water, thickly wooded, as on the borders of some Scotch lake. The river narrows strangely here, and seems shut in with hills. I sat down on the beach to sketch, when I heard the men calling out that "Juma" was coming. Juma was a Zanzibari whom Janssen had recently sent to Léopoldville with letters to Mr. Stanley, and was now returning to Msuäta. I had but little hope of news, having been so often disappointed, so I was proportionately pleased when Juma came and placed a large packet in my hand which contained such, to me, priceless treasures. Letters from Europe I had not had for many months, and here there were dozens in my lap. *Graphics, Punches* and other newspapers stared at me from their battered postal covers, as if surprised to find themselves, probably for the first time, on the Upper Congo. I passed subsequently a very happy evening, and so did my men, for I had given largesse with an ample hand in consideration of my good fortune.

Our journey the next morning was comparatively uneventful. The flies were peculiarly annoying, especially a large brown one that gives a very cruel bite. They seemed to increase in numbers as we approached the Pool.

I stopped for a short time to draw some white lilies * that grew by the borders of the river in great numbers, and were very noticeable at this season of the year, with their tall clusters of delicate white flowers. We rowed into the Pool towards the afternoon, and I was more than ever struck with its imposing aspect. I can quite imagine that Stanley, on descending the Congo in 1877, must have thought himself entering here on some great lake or inland sea, as he saw the clear horizon of water expanding before him.

The vegetation which clothes the precipitous shores on the south side of Stanley Pool, near the entrance from the Upper River, is one of the most magnificent spectacles the Congo offers. Rising nearly perpendicularly from the water, the forest climbs the hillsides, higher than the eye can reach, without a single break in its luxuriance. The variety of colours, too, at this season, when most of the trees are in blossom, is particularly striking. One tree-top will be covered with scarlet flowers scattered with a liberal hand; another has pendulous flowers of a pinky-white hanging gracefully by their long stalks amid the sombre masses of foliage; while errant creepers in exuberant growth trail their yellow and purple blossoms over the victims they entwine. There is every note struck

* *Crinum zeylanicum.* A common lily in equatorial Africa, giving a most fragrant scent, and much thronged by the flies and bees.

in the gamut of green, and the trees that form this mass of foliage may vary in tone from blue-green to greenish-

CRINUM ZEYLANICUM.

yellow, and from greenish-white to russet-red, and they will differ equally in form and aspect. While some are compactly massed in their leafage, others grow erratically and in disordered tufts. Beautiful *Albizzias* dominate their fellows, clothed in foliage of dark-green velvet; *dracœnas* raise their spiky heads here and there from out of the soft verdant mass. The large flat leaves of a fig alternate with the feathery palm fronds, while many stems are completely disguised by the network of graceful creepers which masks them like a vegetable cobweb. The calamus palm makes a sort of lattice-work fence, rising straight up from the water's edge, and seems effectually to forbid trespassing in these fairy forests, while along the river's brim lines of white lilies stand like sentinels to see the barrier is not passed.

Before evening we had arrived at Kimpoko, a newly-founded station at the northern entrance to Stanley Pool. Here the pleasant face of Lieutenant Coquilhat * was greeting me as I landed, and after four months' absence from anything connected with the outside world this return to the outskirts of civilization (which, owing to Mr. Stanley, Stanley Pool has now become) completely prevented my sleeping till a late hour in the night, and I kept up poor Coquilhat talking all the time, and discussing the European news of half a year.

The following day I again set out on my journey towards Léopoldville, and voyaged for three hours amid the islands and sand-banks, and the great placid waters of the Pool. The "Dover Cliffs" glittered in the morning sunlight in all their chalk-like brilliancy, and, with the soft green grass that crowned their scarped summits, looked singularly English. I arrived at Kinshasha towards mid-day, and saw there the *Royal*, and quite a fleet of other boats. Stanley was here, they told me, conducting a palaver. I landed, and walked up through the tall, luxuriant grasses, and past the many native houses, deserted by their inhabitants, to the focus of attraction, which was a large enclosure between high palisades,

---

* Since—like many other gallant and enthusiastic men—dead from fever and overwork; but not before he had risen to high eminence in the Congo Free State.—H. H. J.

where, under the shade of splendid baobabs, and amid a green tracery of palm fronds and creepers, a most imposing palaver was going on. A rough circle or amphitheatre of human beings was formed, those of the inner ranks seated and attentive, and they whom an inferior grade in society relegated to a less prominent position standing up, their

THE ISLAND OPPOSITE KINSHASHA.

arms round each others' waists and necks in the limply caressing way so natural to these people. But seated opposite to each other in the circle were two important groups which attracted alternately supreme attention. All that was chiefest in Black and White was engaged in earnest deliberation. On two superb leopards' skins sat the two principal kinglets of the neighbourhood. One, an

P

old man, with sunken jaws, but a refined-looking face; the other, a very heavy, vulgar-looking person, who spoke but little, and whose stolid silence evidently covered a want of mental force. In face of them was "Bula Matadi," looking his most chieflike, with his resolute face and grey hair, and the sword of state at his side. On his left sat a young Belgian officer, awaiting the favourable result of the palaver to found a station at Kinshasha; and at Stanley's feet Dualla, prime minister, interpreter and counsellor, argued, persuaded, and cajoled the black brothers of the "Stone-Breaking" chief into concordance with his wishes. When I had exchanged a hasty greeting with Stanley, and taken a seat by his side, the palaver, which I had momentarily interrupted, went on again. Bankwa, a chief who was opposed to Stanley's building and founding a station at Kinshasha, rose to his legs and made a lengthy speech, strongly advising the two chiefs on the leopard-skins to have nothing to do with white men. "To-day," he said, "they will send one white man here, but next year twenty more will come, and because we have given land to one, we must do so to all the others; and so, soon, Kinshasha will belong to the white man, as Kintamo (Léopoldville) does already." There was a great deal of truth in Bankwa's remarks, but unfortunately he could not look beyond the immediate present, and conjure up from his inner consciousness a picture of the material advantages that would accrue to the people of Kinshasha from the settlement of civilization in its midst. However, his opposition was overruled, and the result of the palaver was favourable to Stanley, permission to occupy land and build a station being given. Then presents were interchanged, and we left the delighted people shrieking "Mbote" at the departing steamer till they were hoarse.

Once more Kallina Point rose before my eyes, and further on I saw the many buildings of Léopoldville and the Baptist Mission surmounting the hill of Ntāmo. As I landed with Stanley at the little port of the station and walked up the steep ascent through the Zanzibaris' village, and the beautiful banana groves, the whole place had a tender, homelike look about it, bathed as it was in the soft afternoon sunlight, and surrounded by so many evidences of comfort and civilization, strange to my eyes, so long accustomed to the wilderness. But all was not the same as when I had left Léopoldville in the early part of the year to ascend the river. New buildings upraised themselves, new faces looked out on me, and many old ones were gone from the scene.

I stayed with Stanley for nearly ten days at Léopoldville, and enjoyed his hospitality to the full. With plenty of books, good food, and a most entertaining host, the time passed but too quickly, and I really felt quite lonely as I once more set out on my journey to the coast.

We took five days returning to Manyanga, and here I paused again, to rest under the roof of my good friend Nilis, for the climate was beginning to tell a little on my health, and a few days of continuous travel brought on great lassitude and fatigue. It took us two days to descend the Congo in a whale-boat to Isangila, where I met many old friends and new arrivals *en route* for the Upper River. Here, too, was the charming and intellectual Abbé Guillot, the pioneer of the Franco-Algerian missions on the Upper Congo, who a few months later was drowned in the fickle stream in company with poor Janssen. I left Isangila after a night's rest, and set out for Vivi, the last stage of my journey to be done on foot. Though we were now in the month of May, the rainy season was still in full vigour; and the first night after leaving Isangila there was a terrific downpour. I had but a few miserable carriers, beside my three faithful Zanzibaris, and these former were sluggish and obstinate Kabindas. When the rain began they quietly stepped out of the path, made themselves shelters of branches, and proceeded to rest for the night there, with my baggage, while I had gone on in front; consequently I was obliged to pass the night with little shelter from the rain, and no food whatever. However, I reached Vivi ultimately after three days' walking, with no more serious complaint than exhaustion arising from fatigue ; and the quiet weeks of continuous rest that I passed there soon restored me to a fair amount of strength.

Whilst stopping at Vivi I visited the Falls of Yelala, as described in Chapter III., and made a few other excursions in the neighbourhood. Then, as the time for meeting the ocean steamer drew nigh, I embarked on board a whale-boat belonging to the station (the little river steamer of the Expedition being temporarily disabled), and, with a crew of Zanzibaris and Kruboys, made my way slowly down to the sea. This journey, usually lasting nine or ten hours, took me three days, and, owing to a continued attack of rheumatism, was not over-agreeable. The first night we had intended to reach Boma at sundown, but, owing to difficult complications, we were still painfully struggling along the broadened stream and threading an uncertain course through the sandbanks at ten o'clock at night.

At length the red and lurid moon arose, having lost a quarter, and looking like a Dutch cheese with the top cut off, and showed us more clearly our course amid the wooded islets that stud the middle of the river. We landed at the first house to be seen on the outskirts of Boma, which fortunately turned out to be a factory of Messrs. Hatton and Cookson's. Here I received, though utterly unknown to the inmates of the house, a most kindly reception, such as I have ever met with from English and Anglo-Portuguese houses in Africa. Although the night was far advanced, the cook was roused from his slumbers, and the gentlemen of the house bestirred themselves to make me comfortable. I went to bed first, as an attack of fever was menacing ; but, later on, the delicious meal of fragrant tea and cold wild-duck, which was spread by my bedside, banished the preliminary shivers, and I afterwards found in sleep a sweet restorative. The next day I breakfasted at another house in Boma, and then proceeded farther on my way to Ponta da Lenha. Here also I arrived late at night, but this time our way was strangely illuminated by the great grass fires which covered the distant hills with sheets of vivid flame.

Soon after leaving Ponta da Lenha the mangroves begin to attest the commencement of brackish water, and the river widens till its opposite bank is well-nigh invisible, and many islands troop in long succession, often seeming to be the mainland on the other side. Then we pass Kisange rapidly, carried on by the current, and, lastly, a whiff of fresh breeze blows the sea smell into our nostrils, and in the far distance the white houses of Banana are seen, and, beyond, the open horizon of the Atlantic Ocean.

I spent three days at Banana, waiting for the Portuguese steamer, and passed my time in choosing presents for my three Zanzibaris out of the stores at the Dutch house. Each man received a blanket, a pipe, a roll of tobacco and a tobacco-pouch, a pocket-knife, a pair of scissors and a looking-glass; and then I further bestowed a little gift of money, with strict injunctions that it was to be kept and spent only on their return journey to Zanzibar.

I received much kindness during these few days at Banana from my old acquaintances at the Dutch house; nevertheless, the approaching return to civilized countries, and the slight foretaste of civilization to be got at Banana, did not strike me as being so enviable as I had hitherto supposed. I felt a positive regret for the quiet, simple life of Msuāta and the Upper River, and grew saddened at the approaching separation from my three faithful followers, with whom my later African wanderings had been so inseparably and happily associated. Ever since the day when I first saw these men in the porch of Stanley's house at Vivi, there had sprung up between us a real sympathy of feeling. These men were to me more than servants; they were friends and confidants, who shared in my mirth when I was gay, bore meekly my ill-humour when I was cross; nursed me when I was sick; washed for me, cooked for me, mended my clothes; watched over my interests, never robbed me of a penny's worth nor told me an untruth. If Faraji, Mafta, and Imbono may be taken as fair samples of the Semitonegroid population of East Africa, then I think this hybrid race is destined to largely help in the opening-up of Africa. The mixture of Arab blood and Arab culture gives a stability and manliness to the Waswahili which is lacking in even the finest race of pure Negro origin. The Congo peoples, for instance, are usually amiable and soft-mannered, but at heart they are seldom to be depended on. There is something so eminently childish in the Negro's character. A love of talking, a desire to thrust himself forward in every matter, a *naïveté* of manner which is at times very amusing, but which becomes somewhat wearisome when you are no longer content to be amused, and seek for something more reliable than mere simplicity of thought. All these traits are found in the black races of Africa that are of purely Negro or Bantu stock; but in the Semiticised people of Zanzibar you find *men* of thought and reflection, whom you may use as counsellors and confidants; men who are really capable of zealous service, of disinterested affection, and to whom gratitude is a concept neither foreign to their intelligence nor their tongue.

Arrived on board the mail steamer *Portugal,* I found myself, after many months' absence from civilization, once more among people that were fashionably dressed. Fresh from Europe, and touching at the African continent for the first time on the voyage, they regarded me curiously as I walked about the deck in my tattered garments and cumbrous boots, and I felt myself morbidly sensitive to their scrutiny. Faraji, Mafta and Imbono had said their last good-byes, and the boat which bore them back to the shore was disappearing fast from my view in the evening mists that swathed the swampy coast; the Krumen who had accompanied me from Vivi had also gone, in haste to spend the little money-presents I had given them; I felt singularly and sadly alone—somewhat like a fallen potentate. Here were people who, far from shrinking from my frown, glared at me unmoved, and calmly reviewed my idiosyncrasies through their insolent eye-glasses. The stewards were anything but deferential, and asked pointedly to see my first-class ticket. However, I ransacked my weather-stained trunks and found in them some remnants of respectable clothing, such as might befit the decent poor ; but when I sat down at the end of a long *table-d'hôte* with the spick-and-span Portuguese officials and their wives, who were carrying with them into their African exile as much flavour of fashionable Lisbon as they could wear on their persons, I felt myself to be a great barbarian, and almost wished to be back in the centre of Africa, where I should once more lead the *ton*. At last, after two days' steaming, the beautiful Bay of Loanda opened out before us, and I knew myself to be among friends. I walked hurriedly up through the sandy streets, to a blue-and-white house situated on an eminence overlooking the town, from whose roof the Union Jack rose proudly into the still air. The consul was looking out of his study window, and thought I was either a beggar or a "degredado" come to solicit work ; but when I looked up at him and laughed, he welcomed me as one come from the dead (perhaps more heartily than in that case), and under his hospitable roof I had a happy foretaste of an English home.

CHAPTER XII.

CLIMATE AND NATURAL HISTORY.

THE UNHEALTHY DISTRICTS — DRINKING-WATER — PRECAUTIONS AGAINST SUNSTROKE—HOW TO LIVE ON THE CONGO—THE EXCESSIVE MOISTURE—THE RAINY SEASON—"SMOKES"—"LITTLE DRIES"—THE DRY SEASON—THE AFRICAN SPRING—EARLY SUMMER—VIOLENCE OF THE STORMS—THE HARVEST—GEOLOGY OF THE DISTRICT—METALS—FLORA AND FAUNA—THE RIVER NOT A NATURAL BOUNDARY — BOTANICAL ORDERS CHIEFLY REPRESENTED—THE PALMS—LIST OF CHARACTERISTIC SPECIMENS COLLECTED—COLOUR AND FRAGRANCE.

THE climate of the Western Congo naturally varies in different degrees of healthiness and temperature, according to the regions through which the river passes, but on the whole it may be said to be infinitely superior to that of the Niger or the Gold Coast. The great absence of low, marshy ground about its banks is doubtless the cause of less virulent fever, and the regular cool breezes from the South Atlantic greatly reduce the tropical heat. The river probably is least healthy between Boma and the sea, owing, no doubt, to the mangrove swamps that inevitably attend the widening out of the embouchure. Boma itself is decidedly insalubrious.* It is the hottest place on the Congo, and surrounded by many marshes. Towards Vivi it becomes decidedly cooler, owing to the greater elevation; and the higher you proceed up the river the healthier the climate becomes. One aid to salubrity is the magnificent drinking water that may be

* I believe extensive public works carried out by the Belgians have quite sanified Boma.—H. H. J.

had everywhere above Boma; not the water of the Congo
—which, though wholesome, has a disagreeably sweet
taste—but the water from the unnumbered rills and
rivulets which are everywhere trickling, wet and dry
season alike, all the year round. Consequently dysentery

CAMOENSIA MAXIMA.

is almost un-
known above
Vivi. The
most preva-
lent form of
sickness is
the ordinary African fever from over-exposure to the
sun and sudden chills. The most dangerous malady
is bilious fever, the "febre perniciosa" of the Portuguese, but this is rarely incurred without much previous
neglect of one's health. Beyond Stanley Pool, I can
only call the temperature delightful. It ranges, at

such a place as Msuāta for instance, from 87° in the
shade at noon to 60° at two in the morning, and this
in the rainy or hot season.   The highest temperature
I have ever observed at Vivi was 98° in the shade, on a
very hot day.   It is quite possible to walk about all
through the middle of the day and not feel the heat
disagreeable, provided you wear a helmet and carry an
umbrella; but when you see, as I have seen, young men
newly arrived from Europe exposing themselves to the
noonday sun with nothing but a smoking-cap on their
heads, you will hardly be surprised that occasionally
deaths from sunstroke take place.   And then the relatives
of these victims of their own imprudence write to the
papers, especially in Belgium, and speak of the cruel
African Minotaur and its meal of white flesh!   The fact
is that under a tropical sun much greater prudence and
care are needed to regulate one's mode of living in
accordance with the surrounding conditions than in the
temperate zones, where the effect follows less rapidly on
the cause.   In the hot regions, more especially in the
countries that are hot and moist, the agencies of nature
are somewhat sudden and violent in their action.   Everything is "forced" and hurriedly urged on to a climax.
What in Europe would be a mere imprudence, only
causing a serious effect if long persisted in, becomes
under an African sun a grave danger.   You over-eat
yourself, for instance (an excess both common and
excusable when entailed by the violent, unhealthy
appetites which the climate often promotes); and, instead
of being quit with an ordinary attack of indigestion, you
find yourself laid up with a sharp attack of bilious
fever, and perhaps, before you or your companions have
time to check the rapid growth of the malady, other
complications set in, and in two or three days you are
dead.   Yet it is possible to enjoy excellent health on
the Congo, if only it be borne upon one's mind to use
moderation in all things.   Abstain from nothing that is
pleasant and innocuous, but abuse no form of enjoyment.
Eat, drink, and be merry, and remember that meagre

abstention is as harmful as riotous excess. Let every man judge for himself and follow implicitly within due bounds the dictates of his stomach—that is when he has no reason to believe he is prompted by unhealthy cravings. If you conceive a great love for jams and sweet biscuits, indulge in them till satiety begins to take the edge off your greediness, and in all probability this desire for " sweets " is prompted by a necessity for sugar in your system. Avoid alcohol as much as you can. It is almost a case in which abstention is excusable, for wine and brandy are dangerous adjuncts to a healthy man's repast in Africa. On the other hand, alcohol is simply invaluable as a tonic when weak from fever or other causes. Beer, in my own case, proved beneficial and agreeable, but with others it provoked biliousness. Wash in warm water rather than cold, dress warmly and sleep well covered; satisfy all reasonable and natural desires, and you will find life on the Congo both healthy and enjoyable.

The great fault of the climate lies in the excessive damp. Even in the dry season there is great moisture in the air, for, though there is no downright rain, yet the mornings and evenings are ushered in by dense white mists, like low-lying clouds, which incessantly filter through the clammy atmosphere a drizzling vaporous spray that descends over everything like a heavy dew. This is the "cacimbo" of the Portuguese colonies and the "smokes" of the Guinea coast. These morning and evening mists are characteristic of the rainy season, and during the rainy months they disappear, and the beginning and closing of the day is generally bright and clear.

The relative length of the rainy season varies as you advance from the mouth of the Congo towards the equator. Near the sea there are about four months of rain—November, December, February, and March—with an intermediate dry season in the month of January; but ascending the river you find this gradually altering, and on Stanley Pool the rains commence in October and continue till about the 20th of May, thus leaving four months of dry season. There is also here no interval in January, no "little dries," as they are called. Higher up the river still, approaching the equator, the natives tell me it rains often in June, August, and September, so that this may be called a true equatorial climate, where rain is seldom absent, and consequently, as we find at Bolobo, this is the region of perpetual forest. The reason this forest belt does not extend more fully over Africa is that, where there is a continuous dry season of four, five, or six months, there is time for the long grass to become thoroughly tindered by the sun, and the natives can then more easily set going the great bush-fires, in which they delight, which clear the ground for their plantations, and at the same time sweep the forest from the hills. In the equatorial regions of perpetual moisture this is impossible, and so the forest country there, with its somewhat peculiar fauna and avi-fauna, continues to represent a condition of things which probably existed more widely over Africa before the advent of man, or, rather, before the period when man first began to give some effect to his growing dissatisfaction with the arrangements of Nature, and to take the law into his own hands. I am sure that the arboreal life of our species dates very far back in its development, and that, like our cousins the baboons, we had, whilst we were yet mere monkeys, begun to prefer the rocks and caverns * and the knolls of observation in an open country to the dense woods in which our degraded relations the gorillas and orangs still skulk in sullen shyness. As a rule man is an enemy of the forest, and has done much to circumscribe his future supplies of coal, but perhaps on the whole he is unconsciously right. The open country is far healthier and brighter than the gloomy mysterious forest depths, and the higher forms of mammals—those that are strongest in intelligence and widest in range—seem to have been evolved from the breezy plateaus and rolling plains.

* Early paleolithic man is constantly associated with caves.

It seems to be hardly realized how wintry is the aspect of the dry season in the tropics. Many more of the trees in Africa are deciduous than we often imagine in our conjured-up mental visions of a fair tropic land, where perpetual verdure reigns, and the vegetation is a vague, indefinite mixture of limp palms, with fronds like ostrich-feathers, and rampant bananas raising their florid greenery above the masses of formless creepers. But nevertheless, when about a month has elapsed after the last rains are over, the aspect of an African hill-side has much of the cheerless desolation of winter about it. The once imposing baobabs, whose masses of verdure were fair to see, are reduced to mazes of leafless twigs; the ground is covered with a brown carpet of fallen leaves; many trees, though retaining their foliage, put forth no fresh shoots, and are yellow and seared with the hot sun; here and there an evergreen stands out, like an English yew or holly, in almost heartless contrast of dark cold green amid its faded, withered fellows, and next to it, perhaps, is a white skeleton of what was a short time since a tufted tree. The tall herbs, erewhile gay with gorgeous flowers, show now nothing but yellow stalks and shrivelled seed-vessels, in which perhaps there still lurks a point of colour in the red or orange seeds that gleam from under the brown husk. The many tiny flowerets, the mosses and fungi, are scarce to find; only certain repulsive plants—things with fleshy, mutilated limbs, weirdly swollen, distorted and covered with malicious prickles—stand forth in disagreeable prominence, screened from view no longer by the fair and delicate creeping ferns and clambering lycopodiums, and seeming to stand unchanged and prosperous when all else fades and dies. In the great meadows through which the path meanders the waving grasses are laid low, and in their place are dismal tracts of black ashes where the bush fires have just swept by.

But the dry season is hardly death as much as recuperation. It is a short pause—a sleep in which the expended forces of Nature are once more gathered in. Just as the earth in its summer solstice spins out from the sun's

control like a restless child, and then, wearied with its
wilfulness, lets itself be slowly drawn in again to run its
sober winter journey, so its tiny children, who have rioted
in all the exuberant excesses of spring and summer, need
the repose of the slack months to restore their energies.
The birds put away their fine clothes, the "season" being
over, and go into *villéjiature* in plain suits of every-
day garments. The whydah-bird especially, who all the
summer long was the veriest rake, and flaunted his long
plumes wantonly before the eyes of his lady friends in a
manner quite disastrous to their virtue, has now lost his
good looks, and assumes the bearing of a cynic wearied
with excess of love and easy conquests, dropping his
beautiful deportment and rich dress, and assuming a
costume that is strictly plain and almost shabby. He
also has to economise for his past expenditure, but it is
also with the view of having "another good time" by
and by.

Whether life's cycle has had a beginning, and will have
an end, we know not, but to our finite comprehension it
seems eternal. Out of life comes death, which is inactivity,
and out of this springs active life again. The perennials
die down to their roots, exhausted with their late display
of vigour, but when the returning rains once more soften
and cool the dry, cracked soil, up spring the bright young
shoots from the old stock to flourish anew and live their
life. And if the annual dies, has it not scattered round it
germs from which a hundred children rise to carry on its
pedigree and spread its race? So, if there is a winter in
Africa, there is also a spring, full of hope and promise and
cheerful activity. The first rains are seldom violent or
long-continued, but they effectually moisten the soil and
cause the dried-up brooks to flow and the rivers to swell.
Then a myriad flowers blow, the sternest, woodiest shrubs
evince an unsuspected tenderness; spiteful euphorbias,
prickly acacias, apopletic baobabs show that some poetic
feeling lurks beneath their forbidding exterior and finds
a vent in innocent and fragrant blossoms. A wealth of
colour fills the woods, the plain, the swamps, and even

covers the harshest rocks and mountains. Tall orchids
spring up by the river-side, proud of their matchless
beauty. Cannas and amomums lurk in all the damp,
luxuriant glades. The largest trees—stern, sober and
business-like all the rest of the year—display a fortnight's
blaze of blossoming in a sudden and abrupt manner, as if
ashamed of the weakness. The very flowering of the
grasses tries to be feebly pretty ; and, as they have no
petals to boast of, they show their purple stamens
apologetically. The birds build. The weaver-birds hang
their pendent nests on all the grass stalks that border the
streams. The coarse, boisterous fishing-eagles furbish up
their dirty, untidy eyries, and carry on and quickly
conclude a soulless courtship : the " am'rous doves " begin
their sickly-sentimental cooing in every shady tree, and
bright, practical couples of parrots may be seen bustling
round the hollows in many a trunk that contains their
intended breeding-place.

About this season the natives will bring you many
young animals—perhaps the cubs of a black-backed
jackal, or the sweet little kittens of a genet cat. In the
still reaches of the river, on some quiet evening, you may
see the mother hippopotamus leaving the water in a
leisurely manner, accompanied by her fine pink baby ;
they are intending to sleep on shore for greater security
from the spiteful crocodiles, whose young ones, by-the-
bye, are just emerging from the egg and running the
gauntlet, not only of their natural enemies, the storks and
ibises and ichneumons, but of their unnatural fathers, who
do not approve of large families.

So the spring advances till it is summer, and then come
a few short weeks of delicious monotony, when the rain
diminishes, and nature in the acme of her beauty stands
still in a sweet content. But on content there follows
a burst of riotous excess. The air is charged with
electricity. The storms recommence with a fury and
violence which never marked them heretofore. The
thunder roars, the wind howls, and the rain descends in
disordered floods that are no longer the gentle revivers of

a thirsty world, but the reckless destroyers of fragile beauty. Against the piled-up banks of sullen cloud the lightning blazes in silent, vivid wrath, or, moved to greater vehemence of anger, tears in zigzags over the hillsides and deals out sudden death. Between these stormy outbursts come intervals of tearful repentance. The battered flowers lie low, branches and leaves strew the rain-pitted strand, the sky is a pale exhausted blue, and Nature, like a passionate woman, seems disposed to regret her violence, and perhaps through the voice of some small piping bird falters out her repentance over the disordered scene. But she is excited by the ardent sun, who is always imbuing the hot air with a feverishness of unassuaged desire. There is a lustfulness now in most things. The crocodiles hoarsely roar at night with strange love promptings. The heavy hippopotami pursue their mates at sundown with amorous gruntings, crashing through the high rank grass. The very grass itself, once, when the rain first came, a tender green and timid bladelet, creeping above the ashes of its predecessor, is now become an insolent obstruction, with strong and knotted stem and razor-bladed leaves, thrusting its many flower-heads in your face, a very upstart in vulgar pride. Man himself seems swayed by this time of orgie. The crops are gathered in, the sugar-cane is cut, and, from its juice a heady spirit is made which furnishes the cause and excuse of many a wild debauch. It is time that Nature put a check upon her· riot; the wanton world must be purified with fire. Then the rain ceases, the ground dries, the river shrinks. Submerged islands reappear, and cut-off pools stagnate. The always-shining sun is quickly preparing the fiery purification. One day a native throws a lighted brand among the withered herbage. The wind springs up, and an awful blaze roars before it, sweeping rapidly over the hills, so rapidly that, while it reduces the grass to tinder, it does little more than scorch the trees. Then, with the increasing drought, life resumes its soberness. The bull hippopotami skulk in groups of celibates apart from their mates, who, with the presentiment of a future maternity, lead a quiet and regular life. The doves relax in their cooing, and devote themselves to a gluttonous repast on the many seeds which are now scattered broadcast on the soil. The baobabs shed their leaves, and everything once more re-enters the winter state of repose and recuperation.

The rain on the Congo not only falls with considerable force and persistence, the downpour sometimes lasting continuously for twenty hours, but also seems to possess some chemical quality which aids it in disintegrating the hard metamorphic rocks, and in forming the deep-red surface soil. The action of water, both falling from the sky and coursing in torrents down the hills, has largely modified the surface in the Congo lands. Strange hollows and ravines are scooped out by the rain wherever it finds a weak spot, and, after every heavy thunderstorm, the water rushing down the hillsides in temporary brooks carries with it quantities of the friable soil, and cuts great channels which in course of time become accentuated and deepened till their sides fall in, and thus the mountain or hillock is slowly but surely being levelled and the valley filled up. Here and there in the hilly cataract region great isolated blocks of quartz lie about, either washed out from the hillside by rain-made landslips, or forming in a plain the last relics of a bygone hill that has long resisted disintegration. In the bed of the river there are many rocks of clay slate. Basalt also enters into the geological formation of the country, and on the river above Stanley Pool the rocks appear volcanic. Iron is abundant throughout the Congo basin—many of the rocks are streaked with ferruginous stains—and is known and used by the natives, who call it *mputo*. Neither silver nor gold are known by the Congo people. When shown gold by a European they take it for inferior copper.

Topazes are said to be found near Bolobo, as I have mentioned in my account of that place. I have never, however, seen any precious stone of any kind in the possession of the natives; flakes of mica I have noticed among some of their charms.

Q

The fauna and flora of the Congo region between the Stanley Falls, which lie almost in the centre of the continent, and the coast, are by no means uniform, and may be said to offer three distinct aspects, caused by the character of the regions through which the Congo flows.

What may be known as the first region extends from the sea-coast some eighty miles at most inland, and belongs to the marshy forest belt that stretches all along the western littoral of Africa from Cabeça de Cobra, fifty miles south of the Congo mouth, to the river Gambia in Upper Guinea. This swampy area, where mammals and birds are remarkable for their peculiar forms rather than for richness in species, prevails along the lower river uninterruptedly from the coast as far as Ponta da Lenha, about fifty miles from the sea, and further extends, somewhat modified in character, to Boma and beyond, where it insensibly mingles with the next, or "cataract" region, which is characteristic of the parallel mountain chains extending from the Upper Ogowé right down the continent into Southern Angola, and separating the central plateau or basin of tropical Africa from the strip of low-lying coast-land bordering the sea. In this mountain district, which commences some little distance beyond Boma, and may be said to include all the cataracts or rapids of the Congo as far as Stanley Pool, the fauna and flora are of a more generalised type than those of the first and third regions, and partake more of the fauna and flora prevailing in Angola and Lower Guinea. Finally, the influence of this somewhat poor region of stony hills and rocky boulders fades away before the splendid richness of the central plateau, and at Stanley Pool new forms characteristic of Central Equatorial Africa make their appearance; and so abrupt is the change, that the upper end of Stanley Pool more resembles the regions of the Wellé and the western littoral of Tanganyika in its natural history, especially in its flora, than the tract of country twenty miles off, which begins with the first cataract at the lower end of the Pool. Though I have not myself penetrated farther than about 2° 30′ south of the equator, yet, by comparing my observations with those of Stanley along the Upper Congo, and Schweinfurth on the Wellé, I have arrived at the conclusion that there is no sensible difference in the fauna and flora throughout the great basin in which the Congo flows between Stanley Pool and the Stanley Falls; nay, that over that vast tract of country there is more uniformity in forms of life than between the cataract region and the coast.

Before describing the most striking features of Congo Natural History, I would like to remove as far as possible the erroneous idea that the Congo is a natural boundary in the distribution of certain forms, or that it even acts as a limitation southwards of the so-called West African region. I have read in many works on Africa, or on the distribution of plants and animals, that the Congo was the southern boundary of the habitat of the grey parrot, the anthropoid apes, and the oil-palm (*Elaïs guineënsis*). Now the grey parrot reaches perhaps its great development in Malanje, a district of Angola nearly 300 miles south of the Congo, and, together with the oil-palm, continues to be found as far as the tenth degree south of the equator; while the anthropoid apes can hardly be said to be limited southward in their distribution by the lower course of the Congo, for they do not reach even to its northern bank, or approach it nearer than Landana, 100 miles away. Near the equator it is possible that gorillas are found both north and south of the Congo, and we know that a species of anthropoid ape is found to the west of the Lualaba at Nyangwé.* Again, the harnessed antelope (*Tragelaphus scriptus*) and the red buffalo (*Bos brachyceros*), both supposed to be purely West African or "Cis-Congo" forms, are found on the Quanza river, which lies about 200 to 300 miles southward of the Congo, while other West African species do not extend beyond the equator, and therefore are unknown along the Congo in its lower course. There are,

---

* And up to the west and south-west shores of Tanganyika and the vicinity of Lake Mweru.—H. H. J.

besides, many West African plants which stretch right
away from the Gambia, across the Congo, into Angola on
the south.   In short, I have never seen any difference
between the fauna and flora of the northern and southern
banks of this great river; nor do I believe that it acts in
any way as a limitation to the range of species.

I will conclude this chapter with a slight sketch of the
Botany of the Western Congo, first noting a few striking
(not rare) genera which form general features in the landscapes.   The Leguminous order is especially prominent,
as represented by its sub-orders *Papilionaceæ, Cæsalpiniæ,*
and *Mimoseæ.*   Among the most noticeable genera of
Papilionaceæ may be mentioned *Lonchocarpus*, with its
ground masses of mauve blossoms (*L. sericeus*), *Rhyncosia*,
with bright red flowers; *Cajanus indicus, Baphia*, and the
really beautiful, poetical *Camoensia*, aptly named, of
which an illustration heads this chapter.   Among the
Cæsalpiniæ, the genus *Erythrophlæum*, represented by a
towering tree, sometimes 60, 70, and even 100 feet in
height, is remarkable for its intensely poisonous bark.
The *Mimoseæ* are of course abundant.   In this sub-order
the genera *Parkia* and *Acacia* furnish many fine forest
trees.   Another large tree is *Parinarium excelsum*, a
member of the *Rosaceæ*, which possesses fruit that are just
edible.   Among the *Connaraceæ, Cnestis* stands out
prominently, with its brilliant scarlet or orange seed-
vessels.   The beautiful *Mussanda* is a large and well-
represented genus of Rubiaceous shrubs, and the large
order of *Compositæ* offer many striking floral displays.
The Mallows can exhibit such remarkable genera as the
far-spread *Adansonia*, the gaudy-flowered *Hibiscus*, and
the great forest trees, *Eriodendron* and *Bombax.*   Among
the Monocotyledons, the orchid group finds a splendid
representative in the genus *Lissochilus*, which grows
abundantly in the marshy regions of the Lower River,
and in a modified form over a portion of the cataract
country.   It is the most magnificent member of the
Congo flora.   The Lilies are not very noticeable on the
Congo.   Their most striking example is *Crinum zeylani-*

cum (see Chapter XI.). Among the *Commelynaceæ*, *Commelyna* is one of the commonest genera, displaying everywhere its beautiful deep-blue flowers, and more rarely a white-petalled form. Aloes are abundant, and here and there a fine form of *Dracæna, D. sapochinowki,* is seen. *Costus* and *Amomum* offer their delicately-coloured flowers constantly to the view, those of the former being surrounded with many scaly bracts, and the inflorescence of the latter appearing, without any accompanying leaves, just on a level with the soil. The Banana, which is so abundantly cultivated by the natives, represents the genus *Musa,* but I doubt whether it is indigenous to Africa, or this part of Africa. There is no truly wild species on the Congo, and all the cultivated ones produce no seed.*

Among the Palms seven genera may be met with— *Cocos, Borassus, Hyphœne, Phœnix, Raphia, Elaïs,* and *Calamus.* *Cocos,* the Cocoanut-palm, is possibly not indigenous to South Africa, though it is abundantly found along the coast. It never penetrates more than a few miles inland. The Borassus palms (*B. flabelliformis*) are also confined to the estuary of the Congo ; farther inland they are replaced by *Hyphœne guincënsis.* In the cataract region proper there are no Borassine or Hyphænoid palms, but at Stanley Pool a new *Hyphœne* appears, differing materially from *H. guincënsis* of the Lower river, and probably identical with *H. ventricosa* of the Upper Zambezi. It has a swollen stem, bluish-green fronds, and yellow fruit about the shape and size of a large apple, with a thin sweet pulp surrounding a hard ivory-like stone. Of this fruit the elephants are immoderately fond. This palm is illustrated at p. 142. The genus *Phœnix,* rendered celebrated by its distinguished representative the Date-palm,† is only present on the extreme Lower Congo in the form of *Phœnix spinosa. Raphia*

---

* I rather question the accuracy of this statement. I think that a species of *Musa* allied to *Musa Ensete* may be found wild in parts of the Congo basin.—H. H. J.

† *P. dactylifera.*

vinifera is met with all along the river, but is not so abundant or largely used by the natives for wine-making as in Western Africa farther north. On the other hand, the sap of *Elaïs guineënsis*, the graceful oil-palm, is largely drunk by the Congo peoples, and is called by the same name throughout the Congo basin, from Nyangwé to the sea : *viz.* "malafu." * A somewhat similar name, "ma-lebu" or "ma-rebu," is given to the sap of the *Hyphæne*. Both these words are plurals, and the singular forms—"ilafu," and "irebu" or "ilebu"—are given to the tree itself. Finally there is the genus *Calamus*, which only appears on the river Congo at and above Stanley Pool. The species there found is *Calamus secundifloris*. It is illustrated in all its stages of growth and fruiting at p. 122.

Amongst the *Gramineæ* there are many important genera, too numerous to describe in detail. *Andropogon, Olyra, Pennisetum* and others are noticeable from their abundance. The Papyrus is found in quantities on Stanley Pool and in all the quiet reaches of the river. *Pistia stratiotes*, a member of the order *Lemnaceæ*, abounds, as on most tropical streams. Lastly, among the Filices there are tree-ferns (I do not know what genus) to be seen in the cataract region, and the bracken (*Pteris*) is omnipresent.

On the whole, the flora of the Lower Congo is, as one might imagine, half-way between that of Upper and Lower Guinea. The mountainous cataract country between Vivi and Stanley Pool is almost identical with Angola, while the low-lying marshy district near the coast is like the littoral of Senegambia and the Niger delta. The Upper Congo between Stanley Pool and Nyangwé is much of the same character, like the Gold Coast and the great forest belt of Western Africa which stretches northward to the Upper Shari, the Benue, the Kong mountains and the Gambia. Although the Congo offers nothing, as we yet know, that is unique as genus or family, yet probably

* *Vide* Stanley, ' Dark Continent,' pp. 77 *et seq.* ; and Chapters III. and IV. of this book.

nowhere in Africa are there such magnificent displays of colour formed by the conspicuous flowering trees and plants. Here, at any rate, no one can maintain that the temperate zone can offer anything equal in the way of flower-shows. Many of the blossoms also exhale strong odours, sometimes very offensive, but also, I am glad to say, in many cases fragrant and delicious. Few perfumes are more pleasing than the clove-like smell of the *Camoensia*, or the balmy scent of the *Baphias*.

CHAPTER XIII.

NATURAL HISTORY.

ENTOMOLOGY OF THE DISTRICT—LEPIDOPTERA—THEIR EASY CAPTURE
—BUTTERFLY BAIT—LIST OF SPECIES MOST COMMON—BEETLES—
LOCUSTS—EPHEMERIDÆ—THE MASON WASP—ANTS—THE JIGGER
—FLIES — SPIDERS — MOLLUSCA — CRUSTACEA — ICHTHYOLOGY —
BATRACHIANS — REPTILES — CROCODILES — THE   SPUR-WINGED
PLOVER—TORTOISES—LIZARDS—SNAKES.

ONE of the prettiest sights as you voyage up the Congo,
and coast some sandy bank or smooth low-lying shore, is
to see the moist ground covered with myriads of brightly-
coloured butterflies, clustered like beautiful blossoms in
some parterre, round the more humid depressions in the
soil, settling there apparently to suck up the moisture and
quench what appears to be a perpetual thirst. So absorbed
are they in this occupation that they seem well-nigh
unconscious of possible danger, and you may walk quietly
up to them, and, selecting your victims, seize them by the
thorax, pinch and pop them into your collecting box ; by
the time this is done, the other butterflies, momentarily
disturbed by your incursion, will have settled again, and
you can pursue your work of slaughter.   Or, if you like a
more wholesale mode of capture, you can drop your net
down on a cluster, and secure about twenty butterflies at
once.   This, however, has its inconveniences.   Not only is
it difficult to prevent the agitated insects from damaging
themselves as they all struggle together, but you may also
include in your netful a number of nasty little wasps or
big droning bees, that will spitefully sting you through the
gauze of the net when you are trying to carefully secure
the best of the butterflies.   Of course, many of the Lepi-

doptera rarely settle on the ground, and are hopelessly high flyers, never pausing for rest, save an the topmost boughs and flowers of the high trees. Others, though flying low, haunt intricate brushwood, where the net can only be manipulated with great difficulty, if at all.

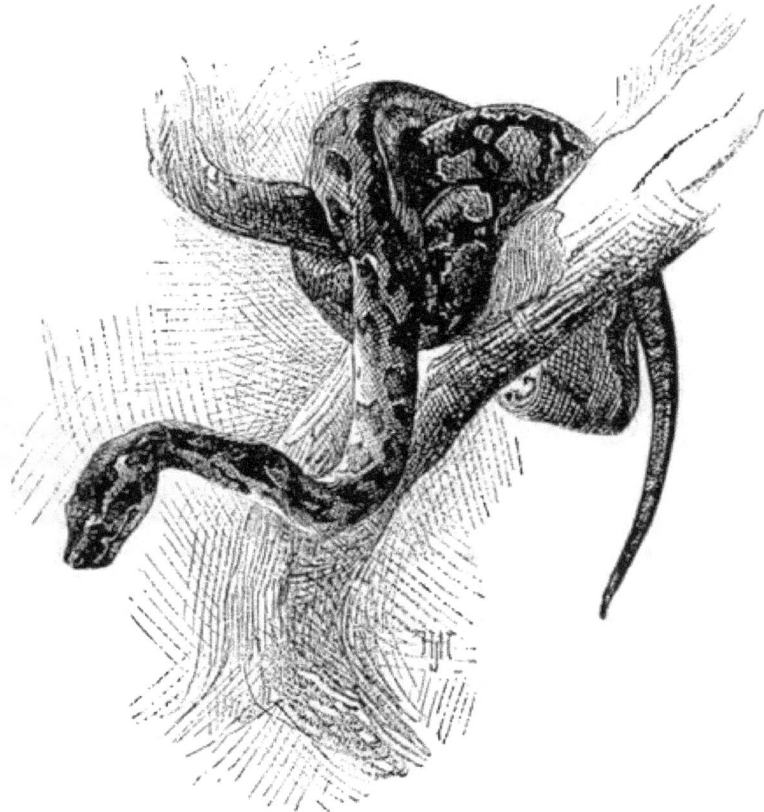

A PYTHON.

This *locale* is very characteristic of a most magnificent crimson moth, a day-flying insect, which I have seen many recurring times, but never been able to secure, for the reason that it enters a tangle thorny bush where capture is impossible. Here it sits complacently, not fearing to

attract attention by the magnificent carmine of the upper
side of the wings, although their underside is leaf-brown
and "protective" in colour, and, if the creature liked,
would, when closed, render it quite indistinguishable from
the dead and scrubby foliage it haunts.

There is one "bait" for butterflies which attracts the
proudest and shyest amongst them—blood. Sprinkle the
gore of a newly-slain animal over any cleared space, and
you will soon reap a rich result in the way of butterflies.
They also flock to most decaying substances, animal or
vegetable, and the deposits of elephant's dung in the forest
will be the frequent resorts of these lovely insects.   The
genus *Papilio* is of course well represented, and by some
very beautiful examples. There is *Papilio Antheus*, tailed,
black, with green spots and stripes ; *Papilio Bromius*, large
and black, with broad bluish-green stripe crossing both
wings (this last is dotted on the underside with dead-gold
spots) ; and *Papilio Tyndarœus*, very scarce species, black
and apple-green, a very handsome insect.

A list of the most prominent species of Lepidoptera to
be met with in the Upper and Lower Congo I here give.
Most of them are represented in my own collection, a few
others have been added from a collection of butterflies
from the Lower Congo in the possession of my brother.   I
might remark that nearly all the species and all the genera
here cited have a wide range, being found on the Gold
Coast, the East of Africa, and even in Natal.   The butterflies of the Upper Congo, above Stanley Pool, seem however to be more purely West African in their range than
those of the Lower river, which extend southwards and
northwards, and right across the Continent, reappearing at
the Cape of the Zanzibar coast and in Senegambia.   One
curious instance of wide distribution is the little species
Eurema Hecabe, which is found all over Africa and India,
specimens from Southern India and the Congo being
identical in size and markings.

Besides the Lepidoptera catalogued below, there are
many day-flying moths observable in the Congo, most of
which are *Bombycidæ*.   There is also a curious genus

(*Paradoxa?*) with delicate, whitish, semi-transparent wings, which frequents the densest forests.

LIST OF COMMON CONGO BUTTERFLIES.

FAMILY I.—Nymphalidæ.

Danais limniaciæ, D. Chrysippus, Amauris Damocles, A. Niavius, Ypthima Asterope, Gnophodes Parmeno, Melatanio Leda, Mycalesis Safitza, Elymnias Phegea, Acræa Zetes, A. Serina, A. Gea, A. Euryta, A. Egina, A. Pseudegina, Atella Phalanta, Junonia Cœnio, Precio Pelarga, P. (? species), Hypanio Ilithya, Cyrestes Camillus, Hypolemnas Misippus, H. dubius, H. Anthedon, Catuna Crithea, Neptio Agatha, Eurephene Sophus, E. Cocalia, E. Plantilla, Euphœdra Eleus, E. Ravola, E. Ceres, E. Themis, E. Medon, E. Xypcte, Aterica Tadema, A. Afer, A. Cupavia, A. (? species), Cymothoë Theodata, C. Theobene, C. Cœnio, Nymphalis Ephyra.

FAMILY III.—Lycænidæ.

Liptina Acræa, L. undularis.

FAMILY IV.—Papilonidæ.

Pontia Alcesta, Eurema Brigitta, E. Hecabe, Trachyrio Saba, T. Sylvia, T. Agathina, Catopsilla Florella, Papilio Leonidas, P. Tyndaræus, P. Demoleus, P. Policenes, P. Antheus, P. Nireus, P. Pylades, P. Bromius, P. Merope, P. Echeroides.

FAMILY V.—Hesperidæ.

Isme Florestan, I. (? species).

Amongst the beetles the Longicorns are well represented, and there appears to be a genus allied to or identical with the *Xenocerus* of Malaysia. There are many species of *Gryllidæ*, some of them with antennæ six inches in length, and all possessing alike in the pupa and imago stages most complicated arrangements for making a hideous noise. There are some of these creatures on the Upper river that absolutely prevent your sleeping with the shrill strident whistle and "skreeking" that they make.

The *Blattidæ* are too well represented. Whether one of them, that is most distinctly *Blatta orientalis* (our black-beetle), has been introduced from the East or is indigenous, I cannot say, but this disgusting insect is everywhere numerous. Fortunately the red ants make it their mission in life to eat these disagreeably odorous pests, and many lizards also make them an article of diet.

Locusts of many species abound, and are often very beautiful in colour. Of course the *Mantidæ* are well represented, and some of them are frequently of great size and fierceness. One small species is a beautiful insect, having on the lower part of each wing a large eye or spot, black and pink, on a green ground, and seeming as if painted in body colour. Walking-stick insects of every size are found, all of them marvellous in their imitation of twigs. The dragon-flies of course are beautiful, and many species of *Calepteryx* (Demoiselles) are banded with chocolate or blue-green on their wings.

In certain places, and on certain nights, there are myriads of *Ephemeridæ* dying round you in such quantities as to cover the surface of everything. In their efforts to die gloriously they completely put the candles out, crowding round the wick and causing it to splutter itself away. I detest these insects—there is something so inane about them. Their pale-green bodies and stupid black eyes have a " cheap " look in their appearance, and give you the idea that so many are turned out by contract that the manufacturers cannot be particular as to finish.

There are many honey-making bees, and wasps of every size and nearly every colour abound, some making paper nests, others, like the mason wasp, building their habitations and storehouses with clay. This mason wasp is, of course, very abundant (as it is everywhere in West Africa), and builds its clay cells on any available support that it can find, especially preferring to place them between the projecting covers of books and in the sleeves of unworn garments. Here it stores away the green caterpillars and little spiders that its newly-hatched wasplings feed on in the larval stage. To those who keep insect-eating birds these storages of the mason wasp are very convenient, as you can always find in their clay cells a constant supply of insect food ready gathered to your hand. The male of this species has for a long time remained undetermined, many supposing it to live parasitically on other insects. I believe, however, that I have seen it in a very tiny black wasp, so small as to be taken for a black fly, but perfectly capable of stinging if caught and much resembling the female in miniature. The white *Termites* are of course as prevalent here as everywhere in tropical Africa, and work the same mischief to all wooden buildings.

Amongst the ants is a species of *Ponera** (perhaps *P. grandis*) and a terrible red ant, called by the Zanzibaris " maji moto " or " hot water," from the terrible scalding sensation its bite produces. When a great army of these ants takes a dwelling-house in its line of march it is wiser to clear out and leave them the road free. At the same time, a cordon of hot wood ashes does a great deal to make them turn from their road. Many species of small ants work terrible mischief amongst one's collections, devouring dried plants, entomological specimens, and skinned birds with equal relish and despatch. Fatal also is it to leave your sugar or sweet things open and unprotected ; once you do so, you must be content to throw them away, or eat them under the form of *compôte de fourmis*, for the masses of gluttonous ants find sweet suicide in these saccharine pitfalls.

I am glad to say that the common flea is unknown on the Upper Congo, or anywhere on this river; in fact, where Portuguese influence has not spread. But, lest this exemption from such an odious pest might make Central African man too contented with his mundane existence, kind Providence has introduced from America into these too happy regions a terrible creature—the " jigger," " chigoe," or " burrowing flea " (*Sarcopsyllus penetrans*). Making its first appearance on the West African coasts at Ambriz in 1855, this horrible little jigger has spread all over Western Africa from Sierra Leone to Mossâmedes with astonishing rapidity. Its progress inland, though as certain, is less speedy than along the coast. However, it

* This large ant exhales a most disgusting odour; especially when crushed.

has now mounted the Congo nearly as far as the equator,* and was beginning already to be a well-known pest at Bolobo at the time of my arrival there, although as yet the suffering natives had hardly given it a name. The "jigger," which is scarcely bigger than a pin's head, burrows under the skin of the feet and hands, and there in its little cell surrounds itself with a sack of eggs. Its presence is soon made evident by the pain and itching it occasions, and it is visible as a small blue point in a circle of white under the skin. If removed soon after discovery it occasions comparatively little inconvenience, but should you delay the eggs will hatch, and a multitude of little fleas will honeycomb your flesh. Neglect may cause the whole foot to rot away and mortify. The jigger is best removed by a sharply-pointed piece of wood, and care must be taken in so doing not to break the egg sack, lest the eggs escape into the wound, and, hatching there, cause it to fester.

There are many fine cicadas on the Congo, especially about Stanley Pool, where one large species is eaten by the natives. This insect is four inches in length, and has "drums" near the base of the abdomen in the male.

Many species of flies add to the small plagues of the Upper river. One, very little and black, sucks the skin until a point of blood as large as itself comes to the surface. Another big dun-coloured fly gives a very painful, itchy bite, especially on the hand. When I was painting studies and sketches in oil-colours this fly

---

* Since the above was written, the Jigger has rapidly advanced across Africa, and even now has reached Zanzibar, it is said. In 1886, it began to be noticed on the Upper Congo, at the Stanley Falls. In 1888, it had reached the west coast of Tanganyika, and in 1892 the north coast of Lake Nyasa and the shores of the Victoria Nyanza. During the past year, 1894, it has spread all over Nyasa-land, and is now to be found on the Lower Zambezi. In a few months all the native postmen in the service of the British Central Africa Protectorate, have been more or less lamed from its attacks. It is always at its worst, however, during the first two or three years after its arrival in a new country; then it seems to be checked, or modified in its increase, or even actually to die out altogether in moist localities.—H. H. J.

annoyed me dreadfully, for it would creep on to the palm of the left hand, which held the palette, and sting or rather probe me so violently with its proboscis that, with my start of pain and surprise, I would often dash the palette away. Other flies that do not bite annoy you fully as much by continually buzzing about your ears and neck, and resisting all your efforts to drive them away.

As a corollary to the abundance of flies are the numerous spiders. I always rather enjoyed seeing a spider kill a fly in England—the spider is so thoroughly cool and practical, and the fly so very weak-minded—but my enjoyment was much enhanced on the Congo, and I looked upon the spiders as my personal friends. Curiously enough, the nickname the natives gave me was " Buï," or' " The Spider," not, I think, from any physical resemblance, but " because I was always catching flies and other insects." There seem to be several species belonging or related to the genus *Mygale*, and some of these are very large and often very beautiful. One big mygaloid spider was velvety blue-black in colour. I also observed many specimens of *Lycosa*, of *Ciniflo* (?), of *Scytodes*, and the terrible *Solpuga* or *Galeodes*. Scorpions are met with, but are not abundant.

Centipedes (*Scolopendra*) are very common and very poisonous. They haunt dry wood, and in the crevices of the logs that the natives collect to make their fires many of these creatures lurk, and sting the native as he drags the wood along. The innocuous millipedes (*Zephronia* ?) are seen everywhere.

Of the molluscs I have little to say, except that some of the snails have most beautifully-decorated shells, and would well repay a collector, and that not a few of the slugs assume very brilliant tints of orange and scarlet, doubtless because they are nasty, and can afford to be bold and showy to warn off possible devourers. There is a kind of fresh-water shrimp in the Lower river much liked by the natives, by whom they are caught, cooked, pounded up in a mortar with salt—shells and all—and used as a seasoning with various forms of vegetable food.

Land crabs are numerous near the estuary of the Congo, especially inhabiting the mangrove swamps along the tidal river.   They are amongst the weirdest things on a tropic shore, as they emerge from their holes in the black mud and march forth in armies after the retreating tide, rushing at the garbage strewn upon the ooze, and devouring everything devourable with unflagging appetite. Then, as the step of a human being approaches, they scuttle back to their many burrows of divers size and depth, and appear and disappear so rapidly that they seem like some formal illusion of the "zoetrope."   It is great fun to intercept an unfortunate land-crab on the way back to his burrow.   He knows perfectly well which is his, and would immediately make for it; but if you urge and exasperate him, and poke him up with your stick (not carrying your humour so far as to hurt the poor crustacean), he will in despair try to enter the retreat of one of his fellows, who will so smartly and spitefully repel him that you may out of pity stand aside, and let him race off to his own hole and pop down it in a trice.   Sometimes a large crab pursued will make for too small a burrow, and get stuck at the opening, in which case, brought to bay, he uses his unequal-sized claws like a boxer, shielding himself with one and nipping with the other.

A river like the Congo naturally abounds in fish, but very little is as yet known about its ichthyology.   It seems, however, from the data we possess, to resemble greatly the Upper Nile, and to offer many identical species and genera.   There are many clupeoid, cyprinoid, and percoid forms.   The siluroid group is represented by several species, among them the huge "bagré"[*] of the Portuguese, a fish with a smooth, shiny skin and a large flat head, in which the eyes, very small and colourless, are placed wide apart.   At each corner of the mouth there is a long reversed tentacle.   Also a ganoid, *Polypterus*, very common and very spiteful.   I give an illustration here, engraved from my original study.   This fish had the

[*] *Bagrus sp.*

lower part of the back armed with nine erectile spines,[*] joined together by a web, and with the fins marked by zebra-like stripes. Then there was one superb creature, a fish with great tusk-like teeth—teeth that resemble in shape, but are somewhat larger than, a dog's canines. This fish is figured in Stanley's 'Dark Continent' under the name of the "Livingstone pike," although I do not myself think it bears any resemblance or affinity to the pike family, but rather approaches *Hydrocyon*,[†] and offers many points in common with *Serrasalmus pirayx* or *Erythrinus macrodon*—fish belonging to the rivers of Guiana and other portions of the west coast of South

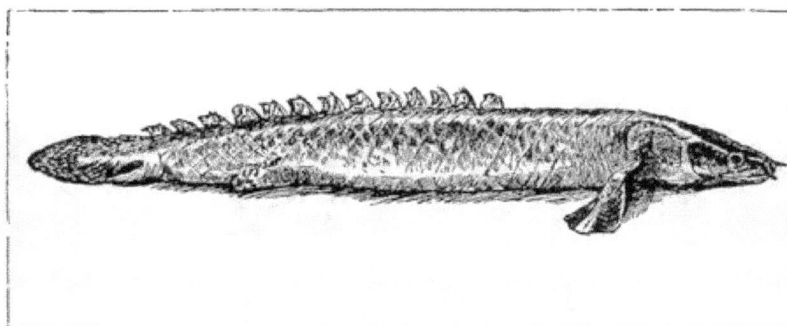

America. This particular specimen of the Congo was a rosy-pink over the upper part of the body, greyish-white below, and was 3 ft. 7 in. in length.[‡] Another curious Congo fish has the jaws prolonged into a sort of proboscis, with a sucker at the end.

Finally, I have often *heard* of *Protopterus* from Europeans, who averred they had seen it, but although I searched in many a muddy stream and pool I was to the end unrewarded by its capture or discovery.

Of the Batrachians I saw but few examples. The African bull-frog is occasionally noticed (*Touropterna*

[*] The number is variable.
[†] Possibly it may belong to this genus.
[‡] See illustration, p. 246.

adspersa ?), and I have also observed *Rana fasciata*, *Cystignathus senegalensis*, and a species of *Discoglossus*. Amongst toads there are *Bufo tuberosus, Brachymerus bifasciatus* (the pretty little two-striped toad), and others which I could not name or identify.

When you come to consider the Reptiles of the Upper Congo, the crocodile is the first to attract your attention, because he is the member of that class with which you most come into contact, and also because he is one of the principal dangers in river travelling, being continually on the look-out for a meal when there appears to be any likelihood of a boat accident. The natives say that when the fearful wind storms or tornadoes take place on the Congo during the rainy season, the crocodiles follow closely in the wake of the wave-tossed canoes, hoping that, ere they can reach the shelter of the bank, the wind, as it often does, may blow them over with their human freight, and throw a choice of limbs in the crocodile's way. It is curious that the crocodiles in this river rarely do more than lop off an arm or a leg from their human victims in the water, leaving the rest of the unhappy creature to attain the shore, if he still live, minus the loss of an arm or leg; that is to say, unless he has to run the gauntlet of other crocodiles and become a limbless trunk. But I do not know so much that it is a curious custom on the part of these monsters as that it indicates a considerable amount of common-sense. Half a loaf is better than no bread, and I think the crocodile does wisely to lop off a limb with his steel-trap-like jaws, and go away quietly with his *bonne bouche*, rather than struggle for the whole body in a fatiguing contest, during which either the native might (as they are traditionally supposed to do) plunge his thumbs into the eyes of his foe, and thus force him to relinquish his hold in agony, or stick his knife into the crocodile's belly; or his friends, having had time for reflection, might decide to interfere and beat off the crocodile with their spears or paddles. Of course if a man is thus maimed he very rarely reaches land alive; but I once saw an individual who, after leaving an arm in a leviathan's jaws, did not succumb to the shock or the rapid current, but reached the shore and lived to tell the tale.

When the sun shines brightly, and the day is still and hot, then the crocodiles by preference leave the water, and repair to some sand-bank or open beach, where they lie and *bake*, rather than bask, in the sun, its fierce heat soon drying up their wet scales, and completely changing their colour from a dark green-brown, tree-like in tone, to a light dust-grey, precisely the colour of the boulders of rock that strew the sandy shore. Indeed, the crocodile's power of assimilation to his surroundings stands him in wonderful stead to deceive his victims and to mislead his only enemy—man. When he lies listlessly floating on the surface of the tepid water, half dreamily enjoying the sun's warmth and his slow motion with the current, it is hard to take him for aught but another of the many torn-up logs and branches that are being carried along by the river; for, like them, he submits to be gently rolled over and over as if an unresisting victim, and he too is dark greenish brown, and somewhat jagged in aspect. It is only when the too regular serration of his back and tail are noticed, or that he attracts your attention by a sudden motion, that you distinguish in him a more interesting and dangerous object than a mere floating log. Again, when the crocodile is lying on the sandy shore, he seems merely a ledge of rock, grey and rough, like the fragments of stone around him. When this reptile lies on the sand he has a way of so tucking his limbs into him and lying prone and flat, with so little variation in his outline that it is small wonder that you take him for an inanimate object; nor does movement on his part quickly undeceive you, for he glides so smoothly towards the water that, before you realize that the "log" is taking itself off, a splash and the wave of a serrated tail enlighten you as to the real character of the phenomenon. The tail of the crocodile is, as you know, a terrible weapon. With it, if effectively employed, he can stun or kill a man in the water, and unwary victims who stand too near the bank may be swept into the water by a sudden sweeping fling of it. I remember on the River Quanza, in Angola, meeting with an illustration of this. The river steamer on which I was travelling was moored close to the shore, and a plank laid just over the water between the deck and the river bank, over which the "krumen" went backwards and forwards with cargo. Towards dusk one of these niggers was crossing the plank with a load on his head, when a hitherto unseen crocodile whisked up his tail and swept the unhappy wretch into the water. He was recovered, for the crocodile himself seemed rather frightened at his own boldness, and abandoned the man after a brief struggle; but the poor wretch had all his bowels crushed by one grip of the crocodile's jaws, and barely lived to reach the shore.

It is really true that the crocodile is accompanied and "protected" by a little wading bird, which utters a shrill warning cry if its mailed friend, sleeping with a peaceful grin of satiety lurking about his cruel jaws, is menaced by approaching foes. This little bird, the spur-winged plover, *Lobivanellus albiceps* (known in Egypt as the zik-zak), lives on terms of the greatest intimacy with the crocodiles, and, when they lie basking on the sand-flats, the birds perch on their backs and hop freely about the recumbent monsters. What return they receive at the hands of their strange allies for the vigilant care they take of them when ashore I cannot say. It used to be supposed that the zik-zak plover was allowed the privilege of acting as the crocodile's toothpick; and other travellers, who thought this a somewhat repellent office, asserted that the bird merely removed the worms and leeches that crept into the soft parts of the crocodile's jaw. I can only say for my part that, although the spur-winged plover is with the crocodile during all the time it spends on land, I have never yet witnessed it taking a meal from out of those formidable jaws.

Before I leave the crocodiles, I might mention that the ordinary and most common species is the common African crocodile (*Crocodilus vulgaris*), but I have seen some species which, from their great concavity of forehead, appeared to be *C. marginatus*. I also once saw, near Bolobo, the half-decayed head of an African gavial with a narrow snout, possibly *Mecistops Bennettii*.

Land tortoises are rarely seen on the Congo; but a curious aquatic species of *Trionyx*, possibly *T. niloticus* (the so-called soft turtle), is commonly found. This is a very curious tortoise, possessing a droll probiscis, which has rather a perky turned-up look. When the animal is in the water he generally sinks entirely below the surface, leaving only his nostrils, at the end of this probiscis, above the water; thus he may remain concealed for a long time ready to pounce on his victims, which may either be insects flying low over the water, small aquatic birds, or even, they say, young crocodiles emerging from the egg. I had one of these curious creatures given me once by a native on the Upper river, and I kept it in captivity during several months, until it became quite tame, and distinctly increased in size, for when I first received it it was only four inches in length. It fed on worms and decaying meat, and throve so well that I fully hoped to bring it back with me to Europe, and had, indeed, started with the trionyx on my homeward journey. One day, however, he had disappeared from my canoe, and, on making inquiries among the men, I found to my horror that one of the krumen, impelled by some unnatural burst of hunger, had roasted and eaten him! Not even the hearty "whacking" I gave the delinquent could console me for the loss of this interesting creature.

The fine monitor lizards are well represented on the Congo. Apparently the two principal species are *Monitor niloticus* and *M. albogularis*. This latter is a really handsome creature, brightly pied with dark-brown and white, and is often six feet in length when adult. The young specimens appear to be much brighter in colour than the adults, the white spots being yellowish and the brown markings greenish black. They are often captured by the natives, despite their ferocity, and brought for sale. Even when quite young they require to be fed on live fowls.

Though, fortunately, these lizards are not provided with any serious means of attack, they prove really redoubtable foes in a contest with men or dogs, using the pliant tail as a terribly efficient swish, and biting savagely with their small teeth. They are capable of killing a dog, and of stripping the skin from a man's leg. In a wild state they eat small mammals, birds, frogs, and insects. I found in the stomach of one that I shot the remains of three squirrels. Amongst other lizards on the Congo may be remarked the following genera, passing over an immense number of species I have been unable to identify : *Acanthodactylus*, the pretty little spine-foot; *Eremias, Zonurus*

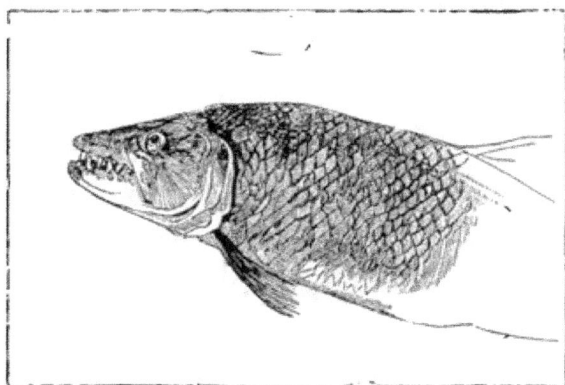

cordylus, Ptyodactylus gecko, Tarentola capensis. Uroprastix, spinipes, and *Agama;* also a very common and handsome lizard of which I do not know the name,* gaudily blue and red in colour, with a short and brittle tail, which is left in your hands should you capture him by that organ. Chameleons are, of course, very common, and exhibit many different species.

Snakes, on the other hand, are decidedly rare, and it is quite possible to voyage right up the Congo and return to Europe without the glimpse of a serpent. I did, however, in the course of my travels along this river, meet with

---

* A species of *Agama.*

three specimens. One was a beautiful species of *Hortulia*, a Boïne snake, quite harmless, and brilliantly marked with brown, yellow, and black rings, over which played a purple bloom or iridescence that faded after death. Then I saw a small specimen of the black African python, and a species of puff-adder, belonging probably to the venomous genus *Clotho*.

CHAPTER XIV.

NATURAL HISTORY—ORNITHOLOGY.

The Fin-foot—Frigate Birds—Gannets—Pelicans—Aquatic Birds at Stanley Pool—Gypohierax Vultures—Hawks—Rails and Plovers—The Crocodile's Friend—A Plover Family—Pigeons—Parrots—Rollers—Crows.

The first bird of any note that I saw after arriving at Stanley Pool was a fin-foot (*Podica*). This curious creature, which is a type of one of those intermediary families from which, as it were, many more specialised forms diverge, is not common in West Africa. I have never observed it but once on the Congo, and that at Stanley Pool; and have only seen it elsewhere on the little Chiluango river, near Landana. The specimen that I examined at Léopold-ville (Stanley Pool) had been shot by a surly German gardener attached to the expedition, who spent his spare time in collecting birds for certain Museums. He had no notion what the bird was; but, seeing I prized it, not only refused to sell it to me, but would not even let me draw it, or dissect its carcase after it had been skinned, fearing lest I might forestall him in the discovery of a new species. Consequently, I am unable to do more than give a super-ficial description of its appearance. The general colour of this *Podica* was a dark mottled brown with green reflec-tions on the whole of the upper surface, while on the throat and belly it was a dirty white. Just above the eye was a streak of light colour, running from the base of the upper mandible to the ear, and beneath this a broader band of dark brown parallel with it. The breast was

spotted with dark brown, and there were a few streaks of
the same colour on the belly. The tail was about four
inches long, and, at the time I saw it, was slightly expanded and resembled very much in general shape the tail

SCHIZORHIS GIGANTEA.

of the darter (*Plotus Levaillanti*). On the central tail-
feathers were a few faint white lines, running transversely.
The beak and the feet were bright orange. The beak
resembled very much in shape the beak of the darter, and
was very sharp at the point. The feet were much like a

grebe's, each toe being lined with a membrane a quarter of
an inch in width. The general appearance of the bird
recalls at once the darters, the herons, the ducks, and the
grebes. When swimming, it lies somewhat low in the
water, and the neck, which is rather long and "kinked,"
moves slowly backwards and forwards, as if poising the
head to dart at a fish. On the river Chiluango, where I
have seen it swimming among the mangrove stalks, little
more than the neck was visible as it swam, and my companions in the boat took it at first for a snake raising its
head from the water. The "darter" (*Plotus Levaillanti*)
is one of the commonest birds on the Congo. It affects
every piece of water, either forming cataracts, tranquil
pools or stagnant marshes. A small cormorant is also
frequently seen, but is not so universally abundant as the
darter. About the Congo region, whether on the Upper
river, the estuary, or the neighbouring coast, types of all
the genera of the sub-order *Pelicani* may be met with.
The frigate-bird (*Fregata aquila*) is not uncommonly seen
off Banana Point, and the tropic-bird (*Phæthon æthereus*) is
of even more frequent occurrence. As this latter breeds
on the island of Sao Thome, he is not so far from home,
off the Congo mouth. Then there is a gannet, *Sula
capensis*, which occasionally visits the estuary of the
Congo in myriads; and, finally, the darters and cormorants
are also represented on the river, together with the pelican.
This giant member of the family is very partial in his
distribution; sometimes you find him in great quantities,
as on Stanley Pool, and about the broadened stream at
Bolobo, at other times he will be absent or unheard of over
a hundred miles of river. On an unapproachable island
above the Falls of Yelala, a colony of pelicans, apparently
Pelicanus onocrotalus, has established itself, and made the
island—which, owing to the rapids, one could only reach
by balloon—a great breeding-place, the shores of which
are white with guano. While I was stopping at the Baptist
Mission at Angu Angu, and afterwards at Vivi, two places
nearly opposite to one another, a strange mortality seemed
to exist among the young pelicans, birds of one year old,

and many of them came floating down the river, and were washed ashore dying or dead. There was no cause easily ascertainable, and this mortality among them reminded me of a similar thing that occurs on the South-West African coast with the gannet (*Sula capensis*), sometimes called the whale-bird, which is often washed ashore dead in incredible quantities. In the Bay of Loanda I have counted often twenty dead gannets round the ship at a glance, and many of them are thrown up on to the beach both at Mossâmedes and at Banana, the mouth of the Congo. After an epidemic like this, the sand is strewn with the carcases of these apparently uninjured birds, which in a few hours are almost consumed by the land crabs and the scapulated crows.

Stanley Pool is a great place for aquatic birds. On the many islands that stud this beautiful expanse of the Congo you may see numbers of crowned cranes, marabou, saddle-billed, and common storks, *Scopus umbretta*, sacred ibises, giant herons, egrets, bitterns, darters, cormorants, spur-winged and Egyptian geese, pratincoles, and large terns with scarlet beaks. Mr. Stanley maintains that he has met with *Balœniceps rex*, the whale-headed stork, on the upper Congo,* and, as he describes the bird very accurately, I see no reason to doubt that he is correct in his assertion. In this case it would certainly extend the habitat of this curious Ardeine bird, hitherto supposed to solely inhabit the waters of the Upper Nile.

A curious feature in Congo ornithology is the absence of all the vultures common to other parts of Africa. Perhaps this may be accounted for by the comparative scarcity of big game, and yet, for all that, there is plenty of animal refuse along the river-side to keep going more than the one species of vulture—if vulture he be—that the Congo possesses. This latter bird is known scientifically as *Gypohierax*, and is sometimes called the Angola vulture, although he is found equally and quite as abundantly in Senegambia or anywhere in West Africa between

* Vol. ii., p. 293, ' Dark Continent.'

the Kunéné and the Senegal. *Gypohierax* is not a true
vulture, but is a form related to the fish eagles, possibly
also to the ospreys, and to that primitive raptorial, *Poly-
boroides.* He is no means a mere scavenger, but goes in
ordinarily for a more refined and respectable line of life,
though it is true that he adapts himself to all circumstances and places, and can, if necessary, get through very
dirty work.   On the Congo, *Gypohierax* is extremely
abundant, and here this accommodating bird has become a
most accomplished fisherman, being much more deft in
catching fish than the proper fishing-eagles (*Hallætus*),
who are to the manner born.   May *Gypohierax* prosper!
He has all my sympathy.   He is one of those clever,
adaptable creatures, like the rat among mammals and the
crow among birds, that can turn their hands, or rather
their stomachs, to anything, and consequently are never
at a loss for a living.   It always annoyed me to see the
way in which Europeans on the Congo massacred poor
Gypohierax.   He is a bold bird, conscious of well-doing,
and in his mature black-and-white plumage (the young
birds are dun-coloured) offers a very good mark to the
neophyte's rifle.   Consequently, scarcely does a party of
newly-arrived Europeans ascend the river without " pop-
ping " at the poor vulture as he sits on the topmost bough
of a dead tree.   The white-headed fishing-eagle is more
often heard than seen.   His vociferous, boisterous screams
greet the rising and the setting sun ; but these birds will
also screech loudly at night or in the day, if anything
occurs to arouse their suspicion.

Amongst noticeable hawks is a very common species of
Milvus (*M. migrans*), a large dark-plumaged bird found
everywhere on the Congo.   Also remarkable is a small
and pretty *Astur* (*A. sphænurus?*), hardly bigger than the
common kestrel, and a dove-coloured grey all over.

Curiously enough, *Helotarsus ecaudatus,* the Bateleur
eagle, is entirely absent from the Congo, although he is
such a common bird in Angola.

Machærhamphus Anderssoni, that curious *bat*-eating
hawk first discovered in Ovampoland and afterwards (an

allied species) in Malaysia, has been shot at Vivi on the Lower Congo, and a specimen may be seen in the Museum of the African International Association at Brussels. In spite of its curiously modified beak, wide gape, and other peculiarities, I think all its affinities are with the accipitrine group. We should certainly admire it for its original taste in food, and one would imagine that it had few emulators in the chase, for bats do not seem to be a favourite article of diet.

There are many plovers and rails found on the Congo, but, in common with most of the wading and water birds, they affect rather the broad stream and many islands of the Upper and Lower river than the straitened region of the cataracts. Of course the species of this great pluvialine group are very numerous. Among them, however, deserve to be noticed certain birds which, from their great abundance and bold demeanour, are common features in the river foregrounds. Such are *Pluvianus Ægyptius*, a pretty little shore-frequenting bird, and the spur-winged plover, whom I have frequently mentioned as the "crocodile's friend." A drawing of him appears at the close of this chapter, but I will also add a word or two of verbal description, so that all my readers who may come across him may recognise him and spare his life, for several reasons: firstly, because he is not at all good to eat; secondly, because he is a bold, independent creature who always speaks or shrieks his mind; and, thirdly, because he is exceedingly common, and it is very wicked to kill a bird unless it is good to eat or new to science. The spur-winged plover, *Lobivanellus albiceps*, is about the size of an ordinary lapwing; has long greenish legs with only three toes; a pendant yellow lobe or wattle, one inch in length, on each side of the head; strong sharp spurs on the "shoulder" or carpal joint of the wings, and is coloured as follows: a large white band runs along the top of the head, from which comes the sub-name *albiceps;* the face, throat, and tail coverts are dove-coloured, merging into fawn on the shoulder; the back and the secondaries are jet-black, and the belly and the pinions snowy-white. The beak is yellow with a black tip, and suggests an affinity to *Œdicnemus,* the "thick-kneed" plover. This latter genus is also another common pluvialine bird. Then there is *Glareola cinerea* and *Nordmani.* I found the young of *G. cinerea* once on a little bare piece of rock, only rising a foot above the water and not more than a few inches square! I used to notice (it was near Msuâta) as I crossed the river every day that a pair of these *Glareolæ* were always perched on this little ledge of rock, and moved not, however near the canoe approached. One day, however, through careless steering, the canoe was driven right up against the rock by the current, and, in putting out my hand to break the shock of encounter, I put it on something soft and warm. Looking down, I saw two little *Glareolæ,* about a week old, pressing themselves flat against the rock. They were covered with blackish down, and were quite invisible when crouched against dark surroundings. There was no sign of a nest, merely a slight concavity or "scoop" in the morsel of rock, which could have retained the eggs. The parents all this time flew round me so close to my head that I made several ineffectual efforts to catch them with my hand. Taking pity on their distress, I left one little one, and took the other home to examine. It was about the size of a day-old chicken, was covered with the afore-mentioned blackish down, and its legs were rather clumsy. The little bird generally rested on its tarsi, with the toes outspread like a squab-pigeon, but it could make an effort to balance itself on its "feet" and shuffle along. It seemed quite unable to feed itself, though it took flies from the hand. As I felt the difficulty of rearing it, and having no spirit to preserve its little carcase for ultimate examination, I took it back the next morning to its rocky nursery, where it nestled down beside its little brother or sister with perfect equanimity, as if nothing particular had happened. I continued to take great interest in this quaint little family, isolated on a point of rock in mid-stream, and paid them several subsequent visits, placing an offering of raw meat (to attract the flies) from time to time in their home. My eventual departure from Msuäta terminated this interesting aquaintance. There are no true bustards on the Congo, although certain species are found not far south in Angola; there are, however, a few small otidine forms, one of which I noticed near Isangila, looking like a very tiny bustard, with some resemblance to a closely-allied family, the coursers. It is a most delicately-coloured little bird—cream, fawn, black, and white. I do not yet know its generic name; but there is a specimen in the Museum of the African International Association at Brussels.

Guinea-fowl are not common on the Congo. I have only met with them to any extent near Bolobo, where the species present was *Numida cristata*. Francolin may be shot from time to time, and make a most agreeable supplement to the traveller's frugal meal.

Among the Pigeons (*Treron*), a common genus, represented by *T. calva*, a fruit pigeon, with green or greenish-grey body, and feet that are very nearly zygodactyle. A beautiful bird, found in the forests all along the Upper river, and in the neighbourhood of Stanley Pool, is the great blue plantain-eater (*Schizorhis gigantea*), with a general plumage of verditer-blue, relieved by a yellow-green stomach, chestnut thighs, and a violet crest. This bird is difficult to shoot, as it is very shy and hides much among the thick foliage of the great trees; but on one occasion I managed to bag him, and, after taking off his beautiful skin, we roasted him for dinner, and his flesh was moist, juicy and delicious. He feeds principally on wild figs and the scarlet dates of a species of *Calamus* palm. A young Belgian officer tried to keep one of these birds alive on bananas, but he refused to eat anything but the above-mentioned fruits, and, the supply of these being scanty, he sickened and died. This bird may be said to be the only one of his group that has the toes distinctly arranged three in front and one behind. All the other plantain-eaters and touracos are either distinctly zygodac-tyle, or else, as in *Schizorhis concolor*, the toes are what one might call "undecided." *Colius*, as we all know, can turn its toes any way; but *Colius*, according to the late Professor Garrod, ought to be separated entirely from the *Musophagidæ*, and to be placed in a group by itself approaching the Cuckoos. Curiously enough, though there are several species of touracos (*Corythaix*) in Angola, that genus is unrepresented on the Congo, the only other member of the *Musophagidæ* group, besides the above-mentioned *Schizorhis*, being the beautiful violaceous plantain-eater (*Musophaga violacea*) which is occasionally met with on the Lower river, especially between Vivi and Isangila. Colies (*Colius*) are most abundant everywhere.

On the islands of Stanley Pool, and indeed everywhere on the Upper Congo, the grey parrot is present—well, it is a moderate estimate to say—in *thousands*. The high trees are covered with them, and their red tails are always enlivening the foliage with bits of scarlet colour. It does not seem to be generally known that the grey parrot has a great variety of note in a wild state. Its whistling is most melodious, especially of an early morning, when the birds fly out from the forest for an airing. The little *Pœocephalus* parrot is common on the mainland round Stanley Pool, and seems a quarrelsome and noisy little bird. It is always quarrelling, more particularly with a species of roller (*Eurystomus*) that appears to invade its haunts and seek unnecessary disputes. The natives say this *Eurystomus* attacks the nests of *Pœocephalus* in the hollow cavities of the baobab-trees, and eats the callow young. If so, this noisy little parrot may have some excuse for its screeching. The species of roller to which I refer is a bird with a large yellow hooked beak, somewhat broad and flattened, and weak toes armed with powerful claws, with the hinder toe directed somewhat forward or "inward," so that the toes appear nearly all four in a row. Its colours are beautiful. The head, back, and mantle are rich chocolate-brown; on the breast this changes to a lovely mauve, while the belly and outer tail-feathers are a pale sea-blue. The quills and central tail-feathers are ultramarine. I wounded one of these birds once, and kept it alive during over three months (having set its broken wing), and, although it never grew tame, it fed voraciously from the hand the moment it was caught. These rollers fly in small flocks, and are much given to mobbing falcons and scapulated crows.

The scapulated crow, one of the commonest of African birds, almost, if not entirely disappears in the cataract region of the Congo, and only makes its reappearance at and beyond Stanley Pool. Is it because the bird really dislikes mountainous regions, or that in this poor country there is too little for it to eat? But this last can hardly be the reason. It is a bird of most accommodating appetite, and would certainly find a means of living round the native villages, especially those near the banks of the river, where there is much fish refuse. On the Upper river he generally builds his nest in the *Hyphœne* palms, and often falls out with a large kite who chooses the same tree for his eerie.

SPUR-WINGED PLOVER.

CHAPTER XV.

NATURAL HISTORY—MAMMALS.

Monkeys—Mandrills—The Gorilla—Lemurs—The Leopard—
The Lion — Tiger-Cats — Hyænas — The Civet Cat — The
Genet Cat—Jackals—The Manatee—The Elephant—Size
of Tusks—The Hippopotamus—A Rogue Hippopotamus—The
Rhinoceros—The Buffalo—Antelopes.

It is strange that a region like the Lower Congo basin, so
richly forested, should be so poor in monkeys. On the
river Kwilu, a little to the north, and on the Quanza, to
the south, the *Simiæ* are abundantly represented, and the
surrounding conditions of nature are much the same.
Nevertheless, just as with the snakes, you might journey
up the Congo from the coast to Bolobo and not see a
single monkey. The only times I ever came across them
myself—that is to say, in a wild state—were in the
uninhabited Inga country, between Vivi and Isangila, in
which district I have frequently seen a large brown
Cercopithecus, whose species I could not determine, that
makes a great unwieldy nest or platform of sticks on the
higher branches of the trees, and sits on it, watching the
passer-by. I have also been able to identify the existence
of several well-known West African species by skins
worn by the natives, or brought for sale. In this way I
have ascertained the presence of the beautiful Diana
monkey,* the Pluto,† the grivet,‡ the sooty mangabey,§
and the *Colobus*.‖ It is possible that all West African

---

* *Ceropithecus Diana.*   † *C. Pluto.*
‡ *C. grisco-virdis.*   § *Cercocebus fuliginosus.*
‖ *Colobus Angolensis.*

genera are represented on the Congo, but they certainly do not show themselves in any abundance. About the mouth of the Congo, in the marshy forest country, monkeys seem to be much more common than up the river, to judge by the numbers brought for sale by the

A GALAGO.

natives. Here I have seen in captivity many mandrills (*Papio maïmon*) and drills (*P. leucophæus*). At the Dutch House in Banana there is, or was at the time of my visit, an admirable collection of West African monkeys, including some very fine male and female mandrills. At Stanley Pool I have heard of baboons * being seen, and

* Probably *Papio Sphinx*.

the natives of Ki-mpoko tell strange tales of large man-like apes in the interior. The gorilla and chimpanzee, which are entirely absent from the Lower Congo, probably approach the Upper river above the falls. Certainly some large anthropoid ape is known to the Ba-teke and Ba-yansi, for they recognised with loud cries an engraving of the gorilla, and said frequently that he was found on the north bank of the river. This has been repeatedly told me by natives of Bolobo (who in speaking of the anthropoid ape used the word "ngina"), by chance visitors at Msuăta, and also at Ki-mpoko and other places on Stanley Pool. The Baptist missionaries at Léopold-ville have also heard of the gorilla from their pupils, who pick out his picture at once in Wood's Natural History. I think, therefore, it is probable that the gorilla, chim-panzee, or both, or some kindred anthropoid ape, is found on the Upper Congo, and is possibly the same as the "soko" of the Lualaba.

Periodicticus potto and *arctocebus* are curious tailless lemuroids which are also found about the Lower Congo. The former is constantly brought for sale by the natives at Banana Point. Parenthetically I might remark that there is no better ground for a collector than this latter place. Possibly its vicinity is no better provided with wild creatures than many other parts of the Congo, but here the natives are accustomed to capture and bring for sale everything they can lay their hands on.

The galago lemur is very common about Stanley Pool, and the natives make "karosses" out of many of its skins joined together, with a fringe of tails. These are very handsome, but the natives resist every temptatiion to sell them unfortunately, or they would be very beautiful and costly souvenirs to bring home.

On the Congo the leopard is the best-known and most dreaded of the *Felidæ*. The natives often call him "great lord," and when a leopard is killed or caught in a trap, a day of public rejoicing is kept in the neighbouring villages, during which the slaves are absolved from all work.

The lion, entirely absent from the coast region between the Congo and Sierra Leone, begins to be heard of at Stanley Pool; and farther into the interior there is no doubt that he exists. Some of the more influential chiefs here have lions' skins. Makoko, the chief of the Ba-teke, received De Brazza seated on one of these, which has now, with other insignia of royalty, passed to his successor. The natives describe his appearance and imitate his roaring so well that there is no doubt that they have come into contact with the king of beasts. I have seen several villages on the north or western bank of the Congo barricaded carefully against the probable attacks of lions, and every night the live-stock was regularly driven into this stockaded fortress. Further, the Zanzibaris aver that once when they went to buy fowls from a village nearly opposite the Kwa River, called Ganchu, they crept into their canoes at night and preferred to sleep on the water, because the lion roared so loudly in their proximity.

Two or three species of tiger-cats are common, and destroy much poultry. One appears to be *Felis serval ;* the others I have not had means of identifying.

The hyæna is often spoken of by the natives, and is, according to their account, the striped species. The civet-cat (*Viverra*) is prized for its scent-bag, but does not seem to be very common. Genets are constantly met with, and make charming house-pets. Their kittens are the most amusing little creatures imaginable, and exhibit more playfulness when young than any animal I know.

The only *Canis* apparently present on the Congo is *C. lateralis*, the side-striped jackal. The black-backed jackal may possibly also be found, but I have never seen any sign of it. *Potamogale*, the curious otter-like insectivore, possibly inhabits the Upper river, to judge by the skins brought down by the natives. I have also seen *Chrysochlorus*, the golden mole.

The manatee (*Manatus*) never passes, as far as we yet know, the cataracts of the Congo, but confines itself to the Lower river. A species of river dolphin, allied possibly to the Amazon species, is occasionally found in the Lower Congo and about the estuary.   I have seen a skull alleged to belong to it.

The elephant is very abundant on the Upper Congo; and every morning, as you ascend the river, traces of their last night's devastations may be seen, for they seem to have a tendency towards wanton destruction and waste, being like parrots and monkeys in only eating about a quarter of the food they procure, and scattering the rest right and left with wanton caprice.   So, on the islands of the Upper river, where the graceful borassus palms grow in their thousands, each blue-green palm with its cluster of orange fruit, the elephant is to be constantly seen— sometimes in broad daylight, but more often towards sun- set—breaking his way through the pillar-like clusters, destroying many a beautiful palm for the sake of those orange-coloured stony dates of which he is so strangely fond.   You may also see them, as I have, in the short hour of tranquil twilight, walking out in Indian file from the sheltering forest into the shallow parts of the river, where they squirt streams of water over their dry heated skins.   Ordinarily it is at nigh-time, and above all when there is a moon, that the elephants come down to drink and bathe.   Moreover, they are much more commonly seen on the Congo during the dry season, as then the many little forest brooks are likely to be dried up, and the elephants are compelled to incur greater publicity in their bath by seeking the great Congo.   Although the elephants are much more frequently met with above Stanley Pool, still in certain districts of the Lower river they are common, especially in the cataract region.   In the country opposite Isangila elephants have often been shot by members of Mr. Stanley's expedition, and at the Livingstone mission station of Banza-Manteka, fifteen miles from the south bank of the Congo, elephants have at times trooped in long succession past the door of the mission-house, whilst the awe-struck missionaries shut themselves up securely within.

The largest Tusk I have yet seen on this river weighed

93 lb., and one from an elephant killed at the station of Msuãta, by one of the Zanzibaris, weighed 79 lb. Of course I have heard of tusks of immense and fabulous weight, 180 lb. and 192 lb. being modestly cited as examples of these prodigies; but I require to see them weighed before believing such statements. The largest tusk I have ever seen in West Africa (at Old Calabar) weighed 140 lb., and looked a monster. Although the elephant is so abundant all along the Congo, from Stanley Pool towards the interior, yet the natives, as far as I have yet ascended the river, never dreamt of attacking him, but received all their ivory from the Bangala of the equator, who are also reported by the Ba-yansi to get theirs from a yet more distant tribe; so that I should not be surprised to learn that the same central region that sends its ivory to the Congo also supplies the merchants of the Shari and the Nile.

The hippopotamus, as will have been gathered from the many previous references to its abundance, is one of the commonest, or at least one of the most noticeable, of the Congo mammalia. During the day-time this great amphibian prefers to frequent the large submerged sandbanks or "shallows" so common in the river. Here he generally stands upright, with his head and backbone rising above the water, and with many of his companions in a line. They yawn constantly, and the huge jaws are lifted in this action high above the water, displaying a pinky chasm of palate and throat. The grunting noise they make, and their great sighs of contentment as they relapse into the tepid water after a momentary inspection of the advancing canoe, may be heard for a long distance across the stream. Hippopotami are distinctly reddish in colour as seen in the water. They generally go in herds of nine and ten together, apparently consisting of one mature bull with four or five cows and their respective calves. The act of coition is said by the natives to take place invariably at night-time, as with pigs. Certainly the activity of the hippopotamus is very much greater after the sun has set, for it is then that he leaves the water and goes to feed amid the great rank grass-fields, where he remains until after sunrise; indeed, if you are smart, you may intercept him there, cut off his retreat, kill him easily, for he offers a huge mark, and then go tranquilly to your breakfast, having first spoilt his. As to shooting them from a canoe on the water, it is a question the utility of which it is difficult to decide. If you do not fire at Hippo, he may come and just wreck you in a spirit of pure play; on the other hand, if you hit and do not kill outright, he will certainly make for you with a vengeance. Fortunately they do not swim very fast, and may easily be out-distanced by a skilfully-paddled canoe. The female hippopotamus is passionately attached to her young, and during the first few weeks of its life lives almost isolated from her fellows, generally on land; I imagine that this is because the baby hippopotami at an early age might form an easy prey to the voracious crocodiles. The males are much given to quarrelling even in the day-time, and, when fighting, utter strange boar-like squeals and grunts. It very often happens that an unfortunate bull, unable to obtain a mate, turns rogue, and lives a solitary life, seeking to wreak his spite on whatever may come in his way. There was one such beast that haunted the neighbourhood of Msuāta. This malicious creature was the terror of the natives in the adjoining villages, for he would lie in wait, amid the rushes, for the canoes returning home with the fishermen at dusk, and then swim out silently under water and wreck them. When I was staying here we sent a canoe with letters to Stanley, who was farther down the river. The canoe started at early dawn, was wrecked close to the station by the demon hippopotamus, and one of its occupants was carried off by a crocodile. On the whole, the hippopotamus may be called the most dangerous animal to man on the river Congo.

The rhinoceros is nowhere heard of in this district, nor is he, properly speaking, found in West Africa at all, merely penetrating into Southern Angola from the Zambezi and South African regions. The red river-hog (*Sus porcus*) is common, and its flesh is greatly appreciated by the natives.

I have seen a skin of *Hyomoschus,* so apparently its range extends to the Congo.

There is only one buffalo on this river, the red species, *Bos brachyceros.* He his much inferior in size to his larger relatives, the buffaloes of Central and Southern Africa, but he seems ordinarily quite as fierce, although at times he shows an opportune mildness of demeanour, as may be judged from the following incident which happened to Mr. Stanley when travelling between Vivi and Isangila. He was at the head of his caravan, and had been ascending a nearly precipitous hill under a hot sun. When he arrived at the top, panting and ready to throw himself down on the grass with fatigue and exhaustion, he suddenly found himself face to face with a red buffalo, who was staring at him in much astonishment. The buffalo lowered his head, and Mr. Stanley fired ; but although he was within a couple of yards of his mark, he was so agitated that he missed. The buffalo, however, merely turned round, and trotted off quietly. As the road in this country is continually taking you up and down abrupt hills, I always used to dread lest, on arriving at the top of some elevation, utterly sick and faint with want of breath, I might find myself in a like predicament, and the buffalo less considerate.

The Congo is very poor in antelopes, as compared with the less forested regions north and south. There are no true gazelles ; *Cervicapra* and *Nanotragus* are found, and frequently go under that name. There are several species of *Cephalophi,* and the large *C. sylvicultrix* is occasionally seen on the Lower river. *Cobus* antelopes are fairly common everywhere, especially on the borders of streams. I give the head of one here, that I do not identify as yet with any of the numerous species of this large genus. The hoofs of this *Cobus* do not offer any great peculiarities, except that they are perhaps somewhat long and wide apart. There is a *Tragelaphus* found on the Congo, *T. gratus* apparently, which has hoofs nearly six inches in length and very pointed. This creature, which is a dark, dun-colour in the male, with white spots and stripes, inhabits the marshes and small streams, being much more at home in the water than on land. The horns are much used by the natives as trumpets (see illustration, p. 296). Other members of the *Tragelaphidæ* are the Kudus,

A COBUS ANTELOPE.

which I have seen near Vivi, the harnessed antelope, common everywhere, and probably also the derbian, or striped eland.

A porcupine is found all along the Congo, and its quills are used for many purposes by the natives. The Ba-yansi call it "nkáké," or "thunder," from the noise it makes rattling its quills in anger. A large rodent, *Aulacodus*, is occasionally captured and eaten by the natives. Small side-striped squirrels abound in the woods, and an infinitude of murine species are met with, one of them a small black rat infesting the native villages.

The curious Edentate, *Manis* is also one of the Congo mammalia, though very rare and shy.

CHAPTER XVI.

THE PEOPLE OF THE CONGO.

The Dwarf Race—The Upper Congo Races—The Ashirongo—
The Bakongo—Conduct and Morality—Phallic Worship—
The Nkimba—The Sacred Language—Art of Medicine—
Domestic Life—Hairiness of African Races—Early Man
— Clothing — Cicatrization — Hairdressing — Features —
Character — Ceremonies — Education—Marriage—Burial —
Food—Domestic Animals—Crops—Houses—Musical Instru-
ments—Population.

The races of man that inhabit the basin of the Congo
throughout its entire course—certainly in all that part of
it that I have visited—belong almost exclusively to that
great Bantu family which, when seen in its purest
exemplars, the Ova-herero and Ova-mpo of the South-
west, the tribes of the Zambezi, the people of the great
lakes of Tanganyika and Nyasa, and the western shores
of Victoria Nyanza, and finally of the Upper Congo, is so
distinct physically and linguistically from the divers
negro, negroid, and Hamitic populations to the north of
it, and from the Hottentot-Bushman group to the south.
I have just written that the inhabitants of the Congo
basin belong "almost" exclusively to this great homo-
geneous Bantu family. The qualifying "almost" is
introduced for two reasons. Firstly, because we know
that about the Upper Congo and Lualaba there are
certain dwarf races, encountered both by Stanley, Wissmann, and many other travellers; and besides this I have
certainly seen myself two specimens of a dwarf type
living as slaves among the Ba-yansi, and differing wholly

1. MU-YANSI.
2. MU-TEKE.
3. MU-SHI-KONGO.

from their masters in physical appearance. Still it is not
quite certain that these dwarfs may not turn out to be a
greatly degraded Bantu tribe. Language is of course by
no means a true guide, as it may often be imposed upon
a conquered or inferior race by stronger immigrants.
Still it is curious that the only recorded words spoken by
a specimen of the Wa-twa, the dwarf race on the Upper
Congo that Stanley encountered,* should be pure Bantu
in character. He is reported by the great traveller to
have said, "Mabi! mabi!" for "bad," "ki-rembo-rembo"
for "lightning," and "Firi Niambi" for "God." Now
"mabi"—meaning bad, poisonous, wicked—is used right
down the Congo as far as Stanley Pool. It is pure
Ki-teke, for example, and is one of the commonest words
employed. "Ki-rembo-rembo" seems to resemble certain
Central African terms for "finger," † and by "Ki-rembo-
rembo, firi Niambi," the dwarf probably meant "the
finger of God," for in using "Niambi" to express "God,"
he simply employed the same word as the "Nyambi,"
"Njambi," "Ndyambi," "Ndambi," "Nzambi," of Angola,
the Western Congo, and the Gaboon.‡ The dwarf-tribes
are reported as being, in the interior, very hairy. Now
hairiness is a feature strangely absent from the Bushmen
and Hottentots of the South, with whom it has been
imagined that these dwarf races might have some distant
relationships; and, on the contrary, the Bantu tribes of
the Congo are very hairy naturally, although most of
them seem smooth-skinned, owing to artificial depilation.
However, there is no doubt these dwarf races sufficiently
differ from their neighbours to justify the qualification I
have introduced into my assertion ; and, besides this first
reason, there is another, in that the Congo tribes, nearing
the coast, begin to lose their distinctive Bantu character,
either through the degradation the coast climate seems to

---

* See Stanley's 'Dark Continent,' vol. ii. pp. 172–3.
† *Lembo, mu-liémo, rémo,* in divers Congo tongues.
‡ Since this was written Mr. Stanley has supplied us with some
vocabularies of the dwarf-tribes in the Aruwimi forests (*vide* "Darkest
Africa") ; these are all Bantu in their affinities.

entail, or because on their migration westward from the
north-east Bantu focus, they originally met and mixed
with, in the low-lying coast-lands, an earlier negro
population. This latter supposition sometimes strikes me
as being the true one, for the reason that, in such a
littoral tribe as the Kabinda or Loango people there are
distinctly two types of Race. One—the Bantu—a fine,
tall, upright man, with delicately small hands and well-
shaped feet, a fine face, high, thin nose, beard, moustache,
and a plentiful crop of hair; the other an ill-shaped,
loosely-made figure, with splay feet, high calves, a
retreating chin, blubber lips, no hair about the face, and
the wool on his head close and crisply curled. The
farther you go into the interior, the finer the type becomes.
Such men as the Bayansi of Bolobo are perfect Greek
statues in the development and poise of their forms, and
two points about them contrast very favourably with
most of the coast races, namely, their lighter colour—
generally a warm chocolate—and their freedom from that
offensive smell which is supposed, wrongly, to characterise
most Africans. Many other details show the comparatively high status of the Upper Congo races: their
small hands and feet, their well-shaped legs with full
calves, and their abundant heads of hair.

The principal tribes to be encountered in ascending the
Congo to the equator are, commencing at the mouth, the
Ka-kongo (Kabindas and others), Ashi-rongo, Ba-kongo,
Ba-sundi, Ba-bwendé, Wa-buno, Ba-teke, Wa-buma, Ba-
nunu, and Ba-yansi.* Of these the Kabindas or Ka-kongo
people have been already touched on; and I might
mention further that they are the Krumen of the south,
hiring themselves out in all directions as servants, sailors,
labourers, and affecting more particularly the Portuguese
colonies, which they overrun as far as Mossâmedes, invariably returning home after a time to spend their

* The tribe which I always knew under the name of "Ba-yansi" is
probably more correctly called "Ba-bangi." Dr. Sims, of the Congo
Free State, has published most interesting Ki-bangi, or Ki-yansi, and
Ki-teke vocabularies.—H. H. J.

earnings. The Kabindas in their dealings with the Portuguese much resemble the relations between the Krumen of the Liberian coast and the English. Both races are largely influenced by their intercourse with the white people, and though in neither case has there been any conquest or previous occupation of territory, yet, on the one hand, every Kabinda knows more or less Portuguese, and few—I might say no—Krumen of the coast are ignorant of English. I think the recent attempt of the Portuguese to establish themselves on the Ka-kongo coast, whatever may be the view taken by the great powers, will meet with the approval of the natives, who have so long served under their new masters abroad that they will take kindly to their dominion at home.

On the southern bank of the Lower river, opposite the Kabinda people, the little-known country of Sonyo or Songo is inhabited by the Au-shi-rongo, as the Portuguese call them, a degraded branch of the great Ba-kongo race which stretches in reality, though it undergoes some variations, from Kabinda to Kinrembo on the coast, and from Stanley Pool to Banana along the river. The Ba-kongo group is split up into several separate tribes, all of which, however, speak more or less the same tongue, which is sometimes called Fiote (meaning "the common people"), and more correctly Ki-shi-kongo. Amongst the Ba-kongo peoples, or inhabitants of the river along its lower course from Stanley Pool to the sea, there are the Ba-shi-kongo already mentioned, who probably represent the van of the Bantu invasion in this direction, mixed with an antecedent negro population; then the Ba-kongo proper, who have their centres about São Salvador and Palabala, the Basundi, the Ba-bwendé, and the Wa-buno. In the names of all these tribes but one, it is curious to notice that the old plural prefix, "Ba," is retained, whereas in the spoken tongue it has degenerated to "Wa" and even "A." The only exception is in the case of the Wa-buno, who are probably a later subdivision from the main stock. The Ba-kongo proper were once the ruling race over all this district, and founded the great Congo empire, which was discovered by the Portuguese at the height of its prosperity, when its ruler's sway extended far beyond the bounds of the Congo districts. Now a small amount of territory between São Salvador and the river is all that remains of a once powerful kingdom. The King of Congo still reigns at São Salvador, and though he is not precisely a Christian, he vacillates between the teachings of the Baptist missionaries at his court, and the dogmas of the Church of Rome, who has once more tried to resume her bygone sway over the Congo peoples. The Ba-kongo tongue, or more properly the Ki-shi-kongo, is spoken in greatest purity at São Salvador, and also about Palabala, and the southern bank of the river opposite Vivi. It is one of the most beautiful and flexible of the Bantu languages, having all the softness of Italian, the precision of French, and the flexibility of English, three qualifications, by-the-bye, well represented in the Portuguese, a language which is for some reason much more easily acquired by African races than any other European tongue. Portuguese has considerably influenced the vocabulary of Kongo, as might be imagined from the four centuries of intercourse between the two peoples. All things of new and exotic origin are expressed by slightly altered Portuguese words, such as *meza* for "table" (Port., *meza*), *di-lalanza* for "orange" (Port., *laranja*), *sabola* for "onion" (Port., *cebola*), and so on. This Portuguese intermixture is much greater at São Salvador and on the coast, and diminishes in proportion as we advance into the interior; still some Lusitanian words have strayed far into the continent from the western coast, and, like the four old muskets that Stanley met with in Rubunga, have taken centuries to enter the vocabularies of tribes to whom Portugal is utterly unknown. Thus, beyond Bolobo, the pine-apple, a Portuguese introduction from Brazil, is called *bi-nasi* or *bi-nanasi*, a corruption of the Portugo-Brazilian name, "ananas." On the coast the pine-apple has been established a sufficient time for it to have changed and varied its name, but among the Ba-yansi the

T

old term has slowly journeyed onward with the extension of the plant.

The Ba-kongo of Palabala are a finer race than the degraded negroid A-shi-kongo or A-so-rongo of the coast. Yet they do not display an entirely Bantu type, such as one sees in the Ba-yansi of the Upper river. Their skin, however, is not the dead coal-black of the coast tribes, but is often a warm chocolate or ruddy brown. They do not practise much personal adornment, either by cicatrization, tatooing or painting the skin with divers pigments. They are naturally a hairy race, especially about the face—some of the chiefs wearing copious beards, whiskers and moustache —but on the body the pile is plucked out from the age of puberty, otherwise their bodies would be partially covered with short curly hair. The two front incisor teeth in the upper jaw are occasionally chipped, but this is not a regular custom, as it is farther up the river. Also among the Ba-bwende of Manyanga and the surrounding district large nose-rings are passed through the septum of the nose, and earrings are frequently worn. Circumcision is everywhere practised on the males, and will be treated of in its place as a semi-religious rite.

In character the Ba-kongo are indolent, fickle, and sensual. They dislike bloodshed as a general rule, and, save for certain superstitious customs, are rarely cruel, showing kindness and gentleness to animals. When their passions are excited, however, by fear of witchcraft or a wish to revenge grave injuries, they can become very demons of fanatical rage; and the people, that in their calmer moments will shudder at an abrasion of the skin in a friend or neighbour, will, when he is convicted of sorcery, leap and shout with frenzied joy around his fiery stake while he frizzles alive. Witch or wizard-burning (as a rule there are more *witches* killed) is very common among the debased tribes of the coast, and the poison-ordeal, already mentioned in Chapter III., prevails largely over the Lower Congo lands. In fact, in many a Ba-konga village, life must be rendered miserable by the constant accusations of sorcery. At Palabala, for instance, for every one—child, woman, or man—who dies, somebody is suspected of having caused the death by supernatural means, and the horrid old *nganga* or "medicine man," who holds the inquest over the corpse, is called upon to detect the guilty person, and generally fixes upon those possessed of worldly goods, in order that they may buy him off from his fell accusation. Should the accused however, either through poverty or the force of public opinion, be unable to evade the charge, he or she is compelled to take the *casca*,* the infusion of a poisonous bark; and according as the potion is regulated in strength by the nganga, so the suspected tamperer with witchcraft either vomits up the poison and recovers, dies at once from its effects, or retains it on the stomach and does not die, in which latter case the natives have rare sport in hacking the ill-doer to pieces with their blunt knives, or in "cooking" their victim over a slow fire. And yet when the fears and passions of these people are not roused they are gentle and effeminate, with many expressive words with which to caress and sympathise.

I have said just now that they are immoral—or, at least sensual—but this is hardly to be taken in the same sense as the word is applied to vicious European communities. Their immorality rather arises from excess of uxoriousness than from a love of vice.

Adultery is not uncommon, and its penalties vary from capital punishment to a trifling fine, according to the station of the offender or the district he lives in. The women have little regard for their own virtue, either before or after marriage, and but for the jealousy of the men there would be promiscuous intercourse between the sexes. Among the Ba-kongo women it is thought something honourable and praiseworthy to merit the position of a white man's mistress, and a woman thus distinguished from her sisters is regarded with respect and consideration by her fellow countrymen. Moreover, though the men evince some marital jealousy amongst

---

* The "Muavi" of East Central Africa.

themselves, they are far from displaying anything but satisfaction when a European is induced to accept the loan of a wife, either as an act of hospitality or in consideration of some small payment. Unmarried girls they are more chary of offering, as their value in the market is greater; but it may be truly said that among these people womanly chastity is unknown, and a woman's honour is measured by the price she costs.

On the Lower Congo as far as Stanley Pool, over a region extending slightly beyond the domain of the Ba-kongo proper, phallic worship in various forms prevails. It is not associated with any rites that might be called particularly obscene; and on the coast, where manners and morals are particularly corrupt, the phallus cult is no longer met with. In the forests between Manyanga and Stanley Pool it is not rare to come upon a little rustic temple, made of palm-fronds and poles, within which male and female figures, nearly or quite life-size, may be seen with disproportionate genital organs, the figures being intended to represent the male and female principle. Around these carved and painted statues, as described in Chapter VI., are many offerings of plates, knives, and cloth, and frequently also the phallic symbol may be seen dangling from the rafters. There is not the slightest suspicion of obscenity in all this, and any one qualifying this worship of the Generative power as obscene does so hastily and ignorantly. It is a solemn mystery to the Congo native, a force but dimly understood; and, like all mysterious natural manifestations—like the great rushing river that upsets his fishing canoes and has the power to drown him—like the blazing lightning, the roaring thunder and the shrieking wind, it is a power that must be propitiated and persuaded to his good.

Connected, no doubt, with this phallic worship are the Nkimba ceremonies which are met with on the Lower Congo between Isangila and the coast, and which in varying forms may be traced among the "manhood-initiation" rites found among most Bantu peoples.

The Nkimba are in all probability males undergoing

circumcision and an initiation into the rites of marriage, and this secret confraternity is generally composed of youths of varying ages, between twelve and fifteen years. Occasionally older men may be seen amongst them, who for some reason have possibly evaded the initiation at an earlier age. These ceremonies last for two native years (twelve months), and there are three or more stages of initiation, said to be marked by changes in their grass coverings. They chalk them- selves all over a ghastly white with some argillaceous earth, and do not wash once during their six months' probation, though they often renew the white colouring. During the whole period of their initiation they live like the lilies of the field, being sustained at the common expense of the village or community. The Nkimba in a great measure live separ- ately from their fellow towns- people, and seem to avoid coming into contact, above all, with the females and children of the community, whose presence, from the fact of their being without the arcana of sacred mystery, is

A NKIMBA.

considered undesirable and contaminating. Consequently, when the Nkimba are on the road they announce their presence by a sort of drumming noise like "dur-r-r!" and then all strangers—all who are not members of their freemasonry—are obliged to clear out of the road. Should they decline to do so they are set upon by the Nkimba, and soundly beaten with the wands these ugly creatures carry. Ugly creatures indeed they are, and they prompt the constantly-recurring question—"Why does man so often make his religious ceremonies frightful?" In addition to the white chalky covering or paste which covers the naturally sooty skins of the Nkimba novitiates, they also decorate their heads, whenever they can afford it, with a curious wicker crown or cage, to which little gaudy strips of scarlet cloth or the feathers of bright-coloured birds are affixed. Then round their waists is a wide wooden hoop or girdle, often quaintly decorated with incised patterns, and from this depends a long and dense skirt of dried grass reaching nearly to the ankles, and being often extended from the body by means of an inner framework like a crinoline. Sometimes there are also tufts and sheaves of grass hanging from the shoulders or the neck, but this addition, I believe, marks the attainment of an advanced grade in initiation.

A curious part of these semi-religious rites is the acquiring of a sacred mysterious language, which is taught by the *nganga*, who presides over these ceremonies, to the disciples who are being circumcised and gathered into the confraternity. This language is never taught to females, and as yet no European has been able to examine its nature. I have heard men discoursing in it, as they do freely, and there were most of the Bantu prefixes and concords recognisable in their speech, though the actual words were unfamiliar. It might possibly be some older and more archaic form of Bantu language conserved for religious purposes—like the Sanskrit, the old Sclavonic, and the Latin—or it may be nothing more than an arbitrary transmogrification of words such as is found in the Mpongwe,* or in such artificial dialects as the Ki-nyume of Zanzibar.†

---

* "Among the elders of the tribe there is a form of speech called the 'Ewiria, or Dark Sayings,' which cannot be understood by the uninitiated, although the council may be held in open assembly. It is formed by changing words in an arbitrary manner, and to no one is the secret confided who has not reached twenty-five years, and then under an oath of secrecy."— *Vide* Cust's 'Modern Languages of Africa,' p. 419, vol. ii.

† *Vide* Steere's 'Handbook to the Ki-suahili Language.'

A Nkimba before initiation is called "Mungwála," and afterwards "Tungwa." I cannot guess at the etymology of these terms in any way, unless a suggestion of a far-off relationship with "Longwa"—*to be taught, to learn*—be of any use.

These Nkimba are not met with among the Congo tribes farther inland than Isangila. Between the latter places and Manyanga there are many eunuchs in the large villages, who seemed to be attached to a vague phallic worship, with which is intricately connected a reverence for the moon. When the new moon appears, dances are performed by the eunuchs, who sacrifice a white fowl, which must always be a male—in its honour. The bird is thrown up into the air and torn to pieces as it falls to earth. I was told that in former days a human victim was offered up on these occasions, but that in later times a white fowl had been substituted.

Naturally, with an imaginative people that refers the explanation of all physical problems to the action of anthropomorphic spirits, diseases are supposed to be due to the malice of demons, who are represented materially, as the embodification of the malady they incite. There is a small-pox bogey, a fever-spirit, and in certain temples about Manyanga you may come across a loathsome representation of the foul demon who is supposed to have inflicted syphilis on the unhappy natives, who bring offerings to his shrine with a view of appeasing his cruel ravages.

Little or no notion of the healing art is present; medicines are represented by vague potions and powders, delivered without any reference to their antiseptic qualities, but merely in regard to their hidden potentialities of magic. The patient undergoes such heroic treatment at times that he may be cured on the principle that one ill drives out another. His friends also, by offering at the shrine, by the intercession of the *nganga*, by loud wailing supplications, seek to appease the disease demon's malice; while on the other hand, with the instinctive feeling that it is "somebody's" fault and that "some one" ought to be punished, they seek to find out who has, by foul witchcraft, egged the evil spirit on to this untoward manifestation of his power. The nganga is of course foremost in this research, and the culprit he fixes on is either mulcted of a heavy fine or, in serious cases, where the accused is poor, is compelled to pass through the "poison" ordeal with varying result. These Ba-kongo people do not seem to suffer from disease to a greater degree than most uncivilized races. Nature is still allowed to exercise a happy selection in the survival of the fittest, and if a child is weakly no efforts are made to save its life. The result is that the physically strong are in the majority, while, *en revanche*, the most cunning secure the greatest number of wives and leave the largest families.

The *nganga* of every community is generally a mean-looking, perhaps puny man, but a glance at his sharp eye will show you that he excels his more brawny neighbours in mental capacity; *ergo*, the "medicine-man" of the village has a large harem, and leaves many descendants.

The daily life of these people must be marked by terrible uniformity. They keep no calendar, and their vague traditions are perpetuated by word of mouth. It is almost like the life of the forest; great calamities, sudden shocks are soon hidden and forgotten, and profound emotions exist not, while fleeing troubles and joys leave little impression on the vacuous mind, which lives and thinks and acts but for the hour.

Before the dawn they begin to grumblingly awake from their sleep, and stir the deadened ashes of the fire into a warming glow. Then they sit on their haunches, with their hands crossed over their shoulders for the sake of warmth, the early morning being the coolest time in Africa; and, whilst the men yawn and rub their eyes at the growing light, the women smack their babies, scold their bigger children, and open their minds on many disagreeable subjects to their lords and masters. Sunrise, that eternal resurrection that gladdens the most brutish soul in Nature, puts an end to these peevish colloquies.

The women issue from the huts with morning greetings to their neighbours, and set about their household duties, while the men polish their weapons and implements of the chase, and set out to visit their bird-snares and fish-traps; or they pack their goods for a neighbouring market, and trudge out to their destination ere the sun shall have risen high.

When they have their regular meals it is hard to say. The children always seem to be gnawing something, and the women are constantly preparing food. I fancy the adults mostly feed at about an hour after sunrise, and just take snacks during the day, perhaps finishing up with another meal at night.

After the morning repast the women go out to cultivate the fields or turn their hands to some industrial employment, such as weaving, making pottery, or constructing coops for their hens and chickens. At noon-time all rest in the shade of their verandahs and indulge in tobacco-smoking, or pass the sultry hours in hair-dressing, personal decoration and friendly gossip. As the sun declines some form of active work is resumed, and after sunset, when the men have returned to the village, dancing and drinking of palm-wine begin, and are kept up, failing other amusement—such as burning a person suspected of scorcery—until a late hour of the night, when all retire, with considerable hilarity and loud talking, to the slumber from which they will wake up very cross the next morning.

I have given a brief description of the tribes inhabiting the Lower Congo from Stanley Pool to the coast. At Stanley Pool, however, just as one meets with new forms of butterflies, birds, and plants, so there is a decided change in the type of man and in the language he speaks.

On the northern bank of the river the Ba-teke extend their range beyond the Pool westwards, to the Jué river, and perhaps even farther into the confines of the Babwende, a tribe speaking a dialect of the Kongo language of the Lower river; but on the south bank of the river the Ba-teke colonies do not commence until we arrive at the district of Ki-ntamo, on the western shores of Stanley Pool.

The Ba-teke, Wa-buma, and Ba-yansi, all tribes of the Upper river,* though they differ each from the other in certain characteristics, and markedly in tongue, yet offer so many mutual points of resemblance and of dissimilarity to the Ba-kongo people below Stanley Pool that they may well be described together in their general features and separated in this description from the races of the Lower river.

These upper Congo people betray little or no inter-

A M-BUMA.

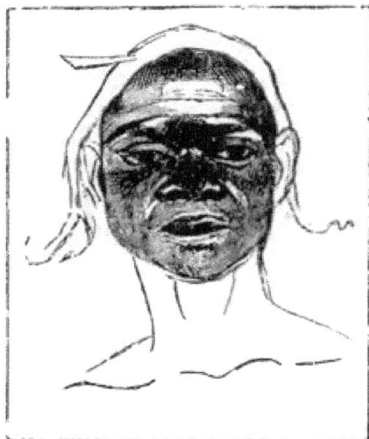

A MU-YANSI.

mixture of "negro" blood. They are pure "Bantu," and consequently greatly resemble other unmixed races of the same stock, such as the Ova-mbo, the Ba-lunda, and the people of Tanganyika and Nyasa. They differ from the more negroid Ba-kongo in having skins of a chocolate brown, and, above all, in their abundant growth of hair. The beard, whiskers, and moustache are always present, but are generally, in common with the hair of the eyebrows and the eyelashes, *plucked* out, from a prejudice

* By *Upper* and *Lower* river I always mean the Congo *above* and *below* Stanley Pool.

against cultivating hair anywhere but on the top of the head. Only in chiefs, as a rule, is the beard allowed to grow, and that only partially. So also on the body, the pile, which would naturally be abundant, and in parts even thick, is remorselessly pulled out by the roots, these people assiduously cultivating that nakedness of skin to which mankind has ever been so partial.

As a fact, most African races are disposed to be hairy, especially on their bodies,* but in so many tribes does the practice exist of rigorously pulling out every hair that makes its appearance, that one conceives the idea that Africans are devoid of hair on their bodies. The only races I know of in which I have failed to detect any trace of pile, or even beard, without being able to explain their absence by the reason that the people prefer naked-ness, are the Bushmen and Hottentots; and yet these are supposed to be the lowest types of man in Africa. It would be interesting to know how this would be explained.

Man in all ages and climes seems to have cultivated a bare skin as a personal attraction. The ancient Greeks and Romans practised the same depilatory processes that are in vogue amongst Africans of the present day. Priests have thought it pleasing to their gods to live smooth-shaven; and the courtiers and counsellors of many an earthly sovereign have trimmed their free-growing beards and curtailed their locks, to acquire a greater air of grave and stately bearing. It is indeed curious that hairiness has always been considered as a sign of ferocity and brutal force, and that soldiers should be allowed to wear the moustache which a rigid fashion might deny to a civilian.

Human nakedness is incipient in the baboons, and in their relative the gelada monkey. These creatures expose their naked parts with evident pride, turning them with

---

* This may be said quite as much of other negroes besides the Bantu. I have seen Krumen on the Gold Coast whose bodies were quite covered with fine curly pile, especially on the breast, stomach, thighs, and back.

complacency to the gaze of foes and friends; not, as has been thought, in a spirit of insult, but rather as the peacock erects his train and rattles his quills to ravish and overawe the looker-on. So in bygone ages the females of incipient man contemplated with satisfaction the growing nakedness of their husbands, much in the same spirit as the she-galada monkey admires and strokes with a tender touch the great bald patch on the breast of her mate. The hands and feet and face are naked in most monkeys of the old world, the hinder parts in baboons are bald and brilliant. Thenceforth, as some aspiring ape struggled on towards humanity, it was rather a gradual diminution of hairiness that supervened than absolute nakedness, for few men's bodies and limbs in a natural state are devoid of hair.

When man had lost all or nearly all the hair which in so many mammals becomes developed into striking ornaments in the male sex, he had attained a sufficient degree of intelligence to abandon the slow workings of nature, and to call in the aid of art or in ministering to his inherent vanity and in decorating his person so as to render it more attractive in the eyes of his women. The beard and moustache, though already existing in less pronounced forms in the higher apes, received a slight ulterior development in man, but beyond this there was little attempt made to secure any striking physical attraction or any analogous development of epidermal colour or excrescence such as we meet in many monkeys.* On the contrary, man seems to have rather degenerated into physical uniformity and insignificance. Looked at from the point of view of an antlered stag or a graceful leopard, a naked man seems a poor sort of creature. The higher beauty of his well-moulded form, and his marked adaptation to his career, is only perceptible to the asthetically-educated minds of his most highly developed examples.

In the very early days of the history of our genus,

---

* As, for instance, the blue-ribbed cheeks of the mandrill, the brilliantly-coloured genital organs of other baboons, the mane of the gelada and colobus, &c.

during that great struggle, not only for existence, but at the same time for dominion, from which some one of the many great apes emerged as man, there must have been little desire or leisure to originate physical adornments by sexual selection. All our energies were at that period directed to the bare necessities of life, to the procuring of food, shelter from enemies, or withstanding the adverse effects of altered climates by artificial means. As, however, these pursuits had the effect of developing and vastly strengthening man's faculties of thought and reflection, so when he had attained such a position of predominance that his existence as a species was assured, the development of physical charms had less attraction for him than it possesses for the lower mammalia. Sexual selection henceforth was applied more prominently to mind than to body, and the most cunning men secured the greatest number of wives. At the same time, though it has lost its old predominance, bodily beauty still exercises, and has exercised greatly in the past, an influence on the minor physical characteristics of mankind. The *rôle* of arbiter in such matters somewhat changed hands. It was the men that began to choose the women, and not the women, always, who had the power of selecting their husbands. The result of this has been that, in one or more of the highest varieties of man, an attempt on the part of the weaker sex has been made to develop attractive facial colouring, and a greatly exaggerated occipital mane. But men or women alike, in their efforts to secure admiration and to satisfy their personal vanity, have had impatient recourse to artificial means of making themselves attractive, awe-inspiring, or ridiculous. Clothing was first adopted as a means of decoration rather than from motives of decency. Clothing also, under climatic influences, derived a greater development than would have arisen from mere motives of decency alone ; and, further, the love of adornment, with the desire of producing an attractive or imposing appearance superadded, has induced man at various times to make himself a very jackdaw arrayed in the borrowed furs and plumes of his fellow-vertebrates. The ermine of a Lord Chancellor may seem a long way removed from the monkey-skin caps and mantles of an old African " medicine-man," just as the ostrich feathers worn at Her Majesty's drawing rooms in England appear to have nothing in common with the parrot-plumes that a Ba-yansi girl sticks in her hair, but all these extraneous decorations are prompted by the same motives. Amongst the natives of tropical Africa, however, clothing is irksome and out of place. A scrap of grass-cloth suffices for the claims of the most prudish modesty. Skins and feathers and shells, ivory, metal, and wood, are all pressed into the people's service to decorate their persons, and still an amount of naked skin remains uncovered and unadorned. Consequently on the Upper Congo, where æsthetic taste is more developed than among the less sensitive tribes of the Lower river and coast, there exist many contrivances for supplementing the insufficiency of nature with the finish of art. The skins of the Ba-teke, Ba-yansi, and Wa-buma are frequently ornamented with broad lines and patterns of pigment, the designs generally following the contours of the body. The colours used are generally white, yellow, red, brown, and black, which are obtained respectively from lime, ochre, " camwood " and charcoal.

This " camwood," which I have already mentioned as the bark of one or more species of *Baphia* (illustrated on page 83), also supplies the Congo people with a red dye like henna, with which their nails, hair, and entire persons are occasionally crimsoned. Besides this coloration of the skin the surface of the epidermis is often varied with incised marks. These are principally tribal in character. Thus the Ba-teke are always distinguished by five or six striated lines across the cheek-bone, while the Ba-yansi scar their foreheads with a horizontal or vertical band.

The Wa-buma do not seem, as a rule, to mark the face with any scars, but, in common with most of the Upper Congo tribes, they practise " cicatrization," which means raising lumps or wheals of skin by slitting it with a knife and rubbing some irritant into the incision. This cicatrization is practised right along the course of the Congo up to the Stanley Falls. I give here an illustration of the torso of a Mu-ngala from the equator (the only specimen of his race I have ever seen) who had nearly the whole of his body thus ornamented.

The Upper Congo people also spend a great deal of

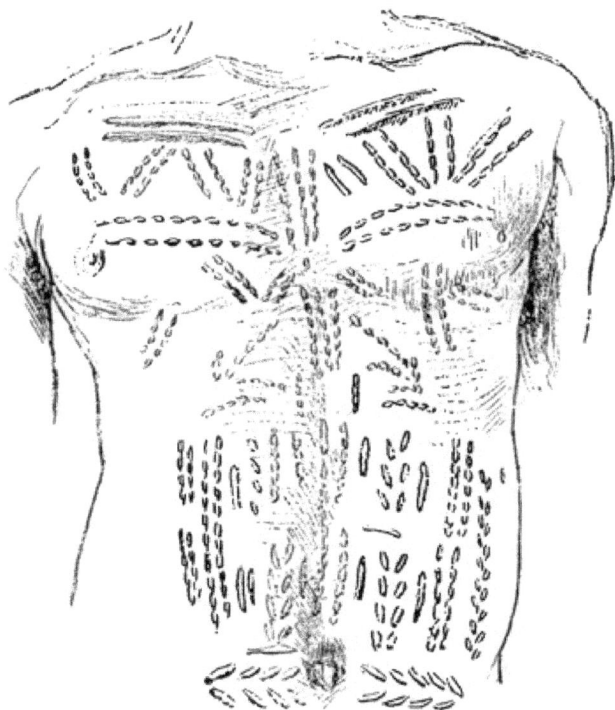

AN EXAMPLE OF CICATRISATION.

time and trouble in dressing their hair. Sometimes the head is shaved all but a small portion of the occiput, on which the hair is allowed to grow long and luxuriantly. On the fore part the *chevelure* is mixed with clay and grease, and is flattened down to the shape of the cranium, while behind is a fuzzy mane like an aureola round the head. But the infinitude of modes of hair-dressing is a subject that demands too much space for a detailed description, so, merely noting that the hair is finer and less crimpy in the newly-born children than in the adults, and that it is generally more abundant in men than in women, I will pass on to other physical features worthy of note.

In the Ba-teke the brow is often prominent, and the frontal ridge very slightly marked. The nose is generally flattened, and always very broad at the nostrils; occasionally, however, one meets with an individual of this tribe possessing a high-bridged, somewhat hooked nose.

The Ba-yansi have as a rule better-shaped noses than either the Wa-buma or the Ba-teke. The mouth in all these people is a variable feature. Sometimes there are thin, well-shaped lips, at other times the mouth is a regular "nigger's," with a wide gape and everted lips. The teeth are always perfect as regards shape and whiteness. There is absolute regularity in their dentition. The canines never project beyond the other teeth.

A BA-TEKE WOMAN.

The chin, like the mouth and the nose, varies greatly in individuals, but there is a great predominance of strong firm ones over those of a weak and receding type.

The eyes are much "clearer" than in most African

races, and the white is less bloodshot. The ears are rather large. The figures of these people are admirably modelled and developed, so that many of them, with their shining glossy skins and their simple nakedness, seem like antique statues cast in bronze. In certain examples the arms are very long, as in this Ba-teke woman here illustrated, but it is not a universal characteristic of the race.

The women usually have better-shaped busts than in the Coast people, and in many of them the nipples have a curious tendency to turn up, and not hang down. The hands and feet are small and well proportioned. The second toe is the longest.

In character the races of the Upper Congo are kindly, lighthearted and full of sensibility to beauty. They are fond of colour and of music, and indulge in dancing that has much meaning and grace. They are decidedly amorous in disposition, but there is a certain poetry in their feelings which ennobles their love above the mere sexual lust of the negro. Husbands are fond of their own wives, as well as those of other people, and many a pretty family picture may be seen in their homesteads, when the father and mother romp with their children, or sit together in a munching group round the supper-pot.

The absence of gloominess in these pleasant folk may be partly accounted for by the absence or dearth of vexatious superstitions. Among them there is, as far as I can ascertain, no ordeal for witchcraft, they are not pestered with initiative ceremonies, indeed, these people are positively lacking in "medicine men"—in the "nganga" of almost universal sway. Whenever this personage is needed for the performance of a few obligatory ceremonies, or for the adjudication of disputed legal questions, he is borrowed from the tribes of the interior. The Ba-yansi, for instance, generally make use of the ngangas of the Ba-nunu, a tribe to the south of them.

In fact these people may be said to be almost without religion. They still retain a mild form of ancestor-worship, and they have a shadowy idea of a god, but,

U

when you ask his name, they always employ a term that is identical with heaven or sky.

They have a vague idea of life after death, and the slaves that are slain at a dead chief's grave are intended to serve him as an escort on his mysterious journey.

When a child is born no particular ceremonies take place. The mother some three months before its birth has lived apart from her husband, and when the time of delivery approaches she is attended by the old women of her acquaintance.

Circumcision is performed twelve days after birth by the "medicine-man," or in his absence by the chief. Hot water is applied continuously to the part till the wound is cicatrized. Occasionaly circumcision is avoided in early youth, either through the caprice of the mother, or because there is no doctor to perform the ceremony. But sooner or later the individual is obliged to submit himself to the operation, and in this case, if he be more or less adult, he is placed close to an immense fire after the excision has been made, and remains crouched before the heat for two or three days until his wound is healed. Circumcision is performed with a sharp knife.

The child is not often weaned until it is two or three years old and all its teeth have come through the gums. All the time it is being suckled the mother remains apart from her husband.

When the child is quite young it is taken down to the river and taught to swim by it parents. If it is a girl it is early instructed in the management of household affairs, and learns to cook and otherwise assist its mother, while the little boys make small bows and arrows, paddle miniature canoes, and ambitiously imitate all the pursuits of manhood.

Marriage is a mere question of purchase, and is attended by no rejoicings or special ceremony. A man procures as many wives as possible, partly because they labour for him, and also because soon after one wife becomes with child she leaves him for two or three years until her baby is weaned.

It is impossible to reckon with any accuracy their average duration of life, but, judging from the experience of missions long established on the coast, I should think the people aged quickly, and that few lived beyond sixty or sixty-five years.

When a slave dies, he is "chucked" without more ado into the river or the bush; but when a person of any consequence departs this life, he is generally buried under the hut he lived in (which is afterwards abandoned), and in his grave are put quantities of cloth, beads, plates, knives, cowries and other things to enable him to start afresh in a new life. The plates are generally broken, and the knives bent, in order to "kill" them, so that they too may "die," and go to the land of the spirits. When a great chief dies four or more slaves are laid transversely in his grave, and his body is placed on the top. The slaves are not buried alive, but are hung first. After the death of a married man, his widow or widows are shut up in his house (underneath which he is buried) for a period of fifty days, during which time they keep their faces blackened with charcoal.

The food of the Upper Congo people is more mixed in character than that of the natives on the Lower river. While their diet is largely vegetable, and bananas, ground-nuts, manioc, Indian corn, and sweet potatoes are staple articles of food, yet other elements vary their repasts. A river like the Congo naturally abounds in fish, and the riverine natives consume quantities of a food at once appetizing and easily procured.

One tribe on the Upper Congo makes quite a traffic in smoked fish, which they sell to the resident tribes along the banks or a little way in the interior. It is a most common sight to see a group of these Ba-yansi people established temporarily on a great sandbank in the middle of the river, smoking the newly-caught fish over immense wood fires. I have often bought and eaten these smoked fish (which are generally large specimens of the *Percidœ* family), and I can only say, provided you get one that is not about a year old and riddled with

worms, they are delicious—yes, emphatically delicious—
for the smoking over some fragrant cedar-like wood lends
a flavour of its own to the solid white flesh.   Sometimes,
too, the natives seem to soak them in brine before
submitting them to the smoking process, and this gives
an agreeable taste of well-cured haddock to the already
appetizing fish.   The natives generally fish with a kind
of seine of different shapes.   Sometimes there is a net
like a huge butterfly net, only with a more oblong
aperture and a very stout handle, but this is only used
for small fry, while monster fish are usually speared.
The Ba-teke, who do a little amateur fishing in a lazy
way, row out to one of the many floating islets of grass
and water-plants, round which the fishes congregate, and,
poising well their little lances, harpoon the fish as they
nibble at the roots just below the surface, gobbling the
larvæ and water insects that cling to them.   The little
Ba-teke boys fish from the banks with prettily-made rods,
lines, and floats.   Then there are the most ingenious
basket-work traps of every size, and it is with these that
the majority of the fish is caught.   Also the mouth of
every narrow bay is netted, so that the fish in the dry
season cannot escape, but fall easy victims to omnivorous
man.

Snares are made for birds, and the smaller mammals
are not despised as food, rats especially being sought for;
but they are chary of hunting large game.   The hippopotamus is occasionally pursued and harpooned, but more
out of revenge for the mischief he wreaks on their canoes
than from a liking for his flesh.   The domestic animals
of the natives also supply them with food, but they are
not so meat-eating as the tribes of Eastern or Southern
Africa, who possess their great herds of cattle.   On the
Upper Congo the ox is unknown, and his old classical
Bantu name, "Ñombu," or "Ñombe," is applied by the
Ba-yansi to the buffalo.   The sheep is rarely met with
beyond Stanley Pool; still it is known and named.   It
belongs to the Central African type—a hairy sheep, with
small horns, and a magnificent mane in the ram, which

extends from the chin to the stomach, and greatly
resembles the same appendage in the aoudad, or wild
sheep of Northern Africa. I do not believe, however,
that this domestic sheep of Central Africa had its origin
in the "mouflon à manchettes" of Algeria. On the
contrary, the ewe, which has no mane, and the young
maneless rams, exactly resemble certain breeds of Persian
sheep, like which they are pied black and white in colour.
The goat of the Congo is a little compactly built animal,

A CONGO SHEEP.

short on the legs and very fat. The females make
excellent milch goats, and their milk is a most delicious
and wholesome addition to one's diet. Unfortunately,
they run dry after three months' milking, and the only
way to keep up a constant supply of this grateful fluid is
to keep four or five of them at once, and arrange that
they all kid at different times. The natives, however,
never take this precaution, as they think it disgusting to
drink milk.

The general type of the dog on the Upper Congo (on
the Lower river it is much mixed with European races

introduced by the Portuguese) is simply the pariah dog of India and the East over again, with a look of the dingo and the wild dog of Sumatra superadded. It has a foxy head, prick ears, a smooth fawn-coloured coat, and a tail slightly inclined to be bushy, and is to my thinking a very pretty creature They have one admirable point in their character in that they never bark, giving vent only, when very much moved, to a long wail or howl. Towards Europeans they are disposed to be very snappish and uncertain, but the attachment between these dogs and their African masters is deep and fully reciprocated. They are considered very dainty eating by the natives, and are indeed such a luxury that by an unwritten law only the superior sex—the men—are allowed to partake of roasted dog. The cats on the Congo are lean, long-legged, and ugly, and offer every diversity and variety of colour. Tabbies, however, are the most commonly seen. These cats are splendid mousers, or rather ratters, and help to rid the native villages of the small black rats which infest them.

The domestic pig is largely kept, and its flesh much eaten by the Congo people. I do not agree with the opinion of those who surmise that the pig was originally introduced into West Africa and the Congo regions by the Portuguese. The pig, in a domestic state, extends among the Bantu races right across Africa, and everywhere possesses a similar name. The pig in Ki-yansi is called "ngulu," and in the Ki-swahili of Zanzibar is known as "nguruwe," or "nguluwe." It is a black, bristly, high-shouldered beast, very like the Irish greyhound pig. Like most African domestic animals, it probably had an Asiatic origin.

The fowl on the Congo is small and mongrel-like. It is however very productive ; and, as its eggs are rarely eaten by the natives, but are allowed to be hatched by the hen that lays them, the domestic fowl swarms in the villages, and is a never-failing article of merchandise.

The Muscovy duck has penetrated to the Upper Congo

from the coast, where it was introduced by the Portuguese
in the seventeenth century.

Among the most usually cultivated plants and trees
may be mentioned the *Cajanus indicus*, the manioc, the
sweet potato, maize, ground-nuts, tobacco, the sugar-cane,
the banana and the oil-palm. Among other Portuguese
introductions that have reached them from the West Coast
are the pine-apple, the orange, lime, papaw, and a small
degenerated cabbage.

It is curious to remark that, while nearly all the

BA-TEKE CHAIR.

domestic animals of Africa can be traced to an Asiatic
origin, the cultivated plants of this region should in a
great measure be introductions from America. It is
difficult to imagine how the people could have lived before
maize, manioc, ground-nuts, and sweet potatoes were
brought to the coast of Africa by the Portuguese and
other European nations since the sixteenth century. The
discovery of America has profoundly affected the later
history of the Dark Continent.

The houses in the Upper Congo villages do not differ
materially in design or material from those already described on the Lower river. They are all rectilinear and

oblong in shape, with slanting roofs and wide verandahs. At Bolobo they exhibit some skill in building, and are

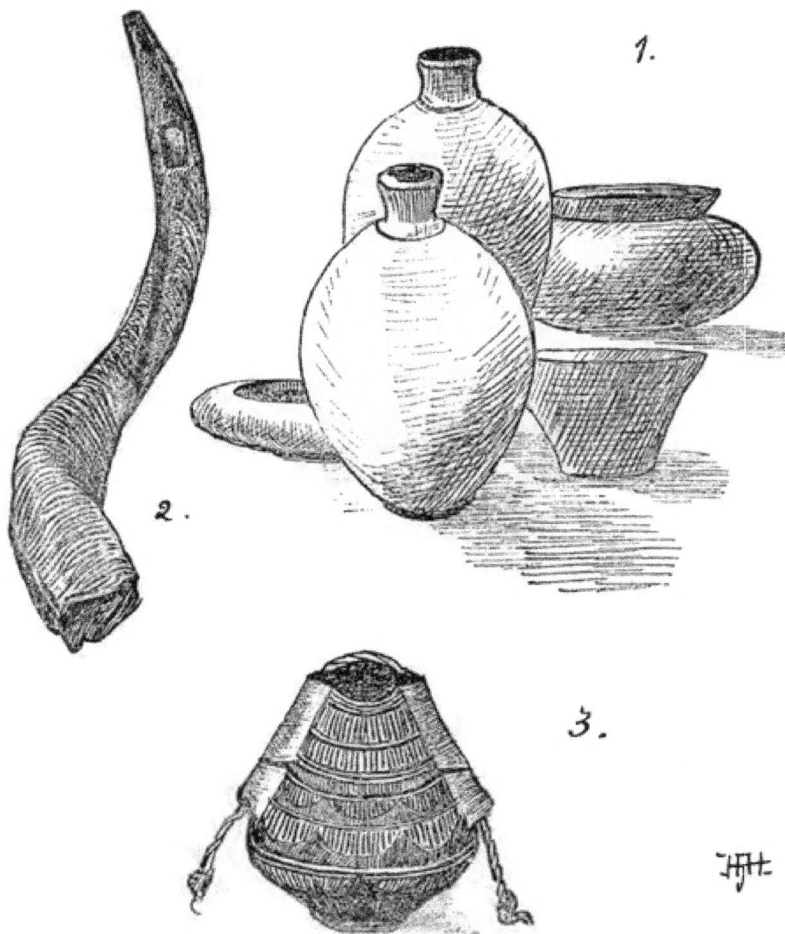

1. POTTERY OF UPPER CONGO.
2. AN ANTELOPE-HORN TRUMPET.
3. A POWDER-FLASK.

divided into several rooms or partitions.   In the attempts at furniture, however, we meet with decided improvement over the Ba-kongo.   Chairs and settees are hewn out of

single blocks of wood without joinery (which art is unknown), and some of them exhibit grace of form and
adaptation to the purpose for which they are made.
Many pretty little things are carved in wood and ornamented with brass-work; pillows or head-rests are made,
much like those used by the ancient Egyptians, and
powder-flasks are hollowed out of soft wood and decorated
with burnt patterns made with a piece of red-hot iron.
Examples of the pottery are here illustrated. There is
no potter's wheel in use. All the utensils are made in
basket-moulds or shaped with the hand.

I have already mentioned the ability these people
display in artistic decoration, and their love of music is
also worthy of notice. Besides the drum, they use the
horns of *Tragelaphus gratus*, and other tragelaphine
antelopes, as trumpets, from which a fine resonant sound
is produced. The Ba-teke children,
moreover, make trumpets from
rolled banana leaves. For the discoursing of melody, they have a
form of " marimba," an instrument
of widespread range, which in principle is so many thin slips or keys
of metal arranged along a sound-
ing-board. When twanged by a
practised touch they yield very
sweet sounds. For real beauty of
tone, however, the five-stringed lyre
on the Congo is remarkable, and
the native musicians produce from
this instrument melodies both
quaint and touching. The penta-
tonic scale is the one in use, and
the notes run thus: C, D, E, G, A,
C, the fourth and seventh being
omitted.

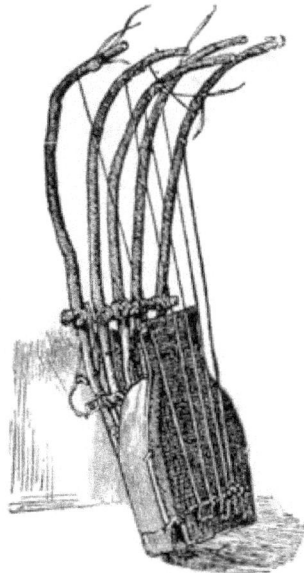

A NATIVE LYRE.

Neither the Ba-teke nor the
Wa-buma appear to be great workers in metal, like the
Ba-yansi. These latter people appear to receive their

X

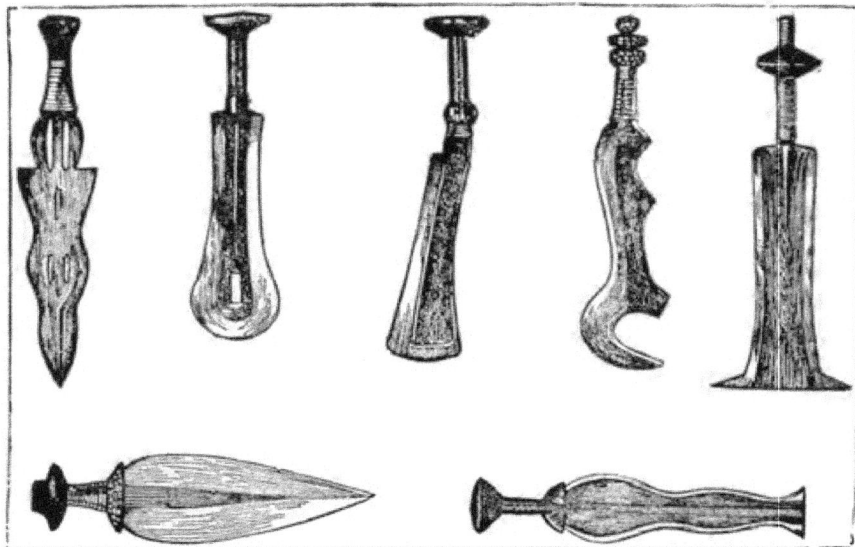

BA-YANSI KNIVES.

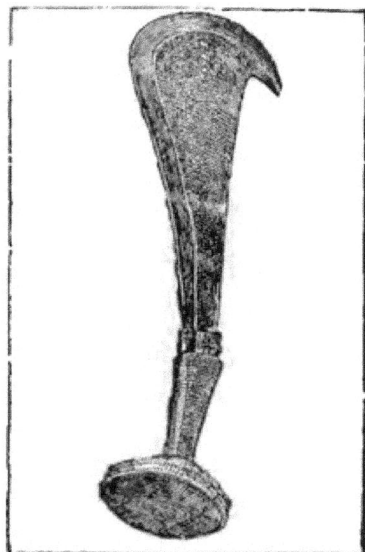

BA-YANSI CHOPPER.

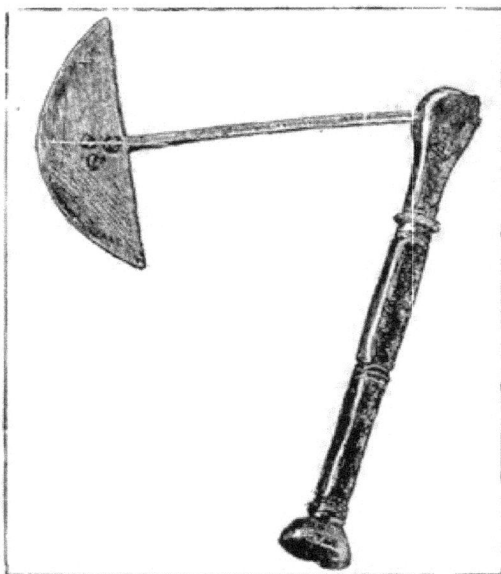

AXE OF AUTHORITY BELONGING TO
A BA-TEKE CHIEF.

iron mostly from tribes farther inland, at any rate there is no sign of its being smelted from the ore near the banks of the Congo, although iron is present in the soil.

The Ba-yansi beat out the iron when red hot, and fashion it into many shapes of knives, hatchets, and axes. They sell most of their knives to the Bateke and Wa-buma.

Most of the chiefs, especially among the Ba-teke, use an axe of a particular shape (see illustration) as a sceptre, or sign of authority. This axe differs entirely from the ordinary chopper form of the tool in daily use, and is purely a ceremonial weapon, being quite blunt at the edges, and useless for cutting. It is always regarded as a sign of authority, and the actual weapon that is here illustrated belonged to De Brazza's friend Makoko, before he was deposed.

The population all along the Congo above Stanley Pool is very dense. Towards Bolobo there is scarcely a river-fronting space clear of villages, and Mr. Stanley reckons from fuller data that the entire population of the Congo basin may possibly amount to 49,000,000, or 55 to the square mile! These masses do not own one great chief or emperor. There is no analogue to the Muata Yanvo, or the negro kingdoms farther north. Such chiefs as Ibaka or Mpumo Ntaba * may rule over a few thousand subjects, but ordinarily every village or settlement is a little independent state. Much has been talked lately about the desirability of introducing some sort of political co-hesion amongst these tribes—of inducing them to band together into one great nationality. This idea has been put forward on high authority, but I must presume to dissent from its advisability. What has hitherto made Mr. Stanley's work so rapid and so comparatively easy has been the want of cohesion amongst the native chiefs; he has had no great jealous empire to contend with, as he would have had farther north or farther south. If one village declined to let him settle among them, the next

* Makoko's successor.

town out of rivalry, received him with open arms.   There has been no *mot d'ordre*, and this has enabled him to effectually implant himself in their midst.   By banding the native kinglets in union—union which would inevitably turn them with race jealousy against the white man, the entry of civilization into the Congo countries will be hindered, and this great work made dependent on the caprices of an African despot.   The black man, though he may make a willing subject, can never rule.   These people are well disposed in their present condition to receive civilization, but the civilization must come not as a humble suppliant but as a monarch.   It must be able to inspire respect as well as naïve wonder, and this is what the expedition as conducted by Mr. Stanley has succeeded in doing.

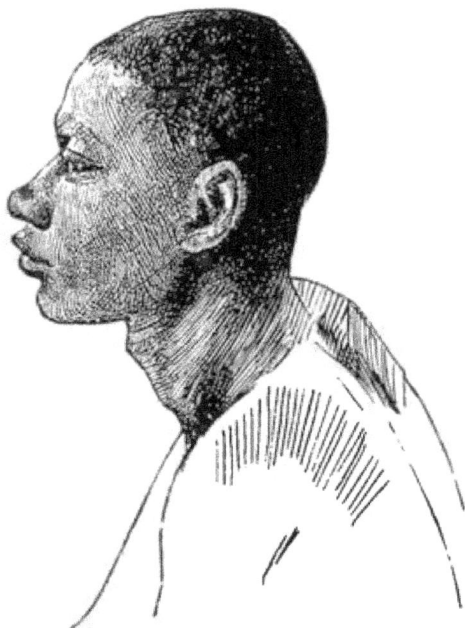

A NATIVE OF THE LOWER CONGO.

LONDON: PRINTED BY WILLIAM CLOWES AND SONS, LIMITED,
STAMFORD STREET AND CHARING CROSS.